SEEKING PLEASURE
IN THE OLD WEST

Seeking Pleasure in the Old West

DAVID DARY

Alfred A. Knopf   New York   1995

THIS IS A BORZOI BOOK
PUBLISHED BY ALFRED A. KNOPF, INC.

Copyright © 1995 by David Dary
All rights reserved under International and Pan-American Copyright Conventions.
Published in the United States by Alfred A. Knopf, Inc., New York,
and simultaneously in Canada by Random House of Canada Limited, Toronto.
Distributed by Random House, Inc., New York.

Owing to limitations of space, all acknowledgments of permission to reprint previously published
material will be found following the index.

Library of Congress Cataloging-in-Publication Data
Dary, David.
Seeking pleasure in the Old West/by David Dary.—1st ed.
p.   cm.
ISBN 0-394-56178-3
1. West (U.S.)—Social life and customs.
2. Amusements—West (U.S.)—History. I. Title.
F596.D3   1995
978—dc20   95-2709
CIP

Manufactured in the United States of America
First Edition

For Sue

Be happy while you're living, for you're a long time dead.

—*Scottish Proverb*

CONTENTS

PREFACE

This is a book about how people in the American West sought pleasure between about 1800 and the early twentieth century. It is the story of what pleasures they found or created, often amid adversity and hardship.

Pleasure, of course, is a very personal matter. What one person considers pleasure may not be gratifying to another, or may even be rejected as harmful or immoral. *The Oxford English Dictionary* defines pleasure as "the condition of consciousness or sensation induced by the enjoyment or anticipation of what is felt or viewed as good or desirable; enjoyment, delight, gratification. The opposite of *pain*."

This book attempts to capture how Americans—some well known, others forgotten—spent their nonworking hours in search of pleasure in the Old West.

Journals, diaries, recollections, reminiscences, and early newspapers contain bits and pieces on how people in the Old West passed their leisure time. Wherever possible, the words of these pioneers have been used to help capture the flavor, setting, and tone of the pleasures they found or sought to provide. A loose time line has been followed to give the reader the necessary historical perspective.

It is my hope that the reader not only will be entertained by what follows but will be reminded of the simple pleasures enjoyed by many Americans in a vanished period of our nation's history—pleasures that helped to shape our national character.

David Dary

Along Imhoff Creek
Norman, Oklahoma
1995

SEEKING PLEASURE
IN THE OLD WEST

CHAPTER I

Early Explorers and Travelers

The great pleasure in life is doing what people say you cannot do.
—Walter Bagehot

A BOUT TWO CENTURIES ago many Americans believed that plea-sure and even leisure were harmful. This belief can be traced to the English middle class of the late sixteenth and early seven-teenth centuries, which put forth the idea that success depended on one's industry and the productive use of time. The Pilgrim fathers—Puritans—brought these beliefs with them to America, preaching that there was no time to play or to pursue pleasure; that everyone should work; that success should be measured by a person's material prosperity. Among other things, they outlawed playing cards, linking them to gambling and idleness. Of course, not everyone agreed. History books tell us that the early New England settlers found recreation in cockfighting, horse racing, and bull-baiting—so much so that one minister implored his congregants to use these diversions "for sauce but not for meat."[1]

This pragmatic philosophy, which has profoundly influenced the Ameri-can character, gave rise to the cults of self-improvement and the self-made person who worked hard, stressed sobriety and thrift, and did not waste God's precious time for fear that idle hands might find work for the devil. The accep-tance of this philosophy grew as the colonies emerged in New England, thanks in part to Benjamin Franklin, who among others sought to build an American tradition. Beginning in 1732, Franklin published *Poor Richard's Almanack* and in the persona of Richard Saunders, supposedly a poor, unedu-cated, pious farmer full of horse sense, offered such preachments as:

Time is money.
God helps them that help themselves.

Dost thou love life? Then do not squander time, for that is the stuff life is
   made of.
Little strokes fell great oaks.
Early to bed and early to rise, makes a man healthy, wealthy, and wise.
He that goes a borrowing goes a sorrowing.

Many colonists related well to Poor Richard and were soon rearing their
children on such sayings. In a letter written in 1748, Franklin advised a
friend, "The way to wealth, if you desire it, is as plain as the way to market.
It depends chiefly on two words, industry and frugality; that is, waste neither time nor money, but make the best use of both. Without industry and
frugality nothing will do, and with them everything." Later Franklin
observed: "If time be of all things the most precious, wasting time must be,
as Poor Richard says, the greatest prodigality; since, as he elsewhere tells us,
lost time is never found again."[2]

Franklin's maxims reflected, for the most part, a simple, straightforward
outlook on life, one that had emerged much earlier, especially in the works
of the English authors Richard Steele and Joseph Addison. But it was
Franklin, largely through *Poor Richard's Almanack,* who gave that outlook
coherent expression and propagated it far and wide. The widespread popularity of "Poor Richard" played a large part in unifying the many diverse
and scattered types of people in America and in molding their character during the latter half of the eighteenth century.

By the time of the American Revolution, the idea of self-improvement
and of not wasting time had helped to shape many second- and third-
generation settlers. These commonsense beliefs soon dominated American
thinking, especially in such trading centers as Boston and Philadelphia.
Laws, religion, and public opinion encouraged diligence and thrift.
Franklin's maxims were still echoing in the minds of many Americans when
President Thomas Jefferson, with the sweep of a pen in 1803, doubled the
size of the United States with the purchase from France of that vast region
called the Louisiana Territory.

In the South, however, a different character was emerging. There the
landowners were developing a philosophy of gracious living that included
leisure and pleasure. James Truslow Adams perhaps expressed the Southern
philosophy best when he wrote:

It was only in the South that the belief in the fully rounded life took
root and flourished. Perhaps no people cared less for mere worldly suc-

cess than the leaders of the old plantation South. The owner of a big plantation, as also its mistress, had ample responsibility, but there was also leisure; and leisure and what to do with it were as important as work, because the Southerner's main preoccupation was how to live a full life.[3]

Meriwether Lewis and William Clark, sent by President Jefferson to explore the Louisiana Territory, both grew up on Virginia plantations and reflected the character of the emerging Southerner who sought a balance between work and pleasure. There is little doubt that their outlook on life and their understanding of human nature were in large measure responsible for their expedition's success. This is reflected in their journals as they traveled up the Missouri River to its source in the Rocky Mountains and westward to the Pacific Ocean. They record that the forty-five men who started up the Missouri River in the spring of 1804 in a fifty-five-foot keelboat and two pirogues encountered many hardships, but also found many pleasures in the unexplored West.

For example, on Monday, August 13, 1804, about three months after leaving St. Louis, the Lewis and Clark party reached a point some distance north of where Council Bluffs, Iowa, stands today. They decided to stop on the south side of a sandbar in the Missouri River. While a few scouts were sent to see if there were any Indians living nearby, the others set up camp. Once it was in place, Lewis and Clark worked on dispatches to be sent to President Jefferson. The other men in camp constructed a "brush drag," or net, out of tree branches, with which to catch fish. The setting was serene as the men worked under a bright sun, amid the peaceful sounds of birds and insects and the muddy river. Perhaps the men talked, hummed, or listened to one of their number whistling while he worked. The next morning ten of them took the brush net and made their way to a nearby creek that emptied into the Missouri. By the afternoon of the following day, August 15, they had caught 318 fish "of different kinds: pike, bass, red-horse, small cat, and a kind of perch." That evening members of the party cooked fresh fish for dinner and then fiddled and danced until it was very late.[4]

This is only one of many accounts of how members of Lewis and Clark's expedition made necessary work a pleasure during their journey of about twenty-nine months. The journals kept by Lewis and Clark describe many other occasions when the men hunted and fished, feasted, drank, danced, made music, and otherwise enjoyed themselves as they became the first group of white men to cross the western half of North America within the present limits of the United States.

Most members of Lewis and Clark's party, and those of other early explorers and travelers in what is now the American West, came from environments in which hunting and fishing were considered both a pleasure and a necessity. Thus the most common way to pass leisure time was to engage in one or the other. On September 19, 1804, the journals of Lewis and Clark note: "Capt. Clark killed a fat buffalo, and York [Clark's black manservant] killed an elk. The hunters got four deer and the boat crew killed two buffalo swimming the river." Two days later Lewis shot some plovers for his dinner, and some of the men fished as the party moved up the Missouri.[5]

The recreations of Lewis and Clark and their men reflected not only their own environment but that of the Indians they encountered. The merging of the white men's culture with the Indians' gave each a better understanding of how the others spent their leisure time. On October 12, 1804, when Lewis and Clark's expedition reached an Arikara Indian village on the Missouri, the explorers exchanged small gifts with the Indians and gave each of the Arikara chiefs sugar, salt, and a magnifying glass. The Indians gave the explorers seven bushels of corn, some tobacco, seeds, leggings, and a buffalo robe. But the Indians then carried reciprocity one step further:

> The Indians have an unusual custom of showing appreciation. They think they cannot show sufficient acknowledgment without offering their guests their handsome squaws. They are displeased if the squaws are not received. The squaws are very insistent about it and followed us to our camp. Our men found no difficulty in procuring companions for the night. York participated in these favors, for the maidens desired to preserve among them some living memorial for this wonderful stranger. An Arikara invited him to his lodge and presented his wife to him, and retired outside the lodge. One of York's comrades came looking for him, but the gallant husband would permit no interruption until a reasonable time had elapsed. Our men traded small articles for buffalo robes. We set off with fiddles playing and horns sounding.[6]

When the expedition reached the Mandans and Minitaris near the mouth of the Knife River in what is now North Dakota, the men built a log fort and went into winter quarters. From November until March the expedition passed the time trading with the Indians, gathering wood, hunting game, maintaining and repairing their tools and weapons, and devising what pleasure they could during their leisure hours. Some of the men told stories for the amusement of others. Others may have enjoyed whittling wood with their knives. Celebrating birthdays and other anniversaries and holidays probably gave some or all of the men the pleasure of anticipation. On Christmas Day 1804, Captain Clark presented a glass of brandy to each of the men. "We prepared one of the rooms for dancing—which was kept up until 8 p.m., all without the company of the female sex, except the three squaws of the interpreters, who only looked on."[7]

A few days later the party welcomed in the new year of 1805. "Two guns were discharged from the swivel to usher in the New Year, and each man of the party fired a round of small arms. A glass of old ardent spirits was given to the men. About 10 a.m., one of the interpreters, Sgt. Ordway and about half of the party, went, at the Mandans request, to the first village to dance. We took fiddles, tambourines, Jew's harps and a sounden horn [probably the expedition's bugle]. Francois Rivet [a French Canadian with the expedition] danced up-side-down [on his hands], and everyone danced around him. The Mandans gave us food and buffalo robes, and were very much pleased to see our dance."[8]

Lewis and Clark's men square-danced to fiddle music provided by Pierre Cruzatte, who was nicknamed "St. Peter." Cruzatte was a small, wiry man with only one good eye. Half French and half Omaha Indian, Cruzatte grew up in St. Louis and had been a trader on the Missouri River before joining the expedition. In their journals Lewis and Clark suggest that the men were rarely too tired to dance when Cruzatte got out his violin. Unfortunately the journals do not tell us what songs were played, although they probably were popular work songs, chanteys, and dance tunes of the day. George Gibson, another member of the expedition, also played the violin, but Cruzatte was clearly the group's chief musician.

THE JOURNALS OF Zebulon Montgomery Pike, who left St. Louis in July 1806 to seek the headwaters of the Arkansas River, also tell us something of how he and his men passed their leisure time during a journey of nearly two years, but his accounts are more subdued than those of Lewis and Clark when touching on the more pleasurable experiences of his expedition. Pike was a Northerner, born in New Jersey in 1779. In all likelihood he grew up hearing the maxims of Ben Franklin, and, in keeping with them, was something of a self-made man. His formal education was meager, but he had read widely and taught himself mathematics and elementary science plus Spanish and French. On one occasion he and his men awoke to a morning rain. They secured their supplies and pitched their tents. "The rain," Pike wrote, "continued without any intermission the whole day; during which we employed ourselves in reading, and in pricking on our arms with India ink some characters which will frequently bring to mind our forlorn and dreary situation, as well as the happiest days of our lives."[9] Another time Pike and his party were caught in a late-afternoon rainstorm. They hurriedly made camp, and the following morning, while drying their supplies and baggage under a warm sun, Pike and his men passed the time with a contest. Pike recorded that they "had a match at shooting: the prize offered to the successful person was a jacket and a twist of tobacco, which I myself was so fortunate as to win; I made the articles, however, a present to the young fellow who waited on me. After this . . . I went out to hunt."[10]

Like Lewis and Clark and company, Pike and his men hunted for both food and pleasure. On November 24, 1806, Pike and two others went after buffalo. Several shaggies were killed. At dusk the party made camp, resuming the hunt at the first light of dawn.

Pike and his men also enjoyed the sport of killing prairie dogs. The prairie dog towns, Pike noted, sometimes covered two or three square miles and were also populated with many rattlesnakes. He and his party killed "great numbers" of the little animals and even ate their meat, but only after it was "exposed a night or two to the frost, by which means the rankness acquired by their subterraneous [sic] dwelling is corrected." Pike observed that as his party approached the prairie dog towns, he and his men were "saluted on all sides by the cry of wish-ton-wish, from which they derive their name with the Indians, uttered in a shrill and piercing manner."[11]

The Pike expedition spent Christmas Day, 1806, in camp because of stormy weather. Pike's description of how they passed their time is one of the more vivid accounts in his journals:

Here I must take the liberty of observing that in this situation the hardships and privations we underwent, were on this day brought more fully to our minds than at any time previously. We had before been occasionally accustomed to some degree of relaxation, and extra enjoyments; but the case was now far different: eight hundred miles from the frontiers of our country, in the most inclement season of the year; not one person properly clothed for the winter, many without blankets, having been obliged to cut them up for socks and other articles; lying down too at night on the snow or wet ground, one side burning whilst the other was pierced with the cold wind; this was briefly the situation of the party: whilst some were endeavouring to make a miserable substitute of raw buffalo hide for shoes, and other covering. We spent this day as agreeably as could be expected from men in our circumstances. Caught a bird of a new species, by a trap made for him.

Pike and his men kept the bird in a small wicker cage for many days and fed it meat.[12]

While the supply lasted, Pike occasionally distributed a dram or cup of whiskey to each of his men.[13] Stephen H. Long did the same for his men as he led an expedition across the plains to the Rocky Mountains in 1820. About forty miles east of what is now Long's Peak in modern Colorado, Long's expedition stopped to celebrate the Fourth of July. Edwin James, a physician who kept the official journal, wrote:

We had hoped to celebrate our great national festival on the Rocky Mountains; but the day had arrived, and they were still at a distance. Being extremely impatient of any unnecessary delay, which prevented us from entering upon the examination of the mountains, we did not devote the day to rest, as had been our intention. We did not, however, forget to celebrate the anniversary of our national independence, according to our circumstances. An extra pint of maize was issued to each mess, and a small portion of whiskey distributed.

The maize was given to Long's men in their soup. Because the expedition's supply of bread was nearly exhausted, maize was thrown into the kettle where the buffalo (bison) meat was boiled. James wrote that the maize took the place of barley in the soup, "always the first and most important dish."[14]

On New Year's Eve, 1819, several Canadians in the employ of the Missouri Fur Company visited Long and his men to dance and sing and welcome in the new year. The Canadians were "adorned with paint after the Indian manner, clothed with bison robes, and had bells attached to different parts of their dress. So completely were they disguised, that three of their employers, who happened to be present, had much difficulty in recognizing them." For their dancing and singing, which included the traditional French country dance La Gineolet, Long gave them whiskey, flour, and meat.[15]

Eight years before, the naturalist John Bradbury had traveled up the Missouri River in a keelboat owned by John Jacob Astor's Pacific Fur Company. In a subsequent account of the journey, Bradbury produced one of the earliest descriptions of music in the American West. He watched and listened as the boat's oarsmen, most of them French Canadians, rowed against the strong current and sang in French. "Sometimes," he wrote, "the steersman sung, and was chorused by the men," and he translated what seemed to him their favorite song. The first three verses were:

Behind our house there is a pond,
Fal lal de ra.
There came three ducks to swim thereon:
All along the river clear,
Lightly my shepherdess dear,
Lightly, fal de ra.

There came three ducks to swim thereon,
Fal lal de ra.
The prince to chase them he did run
All along the river clear,
Lightly my shepherdess dear,
Lightly, fal de ra.

The prince to chase them he did run,
Fal lal de ra.
And he had his great silver gun
All along the river clear,
Lightly my shepherdess dear,
Lightly, fal de ra.[16]

Bradbury and other early travelers and explorers in the West usually ate well, provided they could kill sufficient wild game. Eating was most times just a necessity, but occasionally it was a pleasure. In describing some of the dishes prepared by Long and his men, Edwin James wrote that those prepared with buffalo meat consisted

of the choice parts of the bison, the tongue, the hump ribs, the marrow-bones, &c. dressed in various ways. The hump ribs of the bison, are spinous processes of the backbone, and are from eighteen to twenty-four inches in length. They are taken out with a small portion of the flesh adhering to each side, and whether roasted, boiled, or stewed, are certainly very far superior to any part of the flesh of the domestic ox.[17]

. . .

John Charles Frémont also left a vivid account of a feast following a buffalo hunt in 1842, as he and his party crossed the plains to the Rocky Mountains. After some buffalo were killed, Frémont wrote, "all hands were soon busily engaged in preparing a feast to celebrate the day. The kindness of our friends at St. Louis had provided us with a large supply of excellent preserves and rich fruit cake; and when these were added to a maccaroni soup, and variously prepared dishes of the choicest buffalo meat, crowned with a cup of coffee, and enjoyed with prairie appetite, we felt, as we sat in barbaric luxury around our smoking supper on the grass, a greater sensation of enjoyment than the Roman epicure at his perfumed feast."[18]

When buffalo could not be found, explorers sometimes turned to other game for food. On July 30, 1820, a day when Stephen Long's expedition was nearly out of meat, one of his men killed a black-tailed deer. But its meat was not enough for all, so one of the expedition's horses was also killed. The men, James recorded, "enjoyed the luxury of a full meal."[19]

William Becknell and his party of Missouri traders probably found some pleasure as they crossed the plains in 1821 to become the first Americans to establish trade successfully between the United States and Mexican Santa Fe. Unfortunately, none of the men who made the journey wrote down his recollections for future generations. Nor did other Santa Fe traders between 1821 and 1831. In what is one of the earliest accounts of Santa Fe travel, George Champlin Sibley, a government trader at Fort Osage on the Missouri River (near modern Kansas City, Missouri), started down the trail in July 1825. He was one of three members of the Santa Fe Road Commission, established by Congress to survey and mark the trail. Like so many other early explorers and travelers, Sibley and his party found some pleasure in hunting to provide meat, and he enjoyed taking time to admire the land they crossed, sometimes going out of his way to reach a good vantage point to view the countryside. For instance, as they neared Pawnee Rock on the Arkansas River (southwest of modern Great Bend, Kansas), on August 30, 1825, Sibley wrote in his journal:

> The morning clear cool and pleasant. . . . After Breakfast . . . we all started. The Waggons and most of the Party kept up the River Bottom. Mr. Gamble and myself rode out upon the high Prairie. We first rode nearly north about a mile to a remarkable Rocky Point [Pawnee Rock] which projects into the Bottom from a High Ridge; these Rocks are

very large and of a glossy Black colour; Towards the River, the face is nearly perpendicular. We rode upon the top which is probably 50 feet above the plain below, and from whence there is a charming view of the country in every direction. After we had sufficiently gratified our curiosity here, we proceeded Northward across several Ridges, about two miles farther, and came in full view of an immense level flat. We halted to note the beautiful prospect that here presented itself.[20]

Sibley spent much of his spare time writing letters to his wife and friends in Missouri. By late September he was also making up packets of wildflower seeds collected on the prairies to send to his wife. When he reached Santa Fe in late November, he attended a fandango, a Spanish dance, but provided no description of the festivities in his journal.[21] It is not known if he ignored the fandango because he was not impressed with what he saw or because he preferred not to describe the activities associated with it. Zebulon Pike was another writer who reported attending a fandango in Santa Fe, and like Sibley he gave no description. In all likelihood, however, the fandangos witnessed by Sibley and Pike were very similar to the one James O. Pattie took part in on New Year's Day, 1827. What Pattie described reflected the different culture of those living in Santa Fe, which Sibley and Pike may have chosen to omit from their accounts for fear of giving offense. Regardless, Pattie and a group of Americans were all invited to attend the fandango, or "Spanish ball," as he called it. His candid description leaves little to the reader's imagination:

> We appeared before the Alcaide, clad not unlike our Indian friends; that is to say, we were dressed in deer skin, with leggins, moccasins and hunting shirts, all of this article, with the addition of the customary Indian article of dress around the loins, and this was of red cloth, not an article of which had been washed. . . . It may be imagined that we did not cut a particular dandy-like figure, among people, many of whom were rich, and would be considered well dressed any where. Notwithstanding this, it is a strong proof of their politeness, that we were civilly treated by the ladies, and had the pleasure of dancing with the handsomest and richest of them. . . . The fandango room was about forty by eighteen or twenty feet, with a brick floor raised four or five feet above the earth. That part of the room in which the ladies sat, was carpetted and carpetted on the benches, for them to sit on. Simple benches were provided for the accommodation of the gentlemen. Four men sang to

A fandango in New Mexico. Illustration from J. H. Beadle's
The Undeveloped West, or Five Years in the Territories,
published in 1873. (Author's collection)

the music of a violin and guitar. All that chose to dance stood up on the
floor, and at the striking up of a certain note of the music, they all commenced clapping their hands. The ladies then advanced, one by one,
and stood facing their partners. The dance then changed to a waltz, each
man taking his lady rather unceremoniously, and they began to whirl
round, keeping true, however, to the music, and increasing the swiftness
of their whirling. Many of the movements and figures seemed very
easy, though we found they required practise, for we must certainly
have made a most laughable appearance in their eyes, in attempting to
practise them. Be that as it may, we cut capers with the nimblest, and
what we could not say, we managed by squeezes of the hand, and little
signs of that sort, and passed the time to a charm. . . . When the ball
broke up, it seemed to be expected of us, that we should each escort a
lady home, in whose company we passed the night, and we none of us
brought charges of severity against our fair companions.[22]

About a thousand miles to the northwest and seven days later, Harrison
G. Rogers, another American, witnessed a fandango at the San Gabriel Mis-

sion in California. Rogers, who accompanied Jedediah S. Smith and the first American party to go overland through the Southwest to California, wrote in his journal that the fandango lasted almost until daylight. He added that "The women here are very unchaste; all that I have seen and heard speak appear very vulgar in their conversation and manners. They think it an honor to ask a white man to sleep with them; one came to my lodgings last night and asked me to make her a blanco Pickanina, which, being interpreted, is to get her a white child, and I must say for the first time, I was ashamed, and did not gratify her or comply with her request, seeing her so forward, I had no propensity to tech [have sex with] her."[23]

Albert Pike, who had left his Massachusetts home for the West because he was too poor to marry the girl he loved, had much the same impression of a fandango he attended the evening after he arrived in Taos in 1831. Pike's description of the affair, first published in an Arkansas newspaper in 1835, noted that the same music, mostly waltzes, was played at all events from funerals to fandangos. "Melody, harmony, fiddle, banjo, and all—all is common to all occasions. They have but little music, and they are right in being economical with it," wrote Pike, who described the fandango in these words: "I saw men and women dancing waltzes, and drinking whiskey together; and in another room, I saw the monti-bank open. It is a strange sight—a Spanish fandango. Well dressed women—(they call them ladies)—harlots, priests, thieves, half-breed Indians—all spinning round together in the waltz. Here, a filthy ragged fellow with half a shirt, a pair of leather Breeches, and long dirty woollen stockings, and Apache moccasins, was hanging and whirling round with the pretty wife of Pedro Vigil; and there, the priest was dancing with La Altegracia, who paid her husband a regular sum to keep out of the way, and so lived with an American. I was soon disgusted; but among the graceless shapes and more graceless dresses at the fandango, I saw one young woman who appeared to me exceedingly pretty. She was under the middle size, slightly formed; and besides the delicate foot and ankle and the keen black eye, common to all the women in that country, she possessed a clear and beautiful complexion, and a modest, downcast look, not often to be met with among the New Mexican females. I was informed to my surprise, that she had been married several years before, and was now a widow. There was an air of gentle and deep melancholy in her face which drew my attention to her; but when one week afterward I left Taos, and went down to Santa Fe, the pretty widow was forgotten."[24]

Albert Pike's interest in beauty was not limited to women. He loved words. It was Pike who was the author of what is widely regarded as the best version of the words to "Dixie." He also found pleasure in writing poetry. His 1834 book *Prose Sketches and Poems, Written in the Western Country,* the result of a visit to New Mexico from 1831 to 1833, seems to have marked Pike as the first Anglo-American poet of New Mexico. His poems, "a quaint mixture of Byronic and Shelleyan influences in conjunction with such subjects as 'The Bold Navaho' or 'The Value of Picuris' [PICARESCOS, or rogues], represent much of the same quality that is found in early romanticized American landscape paintings."[25]

Josiah Gregg, author of the classic *Commerce of the Prairies* (1844), was another witness to fandangos. Gregg noted that the term *fandango* "is never applied to any particular dance, but is the usual designation for those ordinary assemblies where dancing and frolicking are carried on." He added, however, that although the Spanish word *baile,* meaning "ball" in English, was applied to those fandangos "of a higher grade," the music at both was the same. "To judge from the quantity of tuned instruments which salute the ear almost every night in the week, one would suppose that a perpetual carnival prevailed everywhere. The musical instruments used at the bailes and fandangos are usually the fiddle and *bandolin* [mandolin], or *guitarra* [guitar], accompanied in some villages by the *tombé* or little Indian drum. The musicians occasionally acquire considerable proficiency in the use of these instruments."[26]

The game of monte, often played at fandangos, was a favorite pastime of the Mexicans in the Spanish Southwest, where, as Josiah Gregg observed, "the love of gambling" was "impregnated with the constitution—in man, woman, and child." Early travelers from the States probably enjoyed the sporting games of *chuza,* which is played with little balls and bears a faint resemblance to roulette, and monte. All classes of people gambled; no one seems to have considered it disreputable to be seen frequently at the monte banks. Gregg tells the story of one young woman of rather loose habits in the Taos area, who was known as La Tules. Finding it difficult to make a living in Taos, she traveled south to Santa Fe, where she plied her trade as a prostitute and played monte with her earnings. For several years she had no luck, but then one night she won several hundred dollars. She opened her own monte game and gradually became wealthy. She eventually became the most expert monte dealer in Santa Fe, and she was openly received "in the first circles of society" as one of the most fashionable ladies in the city, where she was called Señora Doña Gertrudes Barceló.[27]

Although Gregg, Pike, and others all fail to describe how monte was played, the game is well known from other sources. Only thirty-two cards

There was joy and much pleasure for these traders arriving in Santa Fe after spending weeks traversing the Santa Fe Trail from Missouri. This drawing appears in Josiah Gregg's 1844 book Commerce of the Prairies. *(Courtesy Kansas State Historical Society)*

were used, with all twos through sixes discarded, and the monte cards were thinner than modern playing cards. The monte banker, or dealer, had his money on the table where the game was played. After shuffling the cards from the bottom of the deck, the banker dealt two or more cards, one at a time, and placed them faceup, side by side on the table. In English this was called the "lay-out." The players then placed their bets on these cards. The banker next turned up the deck of cards and displayed the bottom, or "port," card. If the card happened to be of the same denomination as any of the cards faceup on the table, the banker took the money bet on the card or cards with the same denomination. The banker then took one or more cards from the top of the deck and placed them faceup on the table, replacing those of the denomination of the port card. Next he took the port card and placed it in the deck, pulling another card from the deck to replace the first as the port card. The players again made their bets and placed money on top of the cards faceup on the table. As the game continued, the banker took cards off

Keno and monte were among the games of chance played in this early Santa Fe saloon and gambling hall. (Author's collection)

A Santa Fe saloon during the middle of the nineteenth century. (Author's collection)

the top of the deck and threw them faceup on the table. If the denomination of the first card did not match that of the cards on which bets were placed, those who placed the bets won. If one or more of the cards faceup on the table had the same denomination as the card tossed faceup onto the table, the banker won. The cards were then reshuffled and the sequence was repeated.[28]

THE ACCOUNTS PROVIDED by early American travelers and explorers, especially those written by Southerners, leave little doubt that life in the West was not all hardship and no play. The influence of the Spanish and Mexican ways of life undoubtedly had an effect on Americans in the Southwest. Even the accounts written by Northern men, who had usually been taught to believe in diligence and thrift and the dangers of idleness, seem to reflect the attitude that both work and pleasure were necessary for the soul and for man's survival in the West. This was also the case among the fur traders and mountain men moving up the Missouri River and into the Rocky Mountains.

CHAPTER II

Among the
♦ Mountain Men

*After you have exhausted what there is in business, politics, conviviality,
and so on—have found that none of these finally satisfy, or permanently
wear—what remains? Nature remains.*

—Walt Whitman

I F ANYONE FROM the nineteenth-century American West is remembered as a notorious pleasure seeker, it is the mountain man. While his span of activity in the West lasted only from about 1822 until 1840, and his numbers are insignificant—probably fewer than a thousand at any given time—his propensity for fun was boundless. But it came in doses, and after his work was done. He made his living by trapping beaver found in western mountain streams. The demand for beaver pelts by hatmakers in the East and Europe made such trapping profitable. At first trappers worked for companies, but later many chose to work for themselves. These free trappers, or freemen, wandered the mountains, often alone, in search of beaver, and sold their pelts to the highest bidder. They were bold men with much courage who came to love the solitude of the mountains and found pleasure in a life of hardship and privation. They were a unique breed.

The typical mountain man was meagerly equipped and supplied. His customary garb consisted of homemade buckskins and perhaps an extra set of leggings in cold weather, and he usually had two horses, one to ride, the other to carry supplies. He carried his rifle, perhaps twenty-five pounds of powder, a hundred pounds of lead, some spare locks and flints, several knives, a pipe, tobacco, sometimes a few books, a cookpot or two, a little flour, tea, and coffee, and a coffeepot. Coffee, costing little in the States, was the principal beverage of the mountain men, and they drank it with pleasure. They obtained it from Indian traders, who bought it cheaply and resold it for "two to six dollars for a half-pint cup."[1]

A nineteenth-century illustration showing two mountain men
exploring a canyon somewhere in the mountain West.
(Author's collection)

Most mountain men also carried and enjoyed a little liquor, which could likewise be obtained from the Indian traders. During the winter months the trappers usually rationed their supply, since it was difficult to obtain. Much of the liquor was "Taos lightning," described as "a raw, fiery spirit," which was produced by distilleries located at Fernandez and El Rancho in the vicinity of modern Taos, New Mexico. Most of the distilleries were operated by Americans who had married Spanish women and settled in the Taos area.[2] For the remainder of their needs, most mountain men found pleasure in living off the land by killing deer, elk, buffalo, antelope, rabbit, and even bobcat for the cookpot. They also supplemented their meals with nuts, wild plums, or wild berries when available.

During the two annual trapping seasons—fall and spring—some trappers might live with an Indian wife or perhaps a few other free trappers and

Artist Frederic Remington's view of a mountain man with his horse.
(Author's collection)

their Indian wives. The fall trapping season began after the beaver's summer fur had become prime, and it lasted until winter snow and ice made trapping and travel impossible. It was not uncommon for free trappers to come together in scattered groups to pass the cold months in winter camp, awaiting the advent of spring. If they were employed by a fur company operating in the northern Rockies, they might go to a trading post or fort operated by the company. Mountain men in the southern Rockies usually wintered in the mountains, but after Bent's Fort was completed about 1835 (east of the Rockies on the Arkansas River, near present-day La Junta, Colorado), some mountain men preferred to winter at the fort.

One authority on the history of Bent's Fort wrote that during the winter mountain men "came in, often with their Indian wives and children, to purchase supplies and to outfit for their spring trapping expeditions, or to visit friends at the fort, after which they returned to their mountain camps. . . . There were amusements of various sorts—hunting parties, games, and not infrequent dances in which the moccasined trappers, in their fringed and beaded or porcupine-quilled buckskin garments, swung merry-faced, laughing Indian women in the rough and hearty dances of the frontier. On holidays, such as Christmas . . . balls were often held at the fort, in which the travelers present, the trappers, employees, Indians, Indian women and Mexican women all took part. Employed about the post there was always a Frenchman or two who could play the violin and guitar. . . . Chipita was the housekeeper and laundress, the principal woman at the post, and the one who, on the occasion of dances or other social festivities, managed these affairs."[3]

As for the mountain men who wintered in the mountains, their pleasures can only be imagined, but on Christmas Day, and again on January 1, they usually celebrated with feasting, drinking, and dancing, and if the weather permitted, they might race their horses and hold shooting and wrestling matches. If winter storms restricted their movements, they remained in their Indian-style lodges, constructed of animal skins and poles, telling stories, reading, or enjoying music.

When ice on streams began to break up in the spring, the mountain men closed down their winter camps and went their own ways to resume trapping, which they continued until the quality of the beaver's fur began to deteriorate because of warm weather. By then most mountain men had accumulated a good supply of beaver pelts and had made plans to meet with traders somewhere in beaver country to dispose of them and to obtain the supplies needed for another year of trapping.

Beginning in 1825, this annual meeting became known as the rendezvous. The first one, held at Henry's Fork (near modern Burntfork, Wyoming), was a mild affair compared with those that followed: The traders from St. Louis had forgotten to bring any whiskey. The observers or travelers who saw the mountain men in action at later rendezvous helped to give them the reputation of being wild pleasure seekers and helped elevate them to the colorful niche they still hold in history and folklore.

The trappers—freemen as well as those working for companies—would arrive at the annual rendezvous, many with their Indian wives dressed in bright clothing and trinkets. Other Indians also came, set up their lodges, and participated in what might be described as a fair, vacation, fiesta, and reunion all rolled into one. Washington Irving, in his classic *Adventures of*

Captain Bonneville, provides what is undoubtedly one of the earliest con-temporary accounts of a rendezvous:

> The three rival companies, which, for a year past had been endeavor-ing to out-trade, out-trap and out-wit each other, were here encamped in close proximity. . . . Never did rival lawyers, after a wrangle at the bar, meet with more social good humor at a circuit dinner. The hunting season over, all past tricks and manoeuvres are forgotten, all feuds and bickerings buried in oblivion. . . . This, then, is the trapper's holiday, when he is all for fun and frolic, and ready for a saturnalia among the mountains. . . . The leaders of the different companies, therefore, min-gled on terms of perfect good fellowship; interchanging visits, and regaling each other in the best style their respective camps afford. But the rich treat for the worthy captain was to see the "chivalry" of the various encampments, engaged in contests of skill at running, jump-ing, wrestling, shooting with the rifle, and running horses. And then their rough hunters' feastings and carousals. They drank together, they sang, they laughed, they whooped; they tried to out-brag and out-lie each other in stories of their adventures and achievements. Here the free trappers were in all their glory; they considered themselves the "cocks of the walk," and always carried the highest crests. Now and then familiarity was pushed too far, and would effervesce into a brawl, and a "rough and tumble" fight; but it all ended in cordial reconcilia-tion and Maudlin endearment. . . . A mania of purchasing spread itself throughout the several bands. . . . The free trappers, especially, were extravagant in their purchases. For a free mountaineer to pause at a pal-try consideration of dollars and cents, in the attainment of any object that might strike his fancy, would stamp him with the mark of the beast in the estimation of his comrades. For a trader to refuse one of these free and flourishing blades a credit, whatever unpaid scores might stare him in the face, would be a flagrant affront scarcely to be forgiven. In a little while most of the trappers, having squandered away all their wages, and perhaps run knee-deep in debt, were ready for another hard campaign in the wilderness.[4]

Another description of a rendezvous is supplied by the Englishman George F. Ruxton, who was impressed by the amount of gambling that occurred, with the stakes, at first, being beaver pelts. "Daring gamblers make the rounds of the camp, challenging each other to play for the trapper's highest stake—his horses, his squaw (if he has one), and, as once happened, his scalp. There goes 'hos and beaver!' is the mountain expression when any great loss is sustained; and, sooner or later, 'hos and beaver' invariably find their way into the insatiable pockets of the traders. A trapper often squanders the produce of his hunt, amounting to hundreds of dollars, in a couple of hours; and, supplied on credit with another equipment, leaves the rendezvous for another expedition, which has the same result time after time, although one tolerably successful hunt would enable him to return to the settlements and civilized life, with an ample sum to purchase and stock a farm, and enjoy himself in ease and comfort the remainder of his days."[5]

Another Englishman, John K. Townsend, witnessed the rendezvous of 1834 on the Green River near present-day Granger, Wyoming. By then Indians were attending the annual rendezvous. Both the mountain men and the Indians, Townsend found, took much pleasure in consuming liquor. In his journal on June 22, 1834, he wrote:

> We are now lying at the rendezvous. W. Sublette, Captains Serre, Fitzpatrick, and other leaders, with their companies, are encamped about a mile from us, on the same plain, and our own camp is crowded with a heterogeneous assemblage of visitors. The principal of these are Indians, of the Nez Perce, Banneck and Shoshone tribes, who come with the furs and peltries . . . to trade for ammunition, trinkets, and "fire water." There is, in addition to these, a great variety of personages amongst us; most of them calling themselves white men, French-Canadians, half-breeds, &c., their color nearly as dark, and their manners wholly as wild, as the Indians with whom they constantly associate. These people, with their obstreperous mirth, their whooping, and howling, and quarrelling, added to the mounted Indians, who are constantly dashing into and through our camp, yelling like fiends, the barking and baying of savage wolf-dogs, and the incessant cracking of rifles and carbines, render our camp a perfect bedlam. A more unpleasant situation for an invalid could scarcely be conceived. I am confined closely to the tent with illness, and am compelled all day to listen to the hiccoughing jargon of drunken traders, and *sacré* and *foutre* of Frenchmen run wild, and the swearing and screaming of our own men, who are scarcely less savage than the rest, being heated by the detestable liquor which circulates freely among them. It is very much to be regretted that at times like the present, there should be a positive necessity to allow the men as much rum as they can drink, but this course has been sanctioned and practised by all leaders of parties

who have hitherto visited these regions, and reform cannot be thought of now. The principal liquor in use here is alcohol diluted with water. It is sold to the men at *three* dollars the pint![6]

At times the drunken mountain men carried their search for pleasure too far. Joseph L. Meek attended several rendezvous beginning in 1832. He recalled that after various contests including horse racing, fine riding, wrestling, and other manly sports, the activities usually degenerated into a "crazy drunk." The trappers freely passed around the brew in small camp kettles. On one occasion one of the mountain men "seized a kettle of alcohol, and poured it over the head of a tall, lank, redheaded fellow, repeating as he did so the baptismal ceremony. No sooner had he concluded . . . [than] another man with a lighted stick, touched him [the redhead] with the blaze, and in an instant he was enveloped in flames. Luckily some of the company had sense enough to perceive his danger, and began beating him with pack-saddles to put out the blaze. But between the burning and the beating, the unhappy wretch nearly lost his life, and never recovered from the effect of his baptism by fire."[7]

When alcohol was not available, mountain men produced a drink called "bitters." Rufus Sage, an itinerant newspaperman from Connecticut, describes its making and its effects:

It is prepared by the following simple process, viz: with one pint of water mix one-fourth gill of buffalo-gall, and you will then have before you a wholesome and exhilarating drink. To a stomach unaccustomed to its use it may at first create a slightly noisome sensation, like the inceptive effects of an emetic; and, to one strongly bilious, it might cause vomiting;—but, on the second or third trial, the stomach attains a taste for it, and receives it with no inconsiderable relish. Upon the whole system its effects are beneficial. As a stimulent [*sic*], it braces the nerves without producing a corresponding relaxation on the cessation of its influence; it also tends to restore an impaired appetite and invigorates the digestive powers. As a sanative, it tends to make sound an irritated and ulcerated stomach, reclaiming it to a healthful and lively tone, and thus striking an effective blow at that most prolific source of so large a majority of the diseases common to civilized life.[8]

When Meek attended his first rendezvous in 1832, he was shocked to see four trappers playing a game of cards using the dead body of another for a table.[9] How the man died is not known, but it may have been in a duel, another type of contest not unknown at the rendezvous. George Ruxton describes "bloody duels" between mountain men, "for over their cups and cards no men are more quarrelsome than your mountaineers. Rifles, at twenty paces, settle all differences, and, as may be imagined, the fall of one or the other of the combatants is certain, or, as sometimes happens, both fall to the word 'fire.' "[10]

The outcome of another contest described by Ruxton was less deadly to the participants, except perhaps to their digestion. At one rendezvous two French-Canadian trappers were seated facing each other. On the ground between them was a dirty saddlecloth of buffalo skin, and on that was a huge coil of fresh buffalo innards looking something like a giant snake. Each man began eating one end of the coil. "As yard after yard slid glibly down their throats, and the serpent on the saddlecloth was dwindling from an anaconda to a moderate-sized rattlesnake, it became a great point with each of the feasters to hurry his operation, so as to gain a march upon his neighbor, and improve the opportunity by swallowing more than his just portion; each, at the same time, exhorting the other, whatever he did, to feed fair, and every now and then, overcome by the unblushing attempts of his partner to bolt a vigorous mouthful, would suddenly jerk back his head, drawing out the same moment, by the retreating motion, several yards of boudin from his neighbor's mouth and stomach (for the greasy viand required no mastication, and was bolted whole), and snapping up himself the ravished portions, greedily swallowed them, to be in turn again withdrawn and subjected to a similar process by the other."[11]

Indians found as much pleasure in attending the rendezvous as did the mountain men. William T. Hamilton, who at the age of twenty was outfitted by his father and sent west into the Rocky mountains to cure a cough, remembered that "a few Utes and Navajos came up [from the southern Rockies] on their annual visit with the Shoshones, to trade and to race horses. Indians and horses were decorated with paint and trappings of finery, according to the taste of the owner. Each man was trying to outdo the others in horsemanship, stopping ponies when in full career, halting at a mark, at a jump—the one who succeeded in stopping the nearest to the mark winning the trophy. The whites and Indians held shooting contests on horseback, and the former showed their superiority. Three posts were set in the ground, about twenty-five yards apart. They stood six feet out of the ground and were ten inches in diameter. The top of the post was squared for a distance of about twelve inches. The arms to be used were Colt's six-shooters. Horses were to be put at full speed, passing the posts not closer than ten feet, and the contestant was to fire two shots at each post. Some of our party put two bullets in each post and all at least one. I tried it twice, and was somewhat surprised to find that the best I could do was to place one bullet in each post. The Indians had several pistols equal to ours, but only three of them hit each post, putting one shot in each. Many Indians hit but one post out of six shots. With rifles the whites defeated the Indians still worse, shooting at all distances from twenty to three hundred yards. In those days the best rifles used were the Hawkins, and they carried three hundred and fifty yards. Wagers were always made, and the Indians always insisted that the white should take the first shot. Nine times out of ten the whites won, and then the Indians as an excuse would claim that 'their medicine was not strong that day.' In riding bucking horses the whites also came out ahead, and it is well known to-day that the Indians never did equal them in this accomplishment."[12]

Mountain men also looked forward to the annual rendezvous as a time to send mail east and to receive anxiously awaited letters and newspapers carried west by the traders. Most of the letters and papers were by then months old, but that mattered little—they all contained news, and the mountain men read and reread them, especially the newspapers, until they were worn out by handling. John Townsend remembered that at the 1834 rendezvous he and others in his party looked anxiously for letters from their families but were all disappointed. Somehow the letters had not reached the traders before they left St. Louis for the rendezvous. "For myself, I have received but one since I left my home, but this has been my solace through many a long and dreary journey. Many a time, while pacing my solitary round as night-guard in the wilderness, have I sat myself down, and stirring up the dying embers of the camp fire, taken the precious little memento from my bosom, undrawn the string of the leathern sack which contained it, and pored over the dear characters, till my eyes would swim with sweet, but sad recollections, then kissing the inanimate paper, return it to its sanctuary, tighten up my pistol belt, shoulder my gun, and with a quivering voice, swelling the 'all's well' upon the night breeze, resume my slow and noiseless tramp around my sleeping companions."[13]

In the absence of white women, some mountain men found pleasure with Indian women. Lewis and Clark and their men observed this at firsthand, as did also John Bradbury, journeying along the Upper Missouri around 1811. In his journal written at Mandan, Bradbury declared he was "surprised on learning that at least two-thirds of our Canadians had experienced unpleasant consequences [apparently venereal disease] from their intercourse with the squaws. . . . I had been informed . . . of the existence of this evil, but found it was of the mildest description, and that here, where the natives do not use spirituous liquors nor salt, it is not feared." (Bradbury apparently believed that the consumption of whiskey and salt somehow contributed to the seriousness of venereal disease.) Bradbury added that among the Indians he encountered, only cowardice and murder were considered crimes and the subject of inquiry by the chiefs. "It scarcely requires to be observed, that chastity in females is not a virtue, nor that a deviation from it is considered a crime, when sanctioned by the consent of their husbands, fathers, or broth-ers: but in some tribes . . . the breach of it, with the consent of the husband, is punished severely, as he may bite off the nose of his squaw if she is found guilty!"[14] In 1824, a year before the first rendezvous was held, John Work, an Irishman who was trapping for the North West Company at Fort George (formerly Fort Astoria, in what is now western Oregon), recalled: "As usual, some women arrived in the evening for the purpose of hiring themselves to the people for the night." Work added that the women were paid with tobacco and buttons, and that before many days passed there were only about two dozen buttons left among the trappers and traders.[15]

It is not surprising that many mountain men bought and sold Indian wives at the annual rendezvous. This practice shocked most visitors, espe-cially the missionaries who began pushing westward toward Oregon during the late 1830s. One evangelist, W. H. Gray, who stopped off at the Green River rendezvous in 1836, was appalled at the open trade he witnessed in Indian women, not to mention the mountain men's drinking and carousing. "No tongue," he declared, "can tell the extent that blasphemy is carried [on] at this place."[16] Washington Irving also observed such trading, and wrote that "the Shoshonie beauties became objects of rivalry among some of the amorous mountaineers. Happy was the trapper who could muster up a red blanket, a string of gay beads, or a paper of precious vermillion, with which to win the smiles of a Shoshonie fair one."[17]

The journals and diaries of those who witnessed the rendezvous occa-sionally refer to music and singing, but provide few details. Certainly singing was popular, but fiddle or violin music was even more so. Fiddles were relatively inexpensive, selling for about ten dollars in frontier settle-ments. When someone who played the fiddle entered the fur trade and headed up the Missouri River or across the plains, the instrument was fairly easy to transport. In at least one instance a mountain man took a guitar with him to the mountains. Reference to guitar music at the 1833 rendezvous is made by William Drummond Stewart, a Scot, who lived among the mountain men from 1833 to 1838 and then wrote of his experiences in an autobiographical novel, *Edward Warren* (1854). Stewart tells of a small group of men sitting in an Indian lodge. On a signal an Indian woman brings forth a guitar with one or two broken strings. The strings are repaired, and a Spanish song is played.[18]

The songs enjoyed most by the mountain men seem to have been jigs and reels to which they could dance. While some of the songs probably could be traced to French settlers in St. Louis and New Orleans, and others were of Spanish origin, many originated in Great Britain. One such song was "Merrily Danced the Baker's Wife," a Scottish jig, and another was "Soldier's Joy," which descended from a popular eighteenth-century English tune titled "The King's Head." Most certainly the chantey "Shenandoah" was popular, since the lyrics tell of the love between a trapper and an Indian maiden. By the late 1820s and 1830s, popular eastern songs made their way westward to the Rocky Mountains, including "Home! Sweet Home!" published in 1823, and Samuel Woodworth's "The Hunters of Kentucky, or the Battle of New Orleans," published in 1824. It became a campaign song for Andrew Jackson, the hero and victor of that battle who was mentioned prominently in the lyrics. "Jessie, the Flower o' Dumblane," a poem written by Woodworth about 1818 but not published until 1834, after it was set to a popular Scottish air, was also popular. Still another favorite was the Scottish song "Commin' Thro' the Rye," not published in the United States until 1828. And it is possible that during the waning years of the fur trade, some mountain men enjoyed "Turkey in the Straw," originally published in 1834 under the title "Zip Coon." Certainly there were other songs, some lost in the passage of time and memory, that reverberated from the camps of the mountain men.[19]

When the men tired of music, they might play dominoes, checkers, or card games. The most popular card games were poker, seven-up, and euchre, a forerunner of bridge.[20] Euchre is played with the thirty-two highest cards in a deck, all twos through sixes being discarded. Although there are rules for two- or three-handed euchre, four persons usually play the game, with partners determined by dealing and turning up one card each. (Those players with the two lowest and two highest cards are partners.) Each player is then dealt five cards in batches of three and two or two and three. The dealer turns the last card of the pack faceup on the table. This turned-up card proposes the trump suit—those cards declared as outranking all other cards for the duration of a hand. The highest trump is the jack, called right bower; the second highest is the other jack of the same color, called left bower. The game consists of five points or the acquiring of five groups, or tricks, of cards, and the first to get all five tricks wins.

The origin of euchre was for a long time a mystery. At one time there was speculation that the word "bower" could have derived from *Bauer,* a German word meaning "peasant" or "farmer," and so the game could have originated in Germany early in the nineteenth century. But even during the mid-1860s the game was unknown in Germany, except where it had been introduced by Americans. Other people thought euchre had a nautical origin, perhaps invented by some old salt, because of the use of words like "deck head," meaning the card turned up as trump, and "bridge," meaning that one side has scored four and the other one or two. But euchre actually originated during the early 1820s in Pennsylvania. It seems that the daughter of a wealthy Pennsylvania Dutch farmer visited friends in Philadelphia, with whom she played a card game called écarté. She carried home a confused memory of the game, and a suitor then re-created it from her description, with the name corrupted to "euchre." With additions and alterations, it grew to be a favorite, and soon found its way west, to be played by mountain men and other Americans.[21]

The game called seven-up, another mountain man favorite, was also known as "all-fours," "old sledge," and "pitch." Unlike euchre, seven-up almost surely originated in England and was brought to North America during colonial times. Although there are several versions of the game, in each a full deck of fifty-two cards is used, and two to four persons may play. The ace is high card, and the deuce is lowest. The players cut for deal, the highest card having the deal, giving six cards to each player, three at a time. The next card is turned up for all players to see, and becomes the trump. The player to the left of the dealer then makes the opening lead. The hands are played out in tricks. The object is to win points in tricks, with a ten card worth ten points, an ace four points, a king three points, and so forth.[22]

Still another game popular among mountain men, and even more so among their Indian wives, originated with Indians and was similar to dice. One eastern traveler provided the following description:

Six plum-stones, smoothly polished, and marked with various parallel, triangular, and transverse lines, are thrown loosely into a small plate-like basket, around which the players are seated with their stores of trinkets. The leader then receives the basket in one hand, and briskly moving it to change the position of the dice, suddenly strikes it upon the ground, tossing the plum-stones from their places and catching them in their descent. The amount won depends upon the number of triangular and transverse lines left uppermost. The loser, having paid the forfeit, next takes the basket and describes the same movements, receives her winnings in like manner, and returns it to her opponent,—and so on alternately. Much cheating and trickery are practised in this game.[23]

Reading was another pleasure of many mountain men. William Hamilton recalled: "We had an abundance of reading matter with us; old mountain men were all great readers. It was always amusing to me to hear people from the East speak of old mountaineers as semi-barbarians, when as a general rule they were the peers of the Easterners in general knowledge." Hamilton remembered two particularly well-educated mountain men, one a Scot and the other a Kentuckian. The Scot gave Hamilton a copy of Shakespeare and an ancient and modern history that he had read and carried with him.[24]

While most mountain men could read and write, James Bridger was an exception: As a boy he had never learned. Then, when he was in his late fifties, he became very interested in reading. While working for the army after the decline of the beaver trade, Bridger heard and was enthralled by Longfellow's story of Hiawatha, which was read to him by Captain J. Lee Humfreville at Fort Laramie. Bridger is said then to have asked Humfreville what was the best book ever written. When Humfreville told him Shakespeare's plays, Bridger lay in wait along the Oregon Trail and sought a copy from emigrants heading west. He reportedly traded some passersby a yoke of cattle for a volume of Shakespeare's plays, and then hired a German boy at forty dollars a month to read the book to him. In time, Bridger could quote copiously from the Bard, sometimes seasoning his quotations with a few cuss words.[25]

In common with his fellow mountain men, James Bridger found pleasure in telling stories. Perhaps to compensate for his inability to read and write, Bridger became quite proficient at this art, gaining quite a reputation as a storyteller. After exploring what is now Yellowstone Park in northwest Wyoming, he told of a lake sixty miles long ringed on the east with high mountains, and of waterspouts seventy feet high, waterfalls thundering down precipices hundreds of feet deep, and springs so hot that meat was readily cooked in them. The stories were true, but when Bridger headed east and told others what he had seen, few people believed him, so he apparently decided thereafter not to let truth stand in his way when telling a story. For example, Bridger told of great herds of buffalo buried in seventy feet of snow that filled the valleys near Great Salt Lake during the winter of 1830.

When spring came, he said, he had only to tumble them into the lake to have enough pickled meat to last him and the whole Ute Indian nation for several years. Another of his tales concerned the great canyon of the Colorado River. Asked if he had ever been there, he supposedly replied, "Yes sir. I have, many a time. There's where the oranges and lemons bear all the time, and the only place I was ever at where the moon's always full!"[26] Another traditional Bridger tale concerned a certain campsite situated opposite a bald, flat-faced mountain. Learning that the mountain was so distant that an echo would take hours to return, Bridger said he would yell, "Time to get up!" before he went to bed at night and six hours later the echo would wake him.

Joseph Meek also mastered the art of storytelling, but he was often the villain rather than the hero of his stories. He told of shooting Indians for amusement, and his tales of Indian women exaggerated their charm and beauty; however, some of his stories were apparently true and told with little embellishment. One such was set early in 1833, when Meek and three other mountain men left their winter camp to hunt for meat, spending several days unsuccessfully looking for game. In desperation they began climbing up the side of a mountain in hopes of finding some mountain sheep. Soon they came to a place where "there were impressions in the snow of enormous grizzly bear feet." Close by was an opening in the rocks, revealing a cavern, and to this the tracks in the snow conducted them. Evidently the bear had come out of its winter den, and made just one circuit back again. At these signs of game the hunters hesitated—certain it was there, but doubtful how to obtain it. At length William Doughty proposed to get up on the rocks above the mouth of the cavern and shoot the bear as he came out, if somebody would go in and dislodge it. Meek volunteered for this duty, and was joined by Antoine Clement and John Hawkins. The three men entered the cave, which was sixteen or twenty feet square, and high enough for a man to stand erect in. Inside they discovered not one but three bears, all standing facing the entrance, the largest one in the middle. The bears did not move, but only gave a low growl as the men approached. The latter kept close to the wall so as not to be silhouetted against the light streaming in from the entrance, and advanced slowly and very cautiously toward their quarry. When Meek got close, he struck the largest bear on the head with his whipping-stick, and it ran from the cave. Doughty shot but only wounded the animal, and it turned and rushed back inside the cave, where it ran around in a circle till the three men inside opened fire and killed it. Hawkins then began to dance around, yelling and laughing, and someone struck the next-largest bear over the head with a stick. This second bear ran from the cave and was killed by a shot from Doughty's rifle. Moments later the men inside the cave drove the last bear out, and Doughty shot and killed it as well. All four hunters, in high spirits, then constructed sleds out of branches of mountain willow and conveyed the carcasses back to camp, where they dined that evening on bear steaks.[27]

Many mountain men also found pleasure in playing jokes on other trappers. One day Joseph Meek and three companions were in Crow Indian country heading to Pryor's River, a branch of the Yellowstone between the Gallatin Fork of the Missouri and the Great Bend of the Yellowstone. As a joke, Meek rode his horse ahead at a fast gallop, and when he reached a point near the entrance to the pass, he suddenly wheeled and came racing back, whooping and yelling, to make the others think he had discovered Indians. Much to Meek's surprise, his actions caused a war party of Crow Indians, hiding in ambush among the rocks and trees near the entrance to the pass, to come charging after the trappers. What had been sport quickly became serious business, and Meek and the three other trappers turned, raced away, and soon lost the Indians. Had Meek not decided to have a little fun, the trappers might have been killed as they entered the pass.[28]

There is no question that the men of the Rocky Mountain fur trade era sought fun and pleasure whenever and wherever they could. When one considers their hardships during many months of the year, and the drudgery of the many tasks they had to perform, it is easy to understand their eagerness for diversion. In this they were no different, moreover, from other people in the West, especially Native Americans.

CHAPTER III

Among the
⚘ Indians

That man is the richest whose pleasures are the cheapest.

—Henry David Thoreau

T HE STORIES TOLD by many early travelers in the American West contributed to the belief among many Easterners that Indians were savages. Certainly some tribes were hostile toward whites, but others were not. The accounts of many early travelers, explorers, and even mountain men attest to this and to the diversity among tribes, making it clear that Indians, like other peoples in the world, sought to fill their leisure time with amusements and pleasures. Unfortunately, few Easterners read such accounts. They were content to believe embellished stories told by people who made little effort to understand Indians, including the writers of dime novels and other publications.

One man who learned the truth of Indian life at firsthand was James Willard Schultz. When he was not quite eighteen, in the spring of 1877, Schultz borrowed five hundred dollars from his mother and took a steamboat ride up the Missouri River to Fort Benton, Montana. He had promised his mother he would be back in the fall to go to school, but he did not return home for three years. By then he had become an adopted member of the Blackfeet and had married one of their women. Later he wrote that Indians "are represented as being a silent, sullen race, seldom speaking and never laughing or joking. However true this may be of some tribes, it is certainly not true in regard to the Blackfeet."[1]

Like children anywhere, Indian children found pleasure in play. During the warm months they might make mud images of men and animals or play games. Colonel Richard Irving Dodge, an army officer who spent many years among the Pawnee, wrote in 1877:

The little girls are very fond of dolls, and their mothers take great pains and show considerable skill in making them. Their dresses are frequently accurately copied, even to the minutest particulars, from the ceremonial dresses of the parents or friends. The baby-houses are miniature tepees, and until large enough to be put to work, most of the waking hours of the girls are spent in their play.[2]

Many games played by Indian children mimicked their parents' activities. Buffalo Child Long Lance, a Blackfoot, whose personal story of his early life was published in 1928, recalled: "We youngsters were given the freedom of the entire prairies on which to carry out our little games. . . . Our mothers never worried about us from morning till night; we could go and come as we chose."

Long Lance described how he and the other boys spent their time:

We knew the game of Indian warfare almost as well as our fathers; for it was the Indian custom for noted warriors to relate and reenact all of their famous battles at the Sun Dance—and we boys had memorized most of our tribal conflicts in every detail.

Sometimes when we were camping in the neighborhood of one of our historic battles with the Crows or Gros Ventres, we youngsters would leave our camp early in the morning, taking along with us a large bag of pemmican for our lunch and our bows and arrows, and go to this spot to "fight." We would divide ourselves into two tribes, and we would look up the old landmarks we had heard our fathers talk about, and station ourselves in the exact positions from which the original battle was fought. Lucky were the boys who were chosen to be the chiefs and medicine-men.

When the "chiefs" had got their warriors lined up in their positions, they would hold separate councils of war, to go over their line of attack. Then we would all strip ourselves as our fathers did when they fought, and paint our bodies the color of the local landscape so that we could not be easily seen by the "enemy." And when the signal was given we would start our battle. We had little arrows, made by our mothers, with blunt, round balls on their striking ends, and whenever a fellow was hit by one of these he was "dead," and had to fall in his tracks and lie there. Our mothers had also tied locks of black horsehair in our hair so that we could be "scalped" when "killed."

When we were at our war games we did not rush at one another blindly as I have seen white boys do. We took the battle very seriously, hiding ourselves as much as possible, creeping up on one another unexpectedly—as the Indian fights. Our fathers made us do that, so that we would be good warriors when we grew up. Our battles sometimes lasted for an hour or more. When the big fight was over, the fellow having the most scalps was the "big brave" of the entire camp of youngsters, and remained so for many days afterward.[3]

A Cheyenne boy named Wikis, whose story was told by George Bird Grinnell, recalled that when his people were together in large camps, the children played many games. "Often the little girls caught some of the dogs, and harnessed them to little travois, and took their baby brothers and sisters, and others of the younger children, and moved off a little way from the camp, and there pitched their little lodges. The boys went too, and we all played at living in camp. In these camps we did the things that older people do. A boy and girl pretended to be husband and wife, and lived in the lodge; the girl cooked and the boy went out hunting. Sometimes some of the boys pretended that they were buffalo, and showed themselves on the prairie a little way off, and other boys were hunters, and went out to chase the buffalo. We were too little to have horses, but the boys rode sticks, which they held between their legs, and lashed with their quirts to make them go faster."[4]

A favorite game of some Indian boys, apparently those living on the prairies and plains, involved carrying a large stone. Buffalo Child Long Lance recalled how he and other youngsters would go out on the prairies with their ponies and look for a big *okotoks*—a stone—around which they would place ropes to drag it back into camp. There they would put it on the ground next to a wooden peg colored red and see which boy could carry the stone the farthest. Wherever each boy had to drop the stone, he would place his own colored stake in the ground. After the boys rolled the stone back to the red stake, another competitor would see how far he could carry it.

Another favorite game described by Buffalo Child Long Lance was throwing a stone to see who had the best back and arms. "We would take a sizable stone and grasp it with both hands and then bend forward and hurl it backward between our legs. We would play this game all afternoon, trying to extend our marks farther and farther; and the fellow who had the longest mark won the 'arm-and-back' championship of the tribal youngsters. But it did not mean that he was the best athlete; for we had yet to try out the legs. . . . We had many foot-races to decide who was the fleetest. We youngsters seldom ran more than two or three miles in our races, but our elders ran as high as 150 and 200 miles in a single race. A favorite race of the Northern Blackfeet, on sports days, was from Blackfoot Crossing, now Gleichen, Alberta, to Medicine Hat and back. That was a distance of about 240 miles. They would start one morning and return the next day—non-stop and on foot. We always ran our foot-races barefoot, not caring to wear out our moccasins, and at the same time wishing to strengthen and toughen our feet. We would tie a buckskin band around our heads to keep our long hair out of our faces, and pull off everything but our breech-cloth, and we ran with our hands down at our hips. It was undignified and a sign of weakness to bend the elbows and run with the hands seesawing back and forth across our chests. After our races we always plunged into the cold river for a swim."[5]

As in the white world, gambling was also a favorite amusement. Schultz describes one popular form of gambling among the Blackfeet:

On pleasant days the men have an outdoor game which is very popular. The small wooden wheel used is about four inches in diameter. It has five spokes, and on these are strung different sizes and colors of beads. At each end of a level space, logs are placed about thirty feet apart. The wheel is rolled back and forth between these logs by two players, who throw arrows at it. Whichever first succeeds in bringing his arrow in contact with a certain spoke, which has been agreed upon, wins the game.[6]

Schultz recalls the similarity of another Blackfoot game to one played by easterners, Kill the Button:

A large lodge is cleared, and an equal number of players take their places on each side of the lodge. In front of them are placed rails on which time to the gambling song is beaten with sticks. Each man bets with the one directly opposite him, and the stakes are piled up in a heap on the ground. Some skillful player now takes two little bones, one white and the other painted red. As the song is begun he deftly tosses the bones from one hand to the other, rubs his palms together and finally holds out both hands for the one opposite to guess which contains the red bone. The winner then takes the bones, and thus the game is kept going, first one side losing then the other, and sometimes it is kept up for a night and day. The bets vary in value from a necklace to two or three horses. This gambling song is the most weird tune the writer ever heard. At first it is a scarcely audible murmur, like the gentle soughing of an evening breeze, then it increases in volume and reaches a pitch unattainable by most voices, sinks quickly to a low bass sound, rises and falls like waves and finally dies away.[7]

Another guessing game was played among the Omahas. A group would first divide into teams. One team would hide small objects in one of several moccasins, and members of the other team tried to discover which moccasin held the objects. Up to forty players, using four moccasins, often participated. Once the objects were hidden by one team, a representative from the other team would hit the moccasin in which he assumed the articles were hidden. If he was wrong, he lost his tally sticks. If he selected the correct moccasin, he continued guessing and winning counters until he missed. At times a hundred tallies won a full-grown horse. Sixty tallies would win a colt, ten tallies a gun, eight tallies a buffalo robe.[8]

Playing dice was another form of gambling, but the dice used were not cubical in shape. Some tribes used sticks with differing faces. Others used plum stones or little pieces of bone with different faces. Among some Pawnee Indians on the plains, cane slips served as dice sets. One piece of cane was painted red on the concave side and had an incised line painted red on the convex side. The second piece of cane was painted blue on the concave side and had featherlike marks on the other. Some Pawnee women used stones instead of cane. They might "toss three large and three small plum stones from a flat twined basket. The smaller stones were burnt black on one side; the large ones, plain on one side, were marked with a curved band and seven dots on the other. The player held her basket near the ground, tossed the stones into the air, and moved the basket smartly against the ground, catching the stones in it. Tallies rested between opposing parties, and each woman laid bets against her vis-a-vis. . . . Every combination of throws scored according to a definite system that seems arbitrary to the outsider."[9]

In 1883 Richard Dodge described a typical game played in a lodge during the winter months.

A blanket will be spread upon the ground, around which the Indians will group until the lodge is packed. . . . Three or four of the men best known as dexterous manipulators, will be seated close on each side of the blanket facing each other. The betting is not confined to the players, almost every looker-on, man or woman, choosing sides, and backing his opinion with whatever he feels like risking. All the articles

wagered are laid out on one side of the blanket, and a most heteroge-
neous agglomeration is sometimes presented.

A fine silver-mounted Mexican saddle is wagered against a war-
bonnet of eagles' feathers, a shield against a bow and quiver full of
arrows, a pair of moccasins against an old hat, or a dollar against a
white shirt. The women bet their necklaces, leg ornaments, bead-work
of every kind. Nothing is too costly or too worthless to minister to this
appetite.

All the bets being up, the game commences. One of the players
will hold up in his fingers a piece of bone, well polished by frequent
use, two to three inches long, by one-quarter inch in diameter. It is then
enclosed between the two hands, and shifted from one to the other,
with inconceivable dexterity and rapidity. His skill consists not only in
completely mystifying his opponents, but by permitting occasional
glimpses of the bone when the hands are together, to make it appear
that it is in one hand while it is really in the other.

The opponents watch carefully and patiently. At last one feels sufficiently sure to warrant a selection, and points quickly to one hand,
which must instantly be stretched out and opened. If the bone is in that
hand, the opponents of the manipulator count a point; if it is not, then
his side counts a point. A man on the other side then takes the bone, and
the process is exactly repeated.

Twenty-one points is game. When it is decided each winner takes
possession of his stake, and the property staked against it, and another
game is started.[10]

When whites arrived, they introduced the Indians to yet another form of
gambling—cards. Colonel Dodge recalled: "I have myself looked on at a
game [of cards] between two Arapahoe chiefs where, it was said, for I could
not understand, 120 dollars depended on a single hand. They are possessed
of the true gambler's passion, and will, if in bad luck, lose ponies, lodge,
arms, robes, blankets, and, finally, wives, and even children (though this is
now rare). I have, however, known, some twenty years ago, more than one
case among the Comanches where an unlucky gambler lost wife, children,
and all. . . . There is no secrecy about the gambling. A blanket spread on the
ground, in the open air in good weather, on the floor of the lodge in bad,
serves as table. Spectators crowd around, and if a man is losing heavily the
whole camp soon knows it. In such case the wives generally put in an
appearance, before things have proceeded to extremities, and break up the

game, either by bullying the husband, or informing the winner that they will not live with him if he won [wins]."[11]

Indians gambling somewhere in Oklahoma Territory. (Courtesy Western History Collections, University of Oklahoma Library)

Henry Boller, a clerk with the American Fur Company on the Upper Missouri between 1858 and 1866, remembered one Indian gambler named Pipe who was "a most inveterate player and usually an unlucky one." Pipe's oldest wife—he had several—"a sour-looking Mandan woman, entirely disapproved of this mode of spending time and would berate him so soundly that he was glad to go with her for the sake of peace, following meekly to the lodge where they stayed, for the poor wretch had none of his own. These exhibitions of conjugal discipline were always very amusing, and greatly enjoyed by his fellow-gamblers."[12]

Gambling was not limited to Indian men. "The women and young girls," Boller recalled, "were equally imbued with it and, sitting down on a smooth place on the ice, they would roll a pebble from one to the other for hours together. Young infants were often kept on the ice all the while, their mothers, or those who had them in charge, being too much engrossed with their play to pay them any attention."[13]

Indian men and women did not play all games separately. About 1860, while at Fort Berthold, Boller observed a favorite game for both sexes, which he describes as rather similar to billiards. A space outside the pickets of the village was beaten as smooth and hard as a floor by those couples wanting to play. "The implements are a round stone and two sticks seven or eight feet long, with bunches of feathers tied on at regular intervals. The players start together, each carrying his pole in a horizontal position, and run along until the one who has the stone throws it giving it a rolling motion, when each, watching his chance, throws his stick. The one who comes nearest (which is determined by the marks on the stick) has the stone for the next throw. Horses, blankets, robes, guns &c., are staked at this game and I have frequently seen Indians play until they had lost everything."[14]

Among the Indians on the Middle Plains there were no games using a ball, or any similar to those played by white children in the East, except tag. But among the Nez Perces and other western tribes, Indian women were fond of a game similar to "shinny" or "hockey" and they played it with great spirit.[15]

Indian women in some tribes found pleasure in their dress. Boller observed young Gros Ventre women dressed in a *metukee,* or petticoat, "of blue or scarlet cloth, some being trimmed with rows of elk's teeth, a scarce and highly prized ornament since it is only the two tushes of an elk that are used. On account of the difficulty of obtaining them the value of a dress ornamented with several hundred teeth is at once apparent. The crease of the hair is painted with vermilion, as is also a round spot on each cheek." On one occasion, Boller wrote, he had seen "three young Indian dandies dressed and painted in the height of fashion, with bunches of shells surmounted with small scarlet feathers fastened to a lock of hair on each side of their foreheads. They wear false hair . . . with spots of red and white clay and ingeniously glued to their own, and sport bright scarlet blankets lavishly garnished with white and black or white and blue beads. The long fringes of their deerskin leggings trail their whole length, and a foxtail dragging from the heel of each moccasin completes the costume."[16]

On the plains and prairies, most Indian men found much pleasure in riding. During good weather perhaps half their waking hours were passed on horseback. Riding was almost second nature. From the youngest age an Indian boy was strapped astride a horse to learn to ride. It was only natural, then, that horse-racing should be a popular form of amusement. One day, Boller noticed much excitement in a Gros Ventre village on the Upper Missouri. He watched as five or six young Indians galloped away from the vil-

*Indian women found pleasure in their dress. This 1901 photograph shows
George and Etta Mapope. Etta is dressed in fringed buckskin decorated
with cowrie shells. (Courtesy Western History Collections, University of
Oklahoma Library)*

lage toward a creek half a mile away. The riders were naked, "with the
scanty exception of a breechcloth," and they controlled their ponies with a
lariat tied around the animals' lower jaw. From the lodges everyone's eyes
were focused on the starting-point. Then someone announced that the riders were on their way back to the village. "In one moment," Boller later
recalled, "the competitors are spread out in line. Next they are hid from view
by an intervening roll of the prairie, but the quick strokes of their horses'

*Two Arapaho women and a child in traditional dress. (Courtesy Western
History Collections, University of Oklahoma Library)*

hoofs grow rapidly more distinct. Now they are close at hand. The excitement is at its height, for the horses are neck and neck. So closely is the race
contested that it is impossible to tell who will be the victor. The friends of
the competitors yield to the impulse of the moment and make bets, throwing
down robes, blankets, and guns in the most reckless manner. The riders lean
forward until they lie almost flat upon their horses, yelling, thumping their
heels into their sides, and using the heavy Indian whip with a will. Fifty
yards more will decide the race, and a breathless suspense prevails. Gathering all his energies for the decisive moment, Crow-that-Flies shoots far

ahead of the rest, amid the wildest exultations of his friends, and careers on at full speed until within a few feet of the edge of the precipitous bank of the river. Then, checking his horse so suddenly as to throw him back upon his haunches, he wheels sharply around and canters back to receive the congratulations of his friends, who are loud in their praises of his black and white spotted steed."[17]

Indian girls also found pleasure in riding ponies, as shown by this turn-of-the-century photo of Shoshoni Indian girls. (Courtesy Western History Collections, University of Oklahoma Library)

Given the opportunity, Indians liked to show up the whites. Richard Dodge recalled in 1877 that once when he was visiting Fort Chadbourne in Texas, a group of Comanches under Mulaquetop were camped nearby, and were frequent visitors to the post. One day some officers who owned several fast purebred horses talked Mulaquetop into a horse race. The officers thought their third-fastest horse could easily beat any Indian entry over a four-hundred-yard track.

The Indians were soon betting robes and other items valued by the soldiers at between sixty or seventy dollars against flour, sugar, and other supplies from the post of like value. At the appointed time a large crowd of soldiers and Indians gathered at the track. As Dodge later wrote: "The Indians 'showed' a miserable sheep of a pony, with legs like churns; a three-inch coat of rough hair stuck out all over the body; and a general expression of neglect, helplessness, and patient suffering that struck pity into the hearts of all beholders."

The Indian rider weighed about 170 pounds and

looked big and strong enough to carry the poor beast on his shoulders. He was armed with a huge club, with which, after the word was given, he belabored the miserable animal from start to finish. To the astonishment of all the whites, the Indian won by a neck.

Another race was proposed by the officers, and, after much "dickering," accepted by the Indians, against the next best horse of the garrison. The bets were doubled; and in less than an hour the second race was run by the same pony, with the same apparent exertion and with exactly the same result.

The officers, thoroughly disgusted, proposed a third race, and brought to the ground a magnificent Kentucky mare, of the true Lexington blood, and known to beat the best of the others at least forty yards in four hundred. The Indians accepted the race, and not only doubled bets as before, but piled up everything they could raise, seemingly almost crazed with the excitement of their previous success. The riders mounted; the word was given. Throwing away his club, the Indian rider gave a whoop, at which the sheep-like pony pricked up his ears, and went away like the wind, almost two feet to the mare's one. The last fifty yards of the course was run by the pony with the rider sitting face to his tail, making hideous grimaces and beckoning to the rider of the mare to come on.

It afterwards transpired that the old sheep was a trick and straight race pony, celebrated among all the tribes of the south, and that Mulaquctop had only just returned from a visit to the Kickapoos, in the Indian nation, whom he had easily cleaned out of six hundred ponies.[18]

Wrestling was a favorite sport, especially among Indian boys, but as Richard Dodge noted, it is done "without rule or science, a mere scuffle." He also observed that Indians did not engage in fistfights. While visiting a military post in Indian Territory during the early 1870s, Dodge witnessed an altercation between an Indian and a white man married to an Indian woman. Their dispute concerned a horse, and the white man finally struck the Indian with his fist. The Indian, however, made no effort to return the blow;

instead, he went to his chief and claimed damages. Dodge wrote: "I have never heard of a fist-fight between Indians."[19]

Aside from a rattle and drum, the flute was the only musical instrument found among many tribes in the West. The Brulé Sioux called the flute a *si-yotanka,* and it was carved from cedarwood and shaped with a long neck and the head of a bird with an open beak, from which the sound came. Used only for love music, the flute was played by young men trying to convey their yearnings for young women.

The drum, however, was used with song and in ceremonies. Nearly all Indians in the West enjoyed singing, but their songs did not necessarily need words. It was the feeling the songs conveyed that was important, and for many tribes the songs were accompanied by the throbbing of the drum, which supposedly represented the Indians' heartbeat. There were appropriate songs for all ceremonies, even funerals. Lullabies were another form of song, sung by mothers to their babies.

Indian songs were usually accompanied by dancing and various forms of celebration. Among many tribes in the Southwest, including the Apaches and Navajos, the onset of a girl's puberty was celebrated by family and friends in a four-day ceremony—four was considered a lucky number—during which time there were ritual chants and dances plus feasts, entertainment, and gift-giving. Traditional dances were passed down from generation to generation because many tribes, including the Navajo and Hopi, believed that all things in nature had specific roles to play in maintaining the world's equilibrium. Thus the rituals—many rather complex—changed little through the years so as not to cause calamity by upsetting nature's delicate balance. On the plains the ceremonial Sun Dance was performed by nearly all tribes, although to European eyes it was hardly a dance. Participants stood more or less in one place, moving up and down on their toes or shuffling backward and forward, focusing their eyes on an object or symbol—often a buffalo skull painted red—attached to a large pole in the center of their dance area. Each participant held eagle bone whistles in his mouth, which sounded with each breath. To those who lasted long enough, a vision might be granted. A Sun Dance might last several days and nights, with the participants going the entire time without water or food.

One of the most popular pleasures among Indians was storytelling, and in many tribes a good storyteller was a person of importance. For example, among the Paiutes the keeper of the legends, called *Narro-gwe-nap,* was viewed almost as a priest because storytelling was more than just an amusement. Among those tribes without a written language, their philosophies of

Cheyenne and Arapaho drummers seated inside the circle at the start of an Indian dance (early twentieth century). (Courtesy Western History Collections, University of Oklahoma Library)

Cheyenne and Arapaho Indians performing the Sun Dance near Clinton, Oklahoma, early in the twentieth century. (Courtesy Western History Collections, University of Oklahoma Library)

life, death, and the world about them were preserved in legends and stories told and retold and passed down from generation to generation with all the reverence of a religious service. Unlike the European literary tale that begins rapidly to arouse curiosity and then shuns repetition, most Indian stories start off in a leisurely fashion and include frequent repetition. As a rule, they stress simplicity in characterization and setting. People are either black or white in character, and only those qualities that directly affect the story are mentioned. It is rare for more than two persons to appear at one time, and the settings are general and have no real interplay with the events or characters of the plot. Simply put, Indian tales center on observed action and way of life. Beyond the characters in the tales, and at the center of Indian beliefs, is a complex spirit concept that includes a Creator, who makes men out of the dust of the earth or the mud of lake or river bottoms. Under the Creator's direction and subject to his guidance are a host of supernatural beings, all great but none supreme. "Sun is father, and Earth is mother. Exposure to the sun and contact with the earth bring strength and blessing. Winds, rain, clouds, thunder, and storms are Sun and Earth's means of communication with each other and with mankind. The importance of moon and stars seems to vary from tribe to tribe, although the variation may be due to the lacunae of time."[20]

Richard Dodge may not have fully understood the importance of storytelling when he observed it at firsthand among Plains Indians during the nineteenth century. Although his Victorian attitudes were present, he certainly captured the scene when, writing in 1883, he described how men, women, and children would go to a storyteller's lodge on a long winter evening to listen. Dodge wrote that the stories were

> as marvellous as the imagination of the inventor can create, jumbling gods and men, fabulous monsters and living animals, the possible and the impossible, in the most heterogeneous confusion. There is little point or wit in them, and scarcely any dramatic power, except the narrator be telling of some personal event, when he also acts the scene with all possible exaggeration. The personal stories are generally very filthy, and the language of the plainest. They have no evasive way of expressing things; a "spade is a spade," with a vengeance. The presence of women and children is not of the slightest consequence, and imposes no restraint, either in words or actions.

Dodge also observed stories being told in sign language:

Sitting or squatting in every position whence a good view can be had, silent and eager, all eyes are intently fixed on the story-teller, who, without a word of speech, is rapidly moving his hands, now one, now the other, now both together. Occasionally a grunt of satisfaction or approval runs around the circle. More and more eagerness of attention, writhing and twistings of body and limbs, show the increase of interest, and finally a burst of uproarious laughter and applause marks the points of the story.[21]

Like people everywhere, Indians in the West sought pleasure whenever and wherever they could. In this way they were no different from other people in America, especially those in New Orleans and northward along the Mississippi River.

CHAPTER IV

Along the Rivers

They talk of the dignity of work. Bosh. The dignity is in leisure.
—Herman Melville

W HEN ESTWICK EVANS, a thirty-one-year-old New Hampshire lawyer, visited New Orleans in June 1818, he found a "wicked" city of forty thousand souls full of "unlimited" pleasures. Evans, whose New England upbringing had undoubtedly steeped him in Puritan views, observed that New Orleans had beautiful women "of fine features, symmetry of form, and elegance of manners," but of loose morals, and there were countless gambling houses open day and night, with the "bewitching influences" of music and drink. "Here men may be vicious without incurring the ill opinion of those around them—for all go one way. . . . There is, perhaps, no place in the civilized world, where the influence of the gospel is more needed than at New Orleans," wrote Evans after returning to his native New England.[1]

First settled by French colonists in 1718, New Orleans was made in the European mold. The old, wooden French town burned down during the late 1780s, and brick-and-plaster buildings were erected over the ashes. By 1803, when New Orleans was purchased as part of the Louisiana Territory, the city was already known as the Paris of America. The Englishman Thomas Ashe wrote that when the sun goes down, "animation begins to rise, the public walks are crowded; the billiard rooms resound, music strikes up, and life and activities resume their joyous career."[2]

Located less than a hundred miles above where the Mississippi flows into the Gulf of Mexico, the Crescent City was the center for commerce on the river and had a distinctly urban character. Evans wrote that:

Perhaps no place in the world, excepting Vienna, contains a greater variety of the human race than New Orleans. . . . Its streets cross each other at right angles, and the side walks of some of them are paved with flat stones or bricks. Most of the streets are narrow. On the river side of the city the buildings are large, and many of them are built of brick and covered with slate and plaster; but those on the back of the place are very small, and consist of wood.

Evans also recalled that one of the buildings housed a theater. Winter "was the principal season for amusement," with carnivals and balls, and even "the Sabbath is devoted to recreation." During the summer months, when the weather was hot and very humid and the population was besieged by bugs and everlasting mosquitoes, "a very considerable proportion of the population leave the city, and during this period but little business, comparatively, is done."[3]

Residents of New Orleans developed a passion for the dignity of home entertainments, good music, the theater, banquets, and a fondness for balls. Lagarde de Montiézant, a Frenchman, visited New Orleans in 1817 and attended a ball. Later he wrote:

The hall was lighted with 200 candles, and sixty young demoiselles, dressed in white were the ornaments. . . . They were simply but elegantly dressed, nearly all had white roses adorning their hair which was artistically cured and plaited with taste and dropped with grace in floating elastic spirals on a virginal forehead around an alabaster neck and upon rosy cheeks. The young mothers, having completed their waltz, would nurse . . . [their] newly born. . . . The ball commenced at eight o'clock and was prolonged up to three o'clock. The women retired afoot with all the dignity of a primitive epoch. Before the city had sidewalks the women had to walk barefoot to the ball room, accompanied by their slaves, carrying the costumes they were to wear at the ball.[4]

The residents' desire for pleasure apparently was passed down from their French and Spanish forebears and instilled in them as children. One visitor to New Orleans in 1814 observed that "children have also their balls and are taught a decorum and propriety of behavior which is preserved through life."[5] One New Orleans historian observed that the original settlers of New Orleans "were, as a rule, law-abiding, sober and moral, and their relationship between themselves was peaceful, amiable and friendly. They all spoke French, worshipped in the same Church, and had the same culture. Vice was to a large extent unknown among them." But after the Louisiana Purchase, New Orleans attracted the attention of the world—and of opportunity-seekers. As the number of American residents increased, "there came a swarm of ruffians, gamblers, adventurers, men of loose morals and of easy conscience, *chevaliers d'industrie,* steeped in the ways of crime and of vice. . . . They were the procurers of misnamed places of amusement and operators of dens of iniquity, grog shops, gambling joints, and vulgar ball rooms."[6]

As a major trade center and the first frontier town along the Mississippi, New Orleans attracted many visitors. Settlers living along the Ohio River shipped their surplus wheat, corn, pelts, whiskey, and other produce by flat-boat down the Ohio and Mississippi to New Orleans, where they found a waiting market—and where gamblers and others waited to fleece the visitors. Timothy Flint, a New England minister who later settled in Louisiana, wrote:

> The instance of a young man of enterprise and standing, as a merchant, trader, planter, or even farmer, who has not made at least one trip to New Orleans, is uncommon. . . . Here they go to inspect, if not to take part in the pursuits of the "roulette, and temple of fortune." Here they come from the remote and isolated points of the west, to see the "*city lions,*" and learn the ways of men in great towns; and they necessarily carry back an impression from what they have seen and heard.[7]

The area in the river district bounded by South Liberty, South Robertson, Julia, and Girod Streets became known as "the Swamp." It was there that one could find liquor, gambling, and prostitutes. According to one account, "For a picayune (six cents) a boatman could get a drink, a woman, and a bed for the night—and the practical certainty of being robbed and perhaps murdered as soon as he fell asleep."[8]

The Swamp was a favorite stopping point for many flatboatmen once they reached New Orleans. But they did not have to wait until they arrived to seek pleasure. Most received a "fillee," or ration of whiskey, usually three times a day, from the captain of their flatboat. Under these circumstances it was not uncommon to see flatboatmen singing and shouting as they floated downstream. Since the water of the Mississippi was of poor quality and usually caused diarrhea, or what became known as "the Mississippi complaint," one may understand why flatboatmen drank whiskey instead of river water on their journey to New Orleans.

Although efforts were made to limit gambling in New Orleans, gambling dens continued to operate. Lotteries were common, too, most of them for charities. Sundays were *the* day for pleasure. During the early 1820s, one visitor wrote: "On the Sunday we arrived, a balloon with a live lamb in the car, and aerial fireworks were to be exhibited by permission of the Mayor. . . . Sunday is a busy holiday, when the theater and the circus have the most spectators, as then they least value the time."[9] There were entertainments of all sorts if one had the price. Early newspaper advertisements reflect the wide range of entertainments offered residents and visitors. In 1818 one newspaper advertisement read:

INTERESTING EXHIBITION

On Sunday next, will be presented in the place where fireworks are generally exhibited, near the Circus, an extraordinary fight of furious animals. The place where these animals will fight is a rotunda of 160 feet in circumference, with a railing 17 feet in height, and a circular gallery well conditioned and strong, inspected by the Mayor and surveyors by him appointed.

    1st Fight—a strong Attakapas Bull, attacked and subdued by six of the strongest dogs in the country.

    2nd Fight—Six bulldogs against a Canadian bear.

    3rd Fight—A beautiful tiger against a Black bear.

    4th Fight—Twelve dogs against a strong and furious Opelousas bull.

If the tiger is not vanquished in his fight with the bear, he will be sent alone against the last bull, and if the latter conquers all his enemies, several pieces of fireworks will be placed on his back, which will produce a very entertaining amusement.

In the circus will be placed two manikins, which, notwithstanding the efforts of the bull to throw them down, will always rise again, whereby, the animal will get furious.

The doors will be opened at 3 o'clock and the exhibition will begin at 4 o'clock precisely. Admittance, one dollar for grown persons, and fifty cents for children. A military band will perform during the exhibition.[10]

Horse racing was another popular pastime. One of the first racetracks was located four miles north of New Orleans. An early classic was run on February 22, 1826, with a purse of six hundred dollars, and was won by a horse called Walk in the Water.

Perhaps the most popular sport, however, was cockfighting. During the first half of the nineteenth century, there were many cockpits in various sections of New Orleans. Everyone—blacks and whites—indulged in the sport. By the 1830s the most popular cockpit, where fights were held each evening, was located behind the Union Hotel. Admission prices ranged from 25 to 50 cents, depending on how close one wanted to be to the action.[11]

From the city's earliest days, most residents of New Orleans enjoyed drinking beer, rum, and especially corn whiskey. Under the French in 1751, intoxicants could not be sold in private homes, and tavern-keepers could not sell to Indians, blacks, or soldiers. Taverns were to close at nine o'clock each evening and during church services every Sunday. However, the laws were not vigorously enforced, because there were so many establishments selling whiskey. Many of the taverns were nothing more than dirty, drab, dusty, and dark rooms where men could gamble or carouse with prostitutes. New Orleans also had many coffeehouses, where the game of dominoes was popular; some had billiard rooms, and nearly all served whiskey.

As in any city, there were fancier establishments too. When Andrew Jackson planned his defense of New Orleans against the British in the War of 1812, he did so in Pierre Maspero's tavern, the Exchange, on St. Louis Street near Chartres. A rather plush establishment, it had a long bar, ornate spittoons, carved woodwork, a sanded floor, and round tables. In its day the Exchange catered to high-class citizens, including bankers, traders, journalists, and soldiers like Old Hickory himself.[12] It is not known whether Henry C. Knight inspected the Exchange when he visited New Orleans in 1824, but, like many other visitors at the time, he observed the planters, merchants, mariners, and others crowding the gambling hells, theaters, and racetracks. As to morals, he wrote, "the word is obsolete."[13]

Many visitors complained that the city's hotels were bad. Thomas Hamilton, an Englishman who visited the city in the early 1830s, was one, but he discovered "an admirable French restaurateur, whose establishment is conducted in a style far superior to anything I had seen in the United States. When not otherwise engaged, I generally dined there," he wrote, without identifying the establishment by name.[14]

By the 1830s New Orleans had two theaters, one French, the other American. Hamilton attended both, and he wrote that the French theater was "tenanted by a very tolerable set of comedians, who play musical pieces and Vaudevilles with a great deal of spirit." But he found the American theater "altogether wretched. I saw Damon and Pythias represented to a full house. Damon was so drunk that he could scarcely stand, and Pythias displayed his friendship in assisting him off stage."[15]

MORE THAN A thousand miles up the Mississippi from New Orleans is St. Louis, first settled in 1764 by a company of merchants who had been given trading rights along the Missouri River by the French. The population of St. Louis increased rapidly after the Louisiana Territory was purchased by the United States, and by 1830 there were about 4,600 residents, and by 1840 nearly 7,000. Early St. Louis had something of the character of New Orleans.

When Samuel Parker arrived there in 1835, he described the town as "a flourishing business place." Located about twenty miles south of where the Missouri River flows into the Mississippi, St. Louis was a fur-trading center, and the influence of the early French fur traders was still visible:

> In the parts of the town built by the French, the streets are narrow. This may have been done to accommodate their propensity to be sociable, so as to enable them to talk from the windows across the streets. The French population, with a few exceptions, are Roman Catholics, noted for indolence and dissipation. Gambling is their favorite amusement; and they have houses devoted to this object, with signs up, like the signs of whiskey venders. As gambling does not increase wealth, there are but a few rich, enterprising men among the French population.[16]

But St. Louis never gained the wicked reputation of New Orleans, perhaps because Americans had a greater hand in shaping its future and in gradually transplanting their traditional institutions and values. By 1820 St. Louis had more than six hundred homes, many business buildings, three or four newspapers, a library association, a fine hotel, an academy, a Catholic seminary, several churches, and a number of schools. But the French influence still existed. The early French residents gave the Americans "a taste for gardening; and there are a number of very handsome gardens in and about the town," wrote Timothy Flint, who observed that St. Louis was a central point in the Mississippi Valley "for immigrants and adventurers of every character."[17]

It was not uncommon during the 1830s for mountain men to travel from the Rocky Mountains to St. Louis to conduct business, enjoy themselves, and perhaps visit friends or relatives. As St. Louis grew, the mountain men provided a striking contrast to the growing sophistication of the wealthier residents who were trying to mirror for themselves life in the East. An early circuit rider in the St. Louis area told the story of a mountain man who came to the city from the Rockies to sell his furs. He got good prices for his pelts and buffalo robes and received in payment three checks drawn on a local bank. When he went to the bank to draw his money, it was filled with nicely dressed men and women, who stared at the trapper in his greasy buckskin hunting shirt and leggings as though they feared he would touch them and spoil or soil their own fine clothing. After sizing up the people around the room, the mountain man stepped up to a window and threw down the first check; it was cashed. Then he threw down the second, and then the third. Each check was cashed. The teller, trying to think of something to say, asked the trapper where he was from. The trapper replied, "Just down from the moon, sir." "How did you get down, sir?" asked the teller. "Why I just greased my hunting shirt, sir, and slid down the rainbow!" The mountain man left the bank smiling, enjoying his ability to have so quickly tested a civilized man.[18]

The residents of St. Louis appear to have found more pleasure in another early traveler than he found in their city. Charles Dickens visited the city in April 1842. The *Missouri Republican* reported that those who "paid their respects to Mr. Dickens and his Lady . . . speak in the highest terms of the gratification afforded them by the visit."[19] Meriwether Lewis Clark, son of William Clark of Lewis and Clark fame, and a number of other prominent residents gave a grand dinner for Dickens and his wife at the Planter's House, a fine hotel that had opened late in 1817. Though Dickens did not like the climate, he found St. Louis to be comfortable and picturesque. What pleasure Dickens enjoyed probably occurred in the Planter's House. In his book *American Notes*, Dickens wrote:

We went to a large hotel, called the Planter's House, built like an English hospital, with long passages and bare walls, and skylights above the room doors for the free circulation of air. There were a great many boarders in it; and as many lights sparkled and glistened from the windows down into the street below, when we drove up, as if it had been illuminated on some occasion of rejoicing. It is an excellent house, and the proprietors have most bountiful notions of providing the creature comforts. Dining alone with my wife in our own room one day, I counted fourteen dishes on the table at once. In the old French portion of the town the thoroughfares are narrow and crooked, and some of the houses are very quaint and picturesque, being built of wood, with tumble-down galleries before the windows, approachable by stairs or rather ladders from the street. There are queer little barbers' shops and drinking-houses, too, in this quarter; and abundance of crazy old tenements with blinking casements, such as may be seen in Flanders. Some of these ancient habitations, with high garret gable-windows perking into the roofs, have a kind of French shrug about them; and being lop-sided with age, appear to hold their heads askew, besides, as if they were grimacing in astonishment at the American improvements.[20]

Later George Ruxton arrived in St. Louis in search of civilized pleasures. After traveling for ten months in Mexico and the Rocky Mountains, Ruxton took a room at the Planter's, anticipating the comforts of a real bed. He wrote:

I that night, for the first time in nearly ten months, slept upon a bed, much to the astonishment of my limbs and body, which, long accustomed to no softer mattress than mother earth, tossed about all night, unable to appreciate the unusual luxury. I found chairs a positive nuisance, and in my own room caught myself in the act, more than once, of squatting cross-legged on the floor. The greatest treat to me was bread; I thought it the best part of the profuse dinners of the Planter's House, and consumed prodigious quantities of the staff of life, to the astonishment of the waiters. Forks, too, I thought were most useless superfluities, and more than once I found myself on the point of grabbing a tempting leg of mutton mountain fashion, and butchering off a hunter's mouthful. But what words can describe the agony of squeezing my feet into boots, after nearly a year of moccasins, or discarding my turban for a great boardy hat, which seemed to crush my temples? The miseries of getting into a horrible coat—of braces, waistcoats, gloves, and all such implements of torture—were too acute to be described, and therefore I draw a veil over them.[21]

Ruxton sought to sample the pleasures of St. Louis but was not impressed. "Apart from the bustle attendant upon loading and unloading thousands and thousands of barrels of grain upon the wharf, St. Louis appeared to me one of the dullest and most commonplace cities of the Union. A great proportion of the population consists of French and Germans; the former congregating in a suburb called Vide Poche, where they retain a few of the characteristics of their light-hearted nation, and the old-fashioned, tumble-down tenements shake with the tread of the merry dancers. The Dutch and Germans have their beer-gardens, where they imbibe huge quantities of malt and honey-dew tobacco; and the Irish their shebeen-shops, where Monongahela is quaffed in lieu of the 'rale crather.' "[22]

The "Monongahela" referred to by Ruxton was Monongahela Rye, first produced in Pennsylvania before the American Revolution by emigrants from Scotland and Ireland. In the late seventeenth and early eighteenth centuries, these emigrants planted barley, corn, and rye, but without good roads they found it difficult to market their grain in eastern cities. So they began to make from it the whiskey that became known as Monongahela Rye, which was easy to transport. Soon they were shipping it down the Ohio to waiting markets in New Orleans and later St. Louis and other settlements on the Mississippi. It is likely that taverns in St. Louis also offered other liquor, including bourbon, which was the product of John Harrod and a group of perhaps forty other Pennsylvanians who had left the Monongahela Valley at some point before the American Revolution. They settled in what is now Kentucky, where they set up their stills and began producing what became known as bourbon, a favorite drink of the wealthier citizens of St. Louis during the 1840s.[23]

By then St. Louis had many such individuals, who had made their fortunes in the fur trade, commerce, or lead mining in the region west of the city. It had also come to offer some of the more sophisticated forms of entertainment found in the East, including theater. One theater, built at Third and Olive Streets and opened in 1837, was designed by the architect and artist Meriwether Lewis Clark, who had become immersed in the spirit of the past. William C. Kennerly, an early St. Louis resident, later recalled that the theater had two tiers of boxes and a gallery. One of its notable features was that the parquet, or main floor, in front of the balcony was laid out better than those in eastern cities. The seats in this part of the theater were chairs, not benches as in other theaters of the day, and there was no crowding and quarreling among members of the audience. Consequently, the parquet was where the respectable people sat, "while the hard customers found their places in the gallery, where they paid half price. It was a large theater, too, for it held fifteen hundred persons." The ceiling, Kennerly remembered, "was decorated with paintings of the Muses. Built by subscription at a cost of sixty-five thousand dollars, the theater was the setting of many an interesting production." Kennerly saw Edwin Booth, the famous actor, perform there as Richard III. Because Booth liked to drink, Kennerly recalled, the management tried to keep the actor away from whiskey during the engagement. On one occasion, however, Booth managed to slip into a bar next door to the theater shortly before a performance. When it came time for the play's hand-to-hand fight between Richard and Richmond, Booth had so taken his role to heart that he not only wounded but tried to kill the unfortunate actor playing Richmond, who backed off the stage and ran out of the theater with "King Richard" in hot pursuit. In the street Booth was restrained by passersby.[24]

Kennerly also remembered the fancy balls enjoyed by some St. Louis residents during the mid-1840s. Many were held in the large mansions of the wealthy.

These parties began early in the evening, and supper was served on a long table, supporting at one end a saddle of venison on which some expert carver was requested to show his skill; while in the center were great pyramids of spun sugar, candied oranges, and nougat, broken at the last amidst much merriment. Chicken bouillon was constantly passed between dances, giving the guests renewed strength to keep up the pace until the small hours. During the winter social season, a great deal of entertaining was done. Many dancing parties were enjoyed through the Christmas holidays, and especially were friends brought together on New Year's Day, when, with many resolutions and much good cheer, *croquecignolles* [a rounded mass of minced meat, fish, or vegetables coated with eggs and bread crumbs and deep-fried], and eggnog, the day was given over to visiting and happy hours of merry-making. Hospitality was then an art, and on Sundays in the country we had many visitors. The old Creole gumbo was often served at dinner; indeed, I've known more than one family who insisted upon eating it twice a day during the tomato season. Gumbo as it was served at my mother's table was a wonderful blend of diced chicken—maybe some crabs and oysters when they were procurable—okra, tomatoes, and I don't know what else; and always with it was a dish of snowy rice. Gumbo can never be made in a hurry, and only one who understands the importance of good living can successfully make it. Its origin has been shrouded in mystery, as one might expect of any creation which bears a touch of the divine. We used to have a visitor who knew the value of romance in life. Venison, grouse, and other wild game were much in evidence at dinner, and we were fond of salad, the dressing for which was made with delicious astregon vinegar.[25]

Kennerly's recollections—among the best—of the lives led by the wealthy residents of early St. Louis, were recorded by his daughter before his death in 1912. He described how the city's concert hall "was rarely without a good musical program or entertainment of some kind," ranging from opera to magicians. "One very popular show was called 'chemical pictures.' These were dioramas lighted up in a special way so that the beholder felt as if he were really in the midst of the scene portrayed. There was a picture of Belshazzar's Feast and views of Jerusalem and Venice and Seville that drew crowds for weeks in the winter or spring of 1845. Exhibits of sculpture, engravings, and paintings were presented. . . . The artists who came were mostly portrait painters. De Franca for years had a studio on Market Street and was painting at least one beauty out of nearly every family. The frontier-life subjects being done by Charles Deas were exciting St. Louis, and George Caleb Bingham, who had long been known in our part of the world for his portraits, was showing some of his Missouri River boatmen pictures. In those winters the river froze solid, permitting us to skate as far as Alton [Illinois], dodging heavily laden wagon teams crossing from Illinois to the Missouri shore with coal. The coldest I remember was later on in the 1850s when the river was frozen solidly over from the middle of January until March. Large horse-drawn sleighs provided a ferry service, and several acres of the rough surface were clear for skating. This sport became very popular, and so many people now thronged the icy river that the levee saloonkeepers put up whiskey tents midway across for the convenience of their customers and profit unto themselves. Sundays were still as dry as the grand jury on which my father served had made them; so most of the male population found it pleasant to do their skating on the Sabbath," said Kennerly, who witnessed the arrival of steamboats on the Mississippi after 1812.[26]

Steamboat travel not only improved commerce and communication between St. Louis and other towns and cities along the Mississippi, but it provided new forms of pleasure. The arrival of steamboats was to travel in the nineteenth century what the arrival of the jet plane was in the twentieth, except that the steamboats provided passengers with a journey and not simply a trip. Timothy Flint, one of the most influential men of letters in the early-nineteenth-century American West, provides one of the better early descriptions of the pleasures found in steamboat travel. He wrote:

A stranger to this mode of traveling would find it difficult to describe his impressions upon descending the Mississippi for the first time in one of these steamboats. . . . He contemplates the prodigious construction, with its double tiers of cabins, and its separate establishment for the ladies, and its commodious arrangements for the deck passengers and the servants. Overhead, about him, and below him, all is life and movement. He contemplates the splendor of the cabin, its beautiful finishing of the richest woods, its rich carpeting, its mirrors and fine furniture, its sliding tables, its bar room, and all its arrangements for the accommodation of a hundred cabin passengers. The fare is sumptuous, and every thing in a style of splendor, order and quiet, far exceeding most city taverns. You read, converse, walk, or sleep, as you choose. You are not burdened by the restraint of useless ceremony. The varied and verdant scenery shifts about you. The trees, the green islands, the houses on the shore, everything has an appearance, as by enchantment, of moving past you. The river fowl, with their white and extended lines, are wheeling their flight above you. The sky is bright. The river is dotted with boats above, beside, and below you. You hear the echo of their bugle reverberating from the woods. Behind the wooded point, you see the ascending column of smoke, rising over the trees, which announces, that another steam boat is approaching you. The moving pageant glides through a narrow passage, between an island, thick set with young cotton woods, so even, so beautiful, and regular, that they seem to have been planted for a pleasure ground, and the main shore. As you shoot out again into the broad stream, you come in view of a plantation, with all its busy and cheerful accompaniments. At other times, you are sweeping along for many leagues together, where either shore is a boundless and pathless wilderness. A contrast is thus strongly forced upon the mind, of the highest improvement and the latest pre-eminent invention of art with the most lonely aspect of a grand but desolate nature,—the most striking and complete assemblage of splendor and comfort, the cheerfulness of a floating hotel, which carries, perhaps, hundreds of guests, with a wild and uninhabited forest, it may be a hundred miles in width, the abode only of bears, owls and noxious animals.[27]

Flint noted the sense of amazement most passengers experienced as they boarded a steamboat and suddenly found themselves "amidst a mass of people, male and female, dressed as much as their means will allow." He wrote that the cards, wine, novels, and many other artificial excitements, including drinking and gambling, were very tempting. "But there are always some graver spirits on the steam boats, whose presence inspires a certain degree of awe and restraint," he added.[28] Other travelers on the Mississippi made similar observations. One compared the larger steamboats to "a world in miniature." He noted that on one journey to New Orleans, a particular steamboat "carried fifty cabin passengers, one or two hundred deck passengers; one negro-driver with his gang of negroes; a part of a company of soldiers; a menagerie of wild beasts; a whole circus; and a company of play actors!"[29] While many travelers seem to have found pleasure in watching other people, Reverend Samuel Parker complained after his 1835 journey that there were few books for the passengers to read. "Some novels are found, but most of them are of a licentious character."[30]

Nearly every town and city where steamboats tied up along the Mississippi catered to the boats and their passengers—selling wood, produce, and other goods—and some offered one or more forms of entertainment for steamboat passengers who might decide to leave their vessel while it was docked. One such stopping point on the Mississippi was Natchez. The town, with its churches and honest merchants, stood atop Chickasaw Bluff, but at the foot of the three-hundred-foot bluff was Natchez-Under-the-Hill, populated by crooked barkeepers, lewd women, gamblers, and robbers. Dangerous enough even during daylight hours, it was still worse after dark. There was one road running from the river's edge up the hill to respectable Natchez, and close to the river's edge, lining either side of this often-muddy thoroughfare, were rows of wooden shanties housing brothels, taverns, and gambling dens. Even before steamboats made their appearance on the Mississippi, flatboatmen often avoided Natchez-Under-the-Hill. Others stopped to drink and to visit one of the many whorehouses, where one can only assume they sought gratification and pleasure. After the arrival of steamboats, male passengers learned to stay aboard their boat at Natchez even though the sounds of fiddle music and merriment coming from the wooden shanties under the bluff must have been most appealing.

Those travelers who did leave the safety of their steamboat to visit such establishments were decidedly tempting fate. Crooked gamblers took their money and prostitutes got them drunk, dragged them into alleys, and robbed them. Often at night, when a steamboat captain rang the bell to signal the boat's departure, all the lights in the shanties would go out, and ruffians would seize, beat, and rob the passengers before those who could still walk could make their way back to their boat.[31] Tyrone Power, a well-known Irish actor (his name was adopted by a 1940s Hollywood leading man), visited the place in the 1830s and described it as the worst "pit of sin" he had ever seen.[32] Natchez-Under-the-Hill continued to prosper until about 1836, when Natchez citizens organized the Adams County Anti-Gambling Society, and a "committee of vigilance" rounded up the gamblers and ran them out of town.

WHEN RICHARD COBDEN visited the United States in 1835, the thirty-one-year-old English businessman was struck by the absence of women in hotels, riding in stagecoaches, and aboard steamboats. He wrote in his diary that either few American men married, or if they did, "they [did] not give much of their company to their wives."[33] Of course, many American men married, but rarely did their wives and children accompany them on trips. During the early part of the nineteenth century, travel was expensive and often filled with hardships. Most women and children enjoyed their pleasures at home in the family setting. But this began to change during the late 1830s, with the onset of what can be called the golden age of pleasure seeking aboard Mississippi steamboats.

Steamboat travel was seasonal. During the months of July, August, September, and sometimes October, a large number of steamboats, especially the larger vessels, did not attempt river travel because of low water. During this period they frequently underwent repairs or remodeling. From October to July, however, steamboat travel was at its peak except on the Upper Mississippi, where during the cold months the river froze. By then many of the steamboats that normally traversed the Upper Mississippi had joined those on the lower river.

Between October and July most steamboat captains took pride in providing passengers, especially those who had booked cabins, with the pleasure of good food. No self-respecting captain wanted to be called a "belly-robber," a term applied to those captains who scrimped on food to increase their profits. "Turkeys, hams, chops, and steaks abounded the tables set by the better captains, and brandy bottles were located at handy intervals."[34] Steamboat dining became quite fashionable until the Civil War, and it was not uncommon for wealthy passengers to take round trips on the steamboats simply to enjoy fine meals, good company, and the atmosphere aboard, which often included music.

The *Excelsior*, a side-wheeler built at Brownsville, Pennsylvania, in 1849, was the first steamboat on the Mississippi to introduce the "steam piano," or calliope, to entertain passengers. Although many people booked passage on the *Excelsior* in order to hear the calliope, and other steamboats also added calliopes, they never really caught on and eventually went out of fashion. Some steamboats tried brass bands, but they were too expensive. George B. Merrick, a steamboat captain, recalled:

> The cabin orchestra was the cheapest and most enduring, as well as the most popular drawing card. A band of six or eight colored men who could play the violin, banjo, and guitar, and in addition sing well, was always a good investment. These men were paid to do the work of wait-ers, barbers, and baggagemen, and in addition were given the privilege of passing the hat occasionally, and keeping all they caught. They made good wages by this combination, and it also pleased the passengers, who had no suspicion that the entire orchestra was hired with the under-standing that they were to play as ordered by the captain or chief clerk, and that it was a strictly business engagement. They also played for dances in the cabin, and at landings sat on the guards and played to attract customers. It soon became advertised abroad which boats carried the best orchestras, and such lost nothing in the way of patronage.[35]

Robert Baird, a frequent steamboat traveler, enjoyed listening to the Negroes on the boiler deck who sang as they stoked the boiler, brought on board a fresh supply of wood, or approached or left a landing. "In these musical fetes, some one acts as the leader, himself oftentimes no mean maker of verses, and the rest join with all their might in the chorus, which gener-ally constitutes every second line of the song. These chorusses are usually an unmeaning string of words, such as 'Ohio, Ohio, O-hi-o'; or 'O hang, boys, hang;' or 'O stormy, stormy,' &c. When tired with the insipid gabble of the card-table in the cabin, or disinclined to converse with anyone, I have spent hours in listening to the boat songs of these men."[36]

Beginning about 1831, a group of eastern entertainers roofed a barge, loaded it with their equipment, and began floating down the Ohio and Mis-sissippi presenting music, farce, and melodrama to frontiersmen and farm-ers, who, in a cash-scarce area, paid admission at river landings with eggs, bacon, apples, potatoes, or other produce. In 1836 someone converted a steamboat into a theater and began touring the Ohio and Mississippi and even some of their smaller tributaries, but the largest entertainment boat of the nineteenth century apparently was the *Floating Palace,* the forerunner of Mississippi showboats. Captain E. N. Shields, a Cincinnati boat designer, built a large barge and two light-draft towing boats for showman Gilbert Spalding at a cost of $42,000. Delivered in 1852, the *Floating Palace* had a forty-two-foot ring in the center, with a mirror at each side, giving the impression of multiple rings. Seating consisted of a thousand cane-bottomed chairs, each numbered, plus five hundred cushioned seats and a gallery of nine hundred less comfortable seats. The *Floating Palace* had hot-water heating and gaslights whose sources were on the towboats. When people arrived for a show, they first passed across the deck of one of the towboats to the barge where Spalding kept a menagerie. After viewing the animals, the customers would move from the towboat to the barge to see the ring acts and main show.[37]

The Floating Palace, *the forerunner of Mississippi showboats, as she probably appeared just after her construction in 1851.*
(Author's collection)

Beginning in the early 1830s, gambling became prevalent on many Mississippi steamboats. Until that time most gamblers dealt their cards in river towns, but with the growth of steamboat travel, they took to the Mississippi, and between 1835 and the Civil War probably as many as eight hundred professional gamblers plied their skills on the paddleboats between New Orleans and St. Louis. The better-regulated steamboats professed not to tolerate gambling, but from all accounts it seems to have existed on just about all of them. By the late 1830s, steamboats were constructed with social rooms as the focal compartment for passengers. Oil paintings sometimes hung on the walls, and one or more billiard tables were often placed in these rooms, along with round tables and chairs to accommodate the gamblers and their "gulls" or "coneys," as neophytes enticed to play were called. Card games, especially poker, whist (a forerunner of bridge), brag (similar to poker), lanterloo or loo (in which each player contributes stakes to a pool), euchre, and twenty-one, or blackjack, were favorites. It was not uncommon for the gamblers to set up roulette wheels. Banking games including chucker luck (played with dice, cups, and a piece of cloth bearing the numbers one through six), *vingt-et-un* (twenty-one), with the cards bearing the same respective values as in cribbage, and faro.

Faro, brought from France to New Orleans, spread northward aboard steamboats and grew in popularity because, when fairly conducted, the game afforded the customer almost an even break, with only a slight percentage in favor of the house. Faro derived its name from "pharaoh," whose picture decorated the cards in France. In the United States the illustration of a Bengal tiger adorned the chips and layout and beckoned all men.

The growing popularity of faro in the West inspired one player to the following verse effusion:

> *'Twas midnight in the faro bank,*
> *Faces pale and cheeks aglow,*
> *A score of sports were gathered,*
> *Watching fortune's ebb and flow.*
>
> *There was one who saw the last turn*
> *With eyes of deep dismay,*
> *And, as the Queen slipped from the box,*
> *Cried, "Broke!" and turned away.*
>
> *For a moment on the table*
> *Down his throbbing head he laid,*
> *Then, looking round him wildly,*
> *He clenched his hand and said:*
>
> *"I'm a pretty slick young feller,*
> *I've been given every deal,*
> *Have often dropped my bankroll,*
> *But was never known to squeal.*
>
> *"But this evening I am weary,*
> *And my socks are hanging low,*
> *My usual gait is 2:13*
> *But to-night I'm trotting slow.*
>
> *"'Tis not for myself I'm kicking,*
> *I've a friend that's near and dear*

Who is lying, worn with sickness,
A couple of blocks from here.

"She's my darling, gents, my darling,
But they say she's got to croak,
And the medicine to save her
I can't get—you see I'm broke."

"Here's a dollar," said the dealer.
A smile lit up his face,
"Thanks, old man,—damn the medicine,
I'll play it on the ace!"[38]

Although a few steamboat captains shared in the profits from gamblers who cleaned the pockets of unsuspecting passengers, many honest ones did not hesitate to put dishonest gamblers ashore at the next landing. In one case the captain of the steamboat *Sea Serpent* was so angry with a gambler that he threw the man off his vessel into the muck and mire of a canebreak while the boat was under steam.[39]

Reverend Parker, who complained about the gambling he observed while traveling by steamboat in 1835, acquired a copy of what he described as "The Gamblers' Constitution." It reads:

Whereas it is admitted by political economists and by some wealthy individuals, that employment of labor, even upon things which in themselves are useless, is praiseworthy, in that it furnishes employment for multitudes;—and whereas this country is so fruitful, that should all be employed in productive pursuits, there would be more than a supply for our markets; and whereas we would be as great philanthropists as those who advocate useless labor to give employment to the lower classes of community, and to keep up our markets; therefore resolved that we whose names are hereunto subscribed, do form ourselves into a society under the following constitution, viz.

Article I. This society shall be called the Fraternal Gambling Society.

Article II. This society shall be composed of all shrewd or silly men, who, to the fortunes of chance, guided by cunning deceit, are willing to risk their money and spend their time in getting rich by short methods.

Article III. It shall be the duty of this society to spend their time in gambling in any such way as they may choose; by cards, dice, billiards, lotteries, horse racing, &c. &c.

Article IV. It shall be lawful and honorable for any person belonging to this society, to cheat and defraud as much as he pleases, provided

Mississippi riverboat gamblers. (Author's collection)

always, he conforms to rules of honor and regulations, specified in the by-laws which may be made from time to time.

Article V. Any person may withdraw from this society when he has lost all, to try his fortune in theft, highway robbery, or to commit suicide; but not to enter upon any labor which might overstock our markets, under the penalty of receiving the scorn and ridicule of all whose interest it is to promote gambling; for it is a principle with us to grow rich by taking from each other's pockets, or in any way except productive labor.[40]

Whether the document was genuine or someone's attempt at tongue-in-cheek humor is not known, although Joseph H. Ingraham, a New Englander who settled in the South, wrote that during the 1830s and 1840s, gamblers on the Mississippi were organized "with local agents in every town, and travelling agents on board the principal steamboats. In the guise of gentlemen, they 'take in' the unwary passenger and unskillful player, from whom they often obtain large sums of money. As the same sportsmen do not go twice in the same boat, the captains do not become so familiar with their persons as to refuse them passage."[41]

Steamboats traveling up the Missouri River from St. Louis were also frequented by professional gamblers, but apparently not to the extent of those
on the Mississippi. Fewer steamboats plied the Missouri, and many of them
carried freight and few passengers. When Francis Parkman, a Boston native,
came west in the spring of 1846, he took a steamboat from Saint Louis up the
Missouri to Independence—then the eastern terminal of the Santa Fe
Trail—and booked passage on the steamboat *Radnor.* On April 29 he wrote
in his journal: "On board the boat are a party of Baltimoreans—flash genteel—very showily attired in 'genteel undress,' though bound for California. They make a great noise at the table, and are waited on by the Negroes
with great attention and admiration. Also a vulgar New Yorker, with the
moustache and the air of a Frenchman, bound for Santa Fe." On April 31:
"The wretched Caw [Kansas] Indians on board were hired, for a pint of
whiskey, to sing. One indulged in a little fooling with a fat Negro, who
danced while the Indian sang." And on May 1, 1846, Parkman observed:
"The Indians are playing cards about the deck. They have a paper for beg-
ging, and one of them sat on the deck collecting contributions yesterday."[42]

When Parkman's steamboat reached Independence (near what is now
Kansas City, Missouri), he found a busy frontier settlement where most merchants sold outfits and supplies to emigrants and to Santa Fe traders and
freighters. There were taverns, brothels, and other places where one could
seek pleasure. Parkman booked a room at the Noland House, then the
largest hotel in Missouri (outside St. Louis), and the westernmost hotel in
the United States. Run by Smallwood Noland, who was called "Uncle
Wood" by his friends, the hotel had a well-known tavern where frontiersmen, traders, eastern businessmen, and anyone else might go for a drink and
conversation. It was considered one of the last outposts of civilized fellow-
ship on what was then the American frontier.

For emigrants about to push westward from the great bend of the Missouri, the "civilized" pleasures of the Noland House at its tavern in Independence, like those found aboard steamboats on the Mississippi and
Missouri, would become scarce and almost nonexistent as they began their
travel overland.

CHAPTER V

With the
Emigrants

A happy life consists in tranquillity of mind.
　　　　　　　　　　　—*Marcus Tullius Cicero*

FINDING PLEASURE was not easy for those who set out overland
during the last century to reach Oregon, Utah, or California.
Every emigrant experienced hardships traveling westward across
the prairies, plains, and mountains, and there were those who died trying to
reach their promised land. Although their diaries, narratives, and recollections attest to struggles to survive, they also describe how many of the emigrants found leisure time and some pleasure on their journeys.

The principal route followed by the emigrants was the Oregon Trail,
later called the Oregon-California Trail. Once they left the jumping-off
towns along the Missouri River, their daily travel of ten to fifteen miles a
day—sometimes less—evolved into a routine. Before dawn they would eat
breakfast, pack their wagons, yoke the oxen or harness the horses, and start
on their way. Each company elected a wagonmaster or captain, who provided some semblance of order by determining, among other things, which
wagon would lead the way. Some companies hired a pilot, someone who had
traveled the trail before. The lead wagons were usually rotated day to day to
give each wagon a chance to avoid the dust kicked up by those that followed.
In much of what is now eastern Kansas and Nebraska, the wagons usually
had to move single file. The trail and terrain provided little extra room, and
those emigrants in (or even walking next to) wagons toward the rear ate a lot
of dust, but on the open prairie and plains, it was not uncommon for two or
more columns to travel together.

As the emigrants established daily routines, many sought simple pleasures. Catherine Margaret Haun, who traveled to California in 1849, was

one. She remembered fondly that during the day, "we womenfolk visited from wagon to wagon or congenial friends spent an hour walking, ever westward, and talking over our home life back in 'the states'; telling of the loved ones left behind; voicing our hopes for the future in the far west and even whispering a little friendly gossip of emigrant life. High teas were not popular but tatting, knitting, crocheting, exchanging receipts for cooking beans or dried apples or swapping food for the sake of variety kept us in practice of feminine occupations and diversions."[1]

Late in the morning the company would stop for the customary midday rest, or "nooning," as it was called. The oxen were unhitched but not unyoked, and permitted to graze along with the horses. While the women prepared the noon meal, called dinner, the men might do chores or simply rest and talk. The midday stop was a favorite time of day for relaxing. One emigrant remembered how her husband would provide shade for her on the open prairie by spreading a saddle blanket upon some sticks placed in the ground. Underneath he made "a rude sofa from saddles, fishamores [oilskin raincoats] and other blankets."[2] Some folks might take a short nap, which oftentimes lasted two or three hours during the heat of the day. After the dishes and pots and pans used for the noon meal were cleaned up, the men would commonly gather in groups and talk among themselves while the women did the same. The children would often play together, and if the company had stopped next to a river or creek, some of the older children and men might go fishing.

In 1850, while one company was camped by Deer Creek in what is now southeastern Wyoming, several emigrants, including George Keller, a physician from Wayne County, Ohio, converted a wagon cover into a fishnet and waded into the creek, which was about thirty feet wide, two feet deep, and had a rapid current. They caught nothing but a cold bath. Later, when Keller and his party nooned on Ham's Fork of the Green River, they found the river too high to ford, and remained in camp and fished and hunted in the vicinity. As Keller wrote, the party "got up a supper." Their evening meal consisted of speckled trout, wild goose, wild duck, dumplings, flapjacks, hard bread, stewed fruit, and coffee. However, such pleasant meals were not everyday affairs for Keller's or other emigrant companies. In late June 1850, when Keller and his party were camped on a grassy meadow near a small stream, he wrote in his diary:

A. Clark, M. Hoover, and ourself were cooking for ourselves and eleven others belonging to the mess. Our stock of provisions, consisted of a lot of musty tea, a few pounds of flour and a few dried elder berries. Hoover made the tea, while Clark and I made the soup and dumplings,—the preparations of the latter articles, being by experimental philosophy, deemed the most economical method of disposing of flour. A handful of berries were put into two camp kettles holding about six gallons of water.—These gave color and consistency to the soup. A small quantity of flour was then made into a stiff batter. This was carefully divided by a spoon into a certain number of pieces, corresponding to the number of individuals in the mess. The result of this ceremony was always announced in order that each one might learn, the amount of his share. I suppose any one might have eaten the entire amount, of course excluding a portion of the six gallons of tasteless soup. Next day, forenoon, travelled two miles, and dined on musty tea alone.[3]

After enjoying what pleasures they could while nooning, most companies would resume travel in the early afternoon, often with a certain distant landmark already decided upon as the evening's camping site. When the first wagons reached the spot, the prime order of business was to corral the wagons—a task presided over by the wagonmaster. The lead wagon stopped at a designated spot, and the other wagons moved into place creating either a circular or elliptical ring of wagons to provide security from Indians, wild animals, and other unwanted guests. The oxen were then unyoked and permitted to graze, as were the horses, and it was not uncommon for the men to take the tongue of each wagon and chain it to the rear wheel of the wagon in front, thereby forming something that resembled a fence between each wagon. The men might leave one or more openings between wagons so that livestock could be moved inside when necessary. Occasionally, if the wagon train was in a peaceful area where no dangers were thought to exist, the wagons might be drawn into a U formation.

Once the wagons were corralled, everyone looked forward to the pleasures they had found on previous evenings around their campfires. Those fires were built with what wood the company carried or could gather around their campsite, but on the open prairies and plains, timber was often scarce. Along the South Platte many emigrants searched for driftwood deposited by the previous year's flood, caused by the mountain snow runoff. In buffalo country it was a common practice to use dried buffalo chips, which resembled rotten wood, to fuel the campfire. When dry the chips made a clear and hot fire, but they burned rapidly, which meant a good supply was needed for each fire. When first exposed to them, the women found them repugnant, but they soon became accustomed and finally came to appreciate them. Wet buffalo chips, however, did not burn, as George Keller found out while camped along the south bank of the Platte River in what is now western Nebraska. Snow began to fall soon after his party made camp. "There was not a vestige of anything resembling fuel, except the buffalo chips, which were so wetted by the melting snow as not to be in very good burning order. A gallon or two of 'cognac,' when applied internally, had the effect of lulling the sensibilities of a number of the company and bringing on a state of happy forgetfulness. But those who drank none felt much better next morning. This example would go far, towards establishing the position, that water is calculated to answer in all kinds of weather."[4]

Most emigrants carried matches in sealed containers purchased at the start of their journey. After several weeks on the trail, matches became highly prized, carefully rationed items. It was not uncommon for an emi-

This nineteenth-century wood engraving depicts two men identified as wagon train captains taking a break on the trail. (Author's collection)

A nineteenth-century illustration of emigrants in camp somewhere in the West, cooking an evening meal around a campfire. The illustration is titled "Night-School of Theology." (Author's collection)

grant to save matches by lighting a stick from a neighbor's fire to start his own, and then the next night use his matches to start a fire and let the neighbor borrow some flame. If emigrants did not have a camp stove, they would usually dig a shallow slit trench two or three feet long, in line with prevailing winds and just wide enough to accommodate a camp kettle. Once the fire was burning well, the women prepared the evening meal, called supper. The basic kitchenware was a cooking kettle, frying pan, coffeepot, tin plates, cups, knives, and forks. Although some diaries and recollections left by emigrants tell of occasional feasts, most evening suppers were usually rather as plain as the midday dinners. Emigrants were advised to take along 200 pounds of flour, 10 pounds of coffee, 150 pounds of bacon, 20 pounds of sugar, and 10 pounds of salt. Other items that were carried included chipped beef, rice, tea, dried beans, dried fruit, saleratus (baking soda), vinegar, cheese, cream of tartar, pickles, ginger, and mustard. The staples of the emigrant's diet, however, were bread, bacon, and coffee. Although every woman knew how to bake bread, it was difficult to knead the dough and bake the bread in Dutch ovens or reflector ovens on the prairies and plains.

So the women came up with a substitute, using cornmeal if they carried no sea biscuits, or hardtack. It was usually quite an event when the women baked pies, using raisins, dried apples, or peaches. There are a few accounts of emigrants bringing along eggs packed in barrels of flour or meal. And some resourceful settlers even took along milk cows to supply milk and butter, and a few chickens to provide eggs. The chickens usually ended up in the cookpot before the emigrants reached their destination, and the milk cows often died after the emigrants reached the alkali regions of what is now Wyoming. The cows then provided meat for the emigrants. The foodstuffs brought along by the emigrants were, of course, sometimes supplemented by wild game—deer and buffalo.

After supper the dishes and pots were washed and put away, and then the emigrants went to bed. A few brought beds, but most soon discarded them. Many slept on mattresses or simply rolled up in blankets for the night. When Margaret A. Frink and her husband set out for California in 1850, they carried an India-rubber mattress that could be filled with either air or water. This is one of the earliest accounts of the modern waterbed, but Mrs. Frink noted in her diary that they usually used air to fill the mattress so that they could empty it out during the day and fold the mattress to provide more room in their wagon.[5] Margaret Haun remembered:

> We did not keep late hours but when not too engrossed with fear of the red enemy or dread of impending danger we enjoyed the hour around the campfire. The menfolk lolling and smoking their pipes and guessing, or maybe betting, how many miles we had covered during the day. We listened to readings, story-telling, music and songs and the day often ended in laughter and merrymaking.[6]

Marian Russell was about seven years old when she traversed the Santa Fe Trail with her mother and brother. They joined a wagon train at Fort Leavenworth, bound for Santa Fe. She recalled:

> Between the two night circles formed by the wagons was a bit of no-man's land which the children used as a playground. The ball games that went on there! The games of leap-frog and dare base. One night I lingered long alone in little no-man's land to gather a species of white poppy that bloomed only at night. To me those prairie poppies were a fascination, blooming only when the evening shadows fell. So I lingered long in no-man's land filling my arms with their white fragrance.

Above me glowed the lights of Captain Aubry's train. I saw how when the lanterns were lighted inside the tents, they turned the tents into Japanese lanterns. The night wind brought to me the sound of voices and laughter. Then I saw little mother standing outside the big lighted circle. She called to me, "Mar-re-an," and there was an anxious note in her voice.[7]

Jesse Applegate, who headed for Oregon in 1843, remembered evening camp life along the trail. He wrote:

Before a tent near the river a violin makes lively music, and some youths and maidens have improvised a dance upon the green; in another quarter a flute gives its mellow and melancholy notes to the still air, which as they float away over the quiet river seem a lament for the past rather than a hope for the future. . . . But time passes; the watch is set up for the night, the council of old men has broken up and each has returned to his own quarter. The flute has whispered its last lament to the deepening night, the violin is silent and the dancers have dispersed. Enamored youths have whispered a tender "good night" in the ears of blushing maidens, or stolen a kiss from the lips of some future bride—for Cupid here as elsewhere has been busy bringing together congenial hearts and among those simple people he alone is consulted in forming the marriage tie.[8]

It was not uncommon for some companies to remain in camp on Sundays to rest and observe the Sabbath. Many emigrants had been regular churchgoers at home, and they tried to continue their religious observances on the trail. Whether a company observed the Sabbath depended on the religious beliefs of those who made it up and was determined by a vote, usually at the start of the journey. When a group voted to "keep the Sabbath," it meant remaining in camp each Sunday and devoting the day to prayers, sermons, and meditations and restricting all other activities to a minimum.

OCCASIONALLY A WEDDING provided emigrants with a reason to remain in camp more than one night. The story of one couple is perhaps typical of those young people who met and fell in love while traveling west. Isaac Decker, of Viraqua, Bodox County, Wisconsin, who left home on April 20, 1853, was bound for California. At about the same time a family named Pond left Beetown, Grant County, Wisconsin, for the same destination. The Ponds had a daughter, Lavina. Although their two wagons reached Council Bluffs, Iowa, independently of each other, they joined the same train, after which Isaac and Lavina met and became close friends. During the midday halt and in camp at night, Isaac and Lavina were frequently seen strolling, talking, and laughing together. Many weeks later, when the wagon train reached Goose Creek in what is now Wyoming, the two announced their intention to marry. The wagon train stopped for two days to prepare for the wedding. The wedding day, August 4, 1853, dawned clear and bright, with a gentle breeze that filled the campsite with the pleasant fragrance of wild-flowers growing nearby. More than two hundred persons, many from other wagon trains camped in the vicinity, greeted the bride, who wore a dark brown dress and a figured nun's veiling. Her hair was combed over her head in coquettish curls. On the bank of the creek, beneath a canopy of willows and wild grapevines, J. M. Robinson, a justice of the peace, pronounced them man and wife. Everyone then congratulated the couple, with many gentlemen from the wagon train seeking the privilege of kissing the bride while an almost equal number of ladies kissed the groom. Nearby some old, greasy wagon sheets had been spread out on the ground for tablecloths. There the wedding dinner was served to everyone in the couple's wagon train. It consisted of bread, beans, roast duck, cake, and custard pie. Some boys had found a duck's nest with fourteen eggs, and killed the duck, and some of the cows provided the milk used to make the custard pies. A dance was held following the dinner, and everyone had a good time until the early morning hours. The next day six Indians came into the camp. Some of the men, including Isaac, fearing trouble, grabbed their guns, but the Indian leader, apparently a chief, soon dispelled their fears. He said he had come to congratulate them on their big "war dance" the night before. It seems that Indians for miles around had heard the music and celebration and thought it was a war dance, which had apparently caused them some concern. As for Mr. and Mrs. Isaac Decker, they eventually settled in Vaca Valley, California.[9]

For G. W. Thissell, who started for California from Iowa, the most pleas-ant part of his journey across the plains was around the evening campfire. When supper was over, as Thissell wrote in his diary, everyone would gather around the fire and relate the scenes of the day and spin long yarns. Some played the violin, others the accordion. A few would play cards, while the young men would sing their favorite California songs. One of the popular songs was "Oh! Susanna," and Thissell recorded the words:

It rained all night, the day I left,
The weather, it was dry.
The sun so hot, I froze to death,
Susanna, don't you cry.

Chorus:—
O Susanna,
Don't you cry for me,
I'm going to California,
Some gold dust for to see.

I had a dream the other night,
When everything was still;
I dreamed I saw Susanna, dear,
A-coming down the hill.

Chorus:—

The buckwheat cake was in her mouth,
The tear stood in her eye,
And all that I could say to her
Was, Susanna don't you cry.

Chorus.[10]

"Oh! Susanna," also known as "Lou'siana Belle," was written by Stephen Foster in Cincinnati about 1847. It quickly became popular in the East, and was brought west by the emigrants. Other popular songs of the day carried over the Oregon Trail include Daniel Decatur Emmett's "Old Dan Tucker" (1843), "My Old Aunt Sally" (1843), "The Blue-Tail Fly" (also known as "Jimmy Crack Corn") (1846), John Hodges's "Lubly Fan" (1844), changed in the West to "Buffalo Gals" ("Won't you come out tonight?"), and other popular songs like "Seein' the Elephant" (1849) and "Sweet Betsy from Pike" (1849). By the early 1850s, Stephen Foster's "Old Folks at Home" (often called "Swanee River") and M. A. Richer's "The California Pioneers" were being sung by emigrants along with such popular folk songs as "Skip to My Lou," "Swing on the Corner," "Old Joe Clark," and "Sourwood Mountains," natural fiddle tunes that had been enjoyed by Americans for decades and were still being played around the emigrants' evening campfires. Many of these songs, especially those by Foster and Emmett, had become popular in the settled areas the emigrants came from because of traveling minstrel shows that showcased the songs, beginning in the middle 1840s.[11]

When wagon trains camped near one another, members of the different companies often visited and sometimes shared meals, especially when two or more trains decided to stop for a day of rest and recuperation. Diaries and recollections suggest that most of the travelers were gregarious and needed no excuse to stop, chat, and make new friends. It was not uncommon for the women to exchange recipes or, as Charlotte Pengra reported in 1853, after another woman she met on the trail admired her sunbonnet in passing, a sun-bonnet pattern.[12]

When Joel Palmer traveled from Missouri to Oregon in the spring and summer of 1845, his company remained in camp on June 15, after a herd of buffalo was sighted nearby early in the morning. Some of the men went buffalo hunting and returned to camp about noon with much buffalo meat. The scene that followed is described in Palmer's own words:

We then commenced jerking it [the buffalo meat]. This is a process resorted to for want of time or means to cure meat by salting. The meat is sliced thin, and a scaffold prepared, by setting forks in the ground, about three feet high, and laying small poles or sticks crosswise upon them. The meat is laid upon those pieces, and a slow fire built beneath; the heat and smoke completes the process in half a day; and with an occasional sunning the meat will keep for months. An unoccupied spectator, who could have beheld our camp to-day, would think it a singular spectacle. The hunters returning with the spoil; some erecting scaffolds, and others drying the meat. Of the women, some were washing, some ironing, some baking. At two of the tents the fiddle was employed in uttering its unaccustomed voice among the solitudes of the Platte; at one tent I heard singing; at others the occupants were engaged in reading, some the Bible, others poring over novels. While all this was going on, that nothing might be wanting to complete the harmony of the scene, a Campbellite preacher, named Foster, was reading a hymn, preparatory to religious worship. The fiddles were silenced, and those who had been occupied with that amusement, betook themselves to cards. Such is but a miniature of the great world we had left behind us, when we crossed the line that separates civilized man from the wilderness. But even here the variety of occupation, the active exercise of body and mind, either in labor or pleasure, the commingling of evil and good, show that the likeness is a true one.[13]

When the first emigrants headed for Oregon during the 1830s, traveling as far as the Rocky Mountains with fur traders, they had to rely on trading posts designed to serve the mountain men. The men who ran these posts usually charged very high prices and had a limited supply of goods, but almost always sold whiskey and offered gambling. Many emigrants tried to avoid these establishments. The first trading post established to capture emigrant trade was Fort Bridger, located in a valley below the snowcapped Uinta Mountains on Black's Fork of the Green River in what is now southwestern Wyoming. Established during the summer of 1843 by Jim Bridger of mountain-man fame, it not only offered a small stock of supplies including whiskey for the emigrants, but it also had a blacksmith shop where wagons could be repaired.

After the discovery of gold in California in 1848, the federal government moved to protect emigrants traveling the Oregon Trail. It established Fort Kearny on the south bank of the Platte River in what is now south-central Nebraska. The trails from the Missouri River towns converged on the site where frame buildings and two earthen fortifications were constructed on four acres of land. Less than a year later, and about 325 miles to the west of Fort Kearny, the government purchased what had been a fur-trading post called Fort William, named for William Sublette, one of two fur traders who established the post in 1843. Located at the junction of the Laramie and North Platte Rivers in what is now southeastern Wyoming, the post was renamed Fort Laramie after the government bought it. Both forts became stopping points for emigrants, who found the surroundings strong reminders of civilized life in the east. The emigrants might purchase supplies from the forts' sutlers or the post quartermaster, receive letters, learn the latest news, sit in chairs, or write letters to friends and family, to be mailed at the forts' post offices.

One emigrant who arrived at Fort Kearny on May 31, 1850, was Madison Berryman Moorman, a twenty-six-year-old cotton broker from Nashville, Tennessee. His company took a full day to unload and repack their belongings. In his journal, which reflects his Southern views toward gracious living, Moorman wrote that he and his party then prepared a "fine dinner" to honor one of the officers at Fort Kearny from Tennessee. "He spent several hours with us after dinner in unrestrained and social conversation, during which a glass of the best quality of old *cognac* was handed around (which was done before dinner, also) and . . . [everyone wore] the best Regalia which had been brought along by our company." A few days after leaving Fort Kearny, Moorman noted in his diary, "We nooned . . . upon the banks of the river, where we rested several hours and had quite a luxury for the *plains*—lemonade." Heading westward toward Fort Laramie, Moorman specially noted in his diary those times when he and his party enjoyed good meals. On June 30, camped a few miles east of Independence Rock, beside the Sweetwater River, many miles northwest of Fort Laramie, Moorman wrote, "We had, in my mess, ham, bread made of flour, by ourselves, (we having had nothing but hard bread for a long time!) in the ordinary way, besides a Yankee dish called dough-nuts fried and well-sweetened—rice & coffee—altogether the best dinner—one that I most relished of any I had had since leaving Fort Kearny."[14]

During the early years of overland travel emigrants devised a simple means of communicating along the trail. If someone wished to leave a message for someone following in another wagon train, he or she would write a short note and place it in a conspicuous place next to the trail. It was not uncommon for the message writer to leave the note in the notched end of a stick stuck into the ground with strips of old cloth tied to it. When paper was not available, the message might be written on wood, rocks, or animal bones, including buffalo skulls. There is at least one account of someone writing a message on a human skull. The emigrants usually were careful not to disturb these messages. One emigrant, George Currey, called them "Bone Express" messages.[15] Looking for messages along the trail helped emigrants to pass the time as their wagons crawled westward.

Although emigrants might indulge in a strictly friendly game of cards while nooning or after supper in camp, gambling along the Oregon Trail was pretty much limited to the trading posts that began appearing along the trail after the discovery of gold in California. Trappers camped on the Green River engaged in stock-trading (to their benefit) and gambling, and during the early 1850s there was probably more gambling at the Green River ferry than at any other point along the trail. Gamblers sought to relieve of their gold not only the emigrants heading west but those who had struck it rich in California's goldfields and were returning east. Emigrant George Belshaw, heading for California, described in his diary what he saw on July 13, 1852: "At the ferry is a set of Gamblers they play cards most of the time at 10 & 20 Dollars a game they take in pockets full of gold from the Emigrants they don't value gold any more than you do so much grain, just kick it around anywhere." A week and a half later the accomplished resident gamblers won three thousand dollars from a drunk.[16]

The gambling, drinking, and decadent living of the trappers on the Green River shocked the more moralistic among the emigrants, as many noted in their diaries. Bernard Reid wrote that he witnessed the game of monte being played in the lodge of one trapper, and John Edwin Banks observed that he never saw gambling equal to what he saw in the Indian-style tent of another. Banks went on to write: "I never despised human nature as I now do. I see many having no claim to humanity but form." Niles Searls, another emigrant who witnessed the gambling in the Green River area, wrote: "Every few days we come across a canvas lodge occupied by some Canadian Frenchman who dignifies his establishment by the name of a trading post, though the title of 'Gambling Hell' would convey a more correct idea of its uses." Searls described the man as "destitute of character." P. C. Tiffany, another emigrant, had much the same reaction when he witnessed the gambling. He wrote that the men who ran the gambling were "not half as honourable as the Indians."

Certainly there were emigrants who did gamble; but overall, diaries, recollections, and early documents suggest that most emigrants did not, and especially not men traveling with their families. They ignored the calls for a "friendly" game and studiously avoided gambling establishments.[17]

Such sinful activities did, of course, provide a subject for conversation among many emigrants, as did the weather, food, birthdays, clothing, and the unusual people encountered on the trail. In one case, members of G. W. Thissell's company, which left Council Bluffs, Iowa, in 1853, soon realized that the young wife of emigrant Jake Fouts was different. Fouts, his wife, and his parents, all from Bellefontaine, Iowa, were bound for California. After a few days on the trail the other women in the train began to avoid Mrs. Fouts. As Thissell later wrote: "She was constantly quarreling with someone, and when not successful in finding a victim to quarrel with, she always had her husband to fall back on, and she did, and then she would make it lively for him." When the wagon train reached Indian country (in what is now central Nebraska) and she saw her first Indians, she became hysterical. "At first we all thought the woman was dying (and some wished she had died). About twice a week she had one of these hysterical fits. Sometimes while walking along the road she would throw up her arms and scream, then down in the road she would go; three or four men would pick her up and dump her into the wagon, where she would lay for two or three hours. After she recovered, she was ready for a fight with the first one who would quarrel with her. During the trip she tried several times to shoot her father-in-law. . . . Thus she kept things lively. On Carson River we met some traders. She took a fancy to one of them. Fouts saw his opportunity, and sold her to the trader for three hundred dollars. It was a day of rejoicing when we saw her leave the train. The trader took her to Hangtown [Placerville, California] and gave her to a gambler, and that was the last we heard of her."[18]

After the Mormons settled in the valley of the Great Salt Lake in 1847 and Salt Lake City was founded, the settlement became a midway stopping point for emigrants, especially those traveling to California during the gold rush. Initially the Mormons had had something of a monopoly on emigrant trade, but after gold was discovered, eastern entrepreneurs began to arrive and set up stores in Salt Lake City to sell goods, supplies, and merchandise to emigrants. Diaries and recollections suggest that many emigrants spent about a week in Salt Lake City before resuming their journey to California, and the settlement not only offered the opportunity to obtain fresh supplies and wagon repairs, but the chance to experience town life, absorb a little religion, and seek some pleasure.

When Madison Moorman and his wagon train of emigrants reached Salt Lake City on July 20, 1850, members of the company were "parcelled out at different houses—private families—there being no such thing as Hotels—to board for a day or two, that we might be relieved from the unpleasant task of cooking, and enjoy the luxuries which this fertile valley produces in such profuse abundance." Moorman's host was a New England couple named Burr.

"They treated us with great civility, and when the supper table was announced as being ready, abundantly furnished with *bacon, beans—peas—coffee—milk—butter—cheese—preserves!* and *hot loaves,* as light as cork, made of new wheat—placed upon a snowy white cloth, the tableware of the plain yet neat delf [*sic*] and good, comfortable chairs to sit in—confirmed me in all the favorable notions I had conceived of them and that I was at the place to live well. After supper, we sat a short time and asked a good many questions relative to the Mormon customs, etc. We bade them good night and returned to where our mules were, and had a fine night's sleep upon a bunk of hay," wrote Moorman.[19]

The following day Moorman and others in his party were invited to Mormon services at their "capacious Bowery," their temple having not yet been finished. The bowery was crowded, and on an elevated stage sat seventy-two elders and Brigham Young. "Singing had commenced before I arrived, and after I got there several tunes, that made me think of bygone days, were sung in good style by the choir composed solely of the dignitaries. . . . When they struck up 'Old Hundred,' 'Coronation,' and 'Sweet home'—vocal and instrumental, a thrill ran through every nerve," wrote Moorman in his diary. When it came time for Brigham Young's sermon— the subject was "The Redemption of Man"—Moorman noted in his diary that Young's remarks were "protracted and disconnected, seldom touching upon his subject. His style was affected—weak and unchaste." Moorman further described Young's manner as "pompous and consequential." Moorman noted that a minister traveling with his party was invited to conclude the services with singing and prayer.[20]

By 1858 Salt Lake City had two hotels and one or more saloons. T. S. Kenderdine, who followed the Oregon Trail to Salt Lake City in 1858 in a wagon train carrying freight, remembered that the saloons served "poisonous concoctions, bearing the names of 'Pure Old Whisky,' 'Prime French Brandy,' 'Superior Port Wine,' etc." Kenderdine said drinks were

> offered to a thirsty public at the rate of two bits [twenty-five cents] a drink, the drinkers little dreaming that they were gulping down a perfect catalog of poisonous drugs at each potation. Each of these establishments had its gambling hell, where newly arrived greenhorns were scientifically fleeced by experienced blacklegs [gamblers], who had flocked here from all parts of the Union in anticipation of a windfall. I visited one of them one evening. Ascending a dark stairway in the rear of the building, I entered a low room densely packed with humanity, and reeking with the fumes of tobacco and bad whisky. The players were seated at their tables and busily engaged in solving the mysteries of *monte,* a game peculiar to Mexico and California, but now introduced into the Mormon Zion by its accomplished and unscrupulous votaries. It was a sad sight, to see the self-satisfied composure with which the blackleg drew in his fraudulently obtained gold; while the plucked victim would utter curses loud and deep at his luck, but would again, lured on by the infernal spirit of gambling, venture another stake, which would be certain to follow in the wake of its predecessors to the coffers of the scientific "dealer." It was odd to see what little value money possessed here, where double-eagles were tossed about like coppers by the excited gamesters. The gambling tables were surrounded by eager lookers-on, who seemed almost as much absorbed in the game as the players themselves, and did one of the latter become tired or "broke," there were numbers ready to take his place. Having staid until my curiosity was fully satisfied, I retired from this aboveground Pandemonium, and wending my way to my lodging-house, I moralized, as I trod the gloomy streets, on the frailties of poor human nature.[21]

After resting in Salt Lake City and perhaps partaking of more genteel pleasures, the refreshed emigrants would continue their journeys toward

California by going north and northwest around the east side of the Great
Salt Lake, hitting the trail that ran southwest from Fort Hall in present-day
Idaho, and then crossing what is now Nevada following the Humboldt River,
aiming toward one of three routes over the Sierra Nevada Mountains to the
goldfields or wherever they were going in California. For many emigrants
this last leg was the most difficult part of their journey. Even then, however,
many still found daily pleasures in such simple things as a good meal, new
friends, relaxing around a campfire, singing or playing games, reading, or
playing with a dog or a cat if they had brought along the family pets.

THERE IS NO question that pets brought pleasure to some travelers, especially those with children. One family took the family dog and cat along on
their journey to California. The animals belonged to James Philly and his
wife and three children, two boys and one girl, whose story captures the
hardships, sorrows, and joys experienced by many emigrants. On April 2,
1850, as they prepared to leave the town of West Point in Cass County, Missouri, the wagon was loaded. Mrs. Philly climbed into the seat. One of the
little boys, George, also climbed in, while Phillip, the other son, stood cling-
ing to old Bose, the family dog. The family had decided to take the dog with
them. As May, the Phillys' five-year-old daughter, was being lifted into the
wagon, she burst into tears. When asked what was wrong, the little girl said
she wanted to take Jip, the family cat. No words or promises could quiet her,
and at last the father relented. Jip was handed to May and the family began
its journey.

When they reached St. Joseph, Missouri, they joined a large wagon train
and on April 25 crossed the Missouri River. James Philly had been a prominent tobacco grower in Missouri, and knowing well that the average tobacco
chewer would rather go without his bread than his tobacco, he loaded a
wagon with it, for which he paid twenty cents per pound. Long before he
reached Fort Laramie, only five hundred miles from the Missouri River, he
was selling tobacco at a dollar per pound. Philly gave some to a few Indians,
and word soon spread among other Indians as the wagon train pushed westward. In exchange for tobacco the Indians left the wagon train alone. When
the group reached Salt Lake City, Philly sold what tobacco he had left for
five dollars a pound.

Before the family reached the headwaters of the Humboldt, many cattle
had died, and others were so poor and weak they gave out and were left by
the roadside. The train was reduced almost to starvation. The child May was

nothing but skin and bones, so weak and frail she could not eat the coarse food. One morning James Philly found a freshly killed rabbit at the door of their tent. They dressed and cooked it, and, oh, how May did relish that rabbit! How it came there none knew, but, strange to say, the next morning there was another rabbit at the tent door. For the next two weeks, while traveling down the Humboldt, almost every morning there was a rabbit at the tent door. All knew now that the faithful cat, Jip, had brought them there, for the willows along the riverbank were full of them. When they reached Ragtown on Carson River, a trader offered a hundred dollars for the cat, but James Philly would not sell Jip.

Tragedy struck the family twenty miles from Ragtown in what is now western Nevada. Young George Philly suddenly fell ill and died. The child's body was wrapped in his blanket and laid in a narrow grave beneath a large pine tree. Two large stakes were driven into the ground, and on the grave were piled huge rocks and stones. A sorrowing family continued on their journey to California, but the next morning the family dog could not be found. On a hunch, James Philly went back to the campsite near George Philly's grave. There he found the faithful Bose, but the animal was seriously injured. As best Philly could determine, the dog had gone back to the grave during the night, surprised a pack of wolves trying to dig it up, and been attacked as he tried to drive the wolves away. The dog's wounds were treated, and he was carried into the wagon, cared for, and soon recovered. Bose lived to be an old dog, and Jip the cat also had a long life at Dutch Flat, in Placer County, California, where the Philly family settled.[22]

The pets carried by other emigrants undoubtedly provided pleasure, too, as did the magnificent western scenery, though most emigrants who kept diaries apparently failed to find adequate words to describe the latter. Some women did make note of seeing beautiful wildflowers, whose seeds they often mailed home or carried to their destination. Nearly all diaries and narratives left by emigrants ignore very personal pleasures. One exception was left by John Lewis, an emigrant who found that sexual intercourse took on a new dimension in the West. Lewis wrote: "Love is hotter her[e] than anywhare that I have seen when they love here they love with all thare mite & some times a little harder."[23]

CHAPTER VI

Among the
🔫 Soldiers

Pleasure's a sin, and sometimes sin's a pleasure.
—*George Gordon, Lord Byron*

THE FIRST U.S. ARMY soldiers sent into the West during the 1820s were in many ways similar to the first emigrants who later set out for Oregon. Most of them were new to the region, unfamiliar with life on the prairies, plains, or mountains that lacked the lush vegetation and undergrowth of mountains in the East. By the nature of their responsibilities and regimented lifestyle, these early soldiers led a rather monotonous existence, devoid of most personal comforts and many simple pleasures enjoyed by emigrants. Like the emigrants, the soldiers learned to adjust, but unlike them, the first soldiers sent west in 1829 from Fort Leavenworth had to *walk* across much of what is now Kansas to the Arkansas River, then the U.S. border with Mexico, to escort traders bound for Santa Fe. Since there were no mounted units in the U.S. Army, the Sixth Infantry was assigned escort duty.

Unfortunately military records tell us little of how these first soldiers in the West found pleasure, but from bits and pieces of information contained in diaries and letters it is obvious that many soldiers *did* find some. When a detachment of Mexican cavalry escorted the traders to the U.S. border many weeks later, the American soldiers, who had been in camp awaiting their return, put on a feast for the Mexicans. Philip St. George Cooke, then a young lieutenant, was there and later wrote:

> Seated cross-legged around a green blanket in the bottom of the tent, we partook of bread, buffalo meat, and as an extraordinary rarity, of some salt pork, but to crown all were large onions for which we were indebted to our arriving guests. A tin cup of whiskey which like the pork was for an unusual occasion was followed by another of water.[1]

The following day the Mexican soldiers put on a feast for the Americans, who were impressed by the many different kinds of wine that were served. The soldiers of the Sixth Infantry escorted the traders back to the Missouri border and then returned to Fort Leavenworth, located on the Missouri River in what is now northeast Kansas. The post had been established in 1827 principally to provide protection for the Santa Fe Trail.

When it became obvious to government officials in Washington, D.C., that mounted soldiers were needed in the West, Congress authorized a six-company battalion of volunteers called Mounted Rangers in the summer of 1832. The following year the horse cavalry became a permanent branch of the U.S. Army. Only then did soldiers patrolling the Santa Fe Trail apparently find life a bit more pleasant. Soldiering, however, did not appeal to most Americans. A private's pay was five dollars a month, which had risen to eight dollars by the time the Mexican War began in May 1846. The salary did not attract quality recruits. Then, too, army discipline was harsh. As a result the army relied heavily on aliens, and by the 1840s not quite half the recruits were immigrants, many of whom could not speak English.

Conditions for officers were a little better. In 1842 a second lieutenant earned forty-two dollars a month. In the spring of that year John Charles Frémont, a lieutenant in the Topographical Corps of the U.S. Army, took a small expedition west to survey the Kansas and Platte Rivers. Frémont enjoyed buffalo hunting both to obtain meat and for the pleasure of the sport, and he and his men often felt the satisfaction that came at the end of a day spent out-of-doors. Their experiences were probably typical of other small military units engaged in exploring areas in the West. For instance, on July 6, 1842, the party stopped at sunset and camped on an island in the Platte River. "We ate our meat with a good relish this evening," wrote Frémont, "for we were all in fine health, and had ridden nearly all of a long summer's day, with a burning sun reflected from the sands." A few days later he and his men came upon the camp of Jean Baptiste Charbonneau, a mountain man and guide. Charbonneau, the son of Toussaint Charbonneau and his Shoshoni Indian wife, Sacagawea, had been born on the Lewis and Clark expedition. He welcomed Frémont and his men to his camp on another island in the Platte. Frémont wrote that Charbonneau sent "one of the people . . . to gather mint, with the aid of which he concocted very good julep; and some boiled buffalo tongue, and coffee with the luxury of sugar, were soon set before us." Continuing westward, Frémont and his party reached South Pass and then moved northwest, exploring the Wind River mountain range before returning east, where they again found buffalo. On August 19, camped on the

Sweetwater River, Frémont and his men enjoyed fresh buffalo meat. They roasted buffalo ribs over an open fire, and they enjoyed, in Frémont's words, "good humor, and laughter and song. . . . Our coffee had been expended, but we now made a kind of tea from the roots of the wild-cherry tree."[2]

On the eve of the Mexican War there were ten frontier military posts in the American West, all of them located along a rough north-south line from Fort Snelling in Minnesota to Fort Jessup in Louisiana. In about the middle was Fort Leavenworth, then the Army's main supply depot for all of the West. It was from there that Colonel Stephen W. Kearny was ordered to take an army and march about eight hundred miles south to conquer New Mexico and then to take California. Kearny and his army of about seventeen hundred men had 1,556 wagons drawn by more than fourteen thousand oxen. In the rush to load supplies at Fort Leavenworth and to start soldiers and wagons toward Santa Fe, some freight wagons were loaded with nothing but tents or cooking utensils or miscellaneous supplies, while other wagons were loaded only with food. For the soldiers traveling with food wagons, nearly every meal was a feast, but there were near-famine conditions for soldiers traveling with wagons not carrying foodstuffs. Still, most of the soldiers were able to overcome the difficulties. The diaries and journals kept by some of them suggest that even some of the soldiers traveling on short rations found pleasure after a long day's march in telling stories, singing, playing cards, smoking a pipe, reading novels, or perhaps just bathing in a creek.[3]

The first elements of Kearny's "Army of the West," as it was called, reached Santa Fe on the Fourth of July. To enable his men to "celebrate as best they might," Kearny permitted them to buy liquor from Hiram Rich, the sutler at Fort Leavenworth, who traveled with the command.[4]

One soldier who went to Santa Fe with Kearny was William Kennerly, then in his twenties. He answered the call in St. Louis and volunteered, becoming an enlisted man in a battalion of light artillery under Major Meriwether Lewis Clark. Each artilleryman furnished his own horse, saddle, uniforms, staples, and everything but arms. Kennerly also took a large knife and a revolver plus two mackinaw blankets on which to sleep. He was fortunate because his unit included an old hunter, Antoine Clement, who knew the West and how to hunt buffalo, keeping the unit supplied with fresh meat. When Kennerly's unit reached New Mexico, he and the others enjoyed the beauty of the mountains as they smoked their pipes and talked and told stories around their campfires under the August stars.

Kearny's army met no resistance when it reached Santa Fe, a town of adobe buildings and about four thousand souls, and the soldiers were put up in public buildings as they occupied the town. Kennerly visited the Plaza and described it as a

> kaleidoscope . . . brilliant serapes of the peons, mingling with our uniforms, vied with the multicolored *rebozos* of the *señoritas* who, sitting on the benches under the *al godón* trees, flashed curious glances from under their mantillas. A few of these charmers responded to the chivalrous approach of the soldiers in this setting where the murmur of fountains merged with the melodious cries of the various vendors, and I soon had a lady upon my arm. I was shortly attracted by a man sitting on a red blanket dealing three-card monte. Recognizing me as a tenderfoot, he continued putting down the cards and singing out in monotonous tones, "No one can put his money on the *cavallo*." [queen card] . . . "Hold on!" I called. "It looks easy to me," and produced a dollar gold piece (to be followed by several others). I put it down, but, when the pasteboard was drawn out, it proved not to be on the *cavallo*. The *señorita* with me seemed horrified to see the good American coin disappear so suddenly. "Ah, *Señor*," she cried, "Had you not bet, you would not have lost your gold!" A profound observation to which there was no argument in any language![5]

Kennerly and other U.S. soldiers in their gold-braided caps and uniforms apparently were quite attractive to the señoritas at the fandangos:

> There we danced as late as the military law allowed with these gay charmers, who kept their red-heeled slippers tapping in perfect time to their castanets. They carried on most of the conversation with their soft, dark eyes; but knowing French, I soon picked up the Spanish language, which I had once studied, and was frequently called upon to interpret for my young companions. Many were the compliments interpolated on my own responsibility that made these gay damsels cast sidelong glances from behind their fans at the innocent ones.[6]

On a hill overlooking Santa Fe, Kearny soon had more than a hundred Mexican laborers and stonemasons helping the soldiers to build a military post called Fort Marcy, named for Captain R. B. Marcy, discoverer of the headwaters of the Canadian River. Kennerly remembered with enjoyment how many soldiers tried to avoid the hard work involved in building the fort, preferring to enjoy the activities in the plaza. Many of them began reporting sick. The officer in charge, convinced the men were shamming, appeared one morning with a black bottle and a large spoon. As the line of soldiers reporting sick lengthened, he gave each man a nauseous dose from the bottle. The number of soldiers on sick call declined rapidly.[7]

When Kearny and his troops started for California in late September 1846, Kennerly's unit was ordered to remain in Santa Fe. Although they drilled almost daily, the soldiers had much leisure time and decided to put on a theatrical performance. "The costumes were made by a tailor in the ranks, a painter furnishing the scenery. The Palace was borrowed for the occasion, the officers taking great interest in the preparations, and on the opening night it was crowded with most of the army and as many of the natives as could be accommodated. The play was 'She Stoops to Conquer' and was followed by a minstrel performance which brought down the house, especially the Mexican contingent, who could understand it better than the play. 'Bravo! Bravo!' they cried, and we had so many requests to repeat our efforts that we had to add several plays to our repertoire. The proceeds were mostly spent on the production, but the surplus was expended on a supper after the play for the general refreshment of the actors," recalled Kennerly.[8]

After Texas joined the Union in 1845, and New Mexico and California were ceded to the United States in 1848, vast new areas opened for settlement. As American settlers moved in, they began to call for increased military protection. By 1849 a dozen military forts were established in Texas, while in New Mexico U.S. soldiers were stationed at Albuquerque, Las Vegas, and Taos in addition to Fort Marcy at Santa Fe. Northward there was Fort Kearny, located on the Oregon-California Trail in modern Nebraska, and Fort Laramie in what is now Wyoming. In California the Spanish presidios at Monterey and San Francisco became U.S. military posts, and in the Far Northwest, Fort Vancouver and Fort Dalles were established on the Columbia River.

For soldiers stationed at the more remote forts, garrison duty was often monotonous. Most soldiers, including Percival G. Lowe, preferred army life in the field to that in garrison. Lowe, a New Englander, enlisted as a soldier at a Boston recruiting office in October 1849. Twenty-one years old, he stood five feet eleven inches high, had a dark complexion, dark brown hair, and gray eyes, and was in good health. Late in life he recalled, "The fact a man would get drunk was no bar to his enlistment, and his moral character was of little interest" to the army of 1849. "Once enlisted, the proper authorities would attend to the rest. Being physically all right, his habits cut little figure. Family trouble, disappointment in love, riots and personal difficulties, making one amenable to the law, often caused men to enlist who proved to be the best soldiers." Lowe was sent to Carlisle Barracks in Pennsylvania, then a school for dragoons and mounted rifles. From there he was sent west to Fort Leavenworth, and in 1851 he and other soldiers were ordered to escort a paymaster to Fort Kearny and to Fort Laramie on the Oregon Trail. Lowe enjoyed the life and recalled that he and others often found pleasure in camp watching another soldier produce sketches of the countryside or listening to some of the men sing. "The infantry had several fair singers, every one could tell a story, and the time passed merrily away from dinner, as soon as practicable after coming into camp, until bed time, soon after dark."[9]

For Lowe, his happiest days as a soldier came after the escort reached Fort Laramie and was ordered to remain there. Lowe and others were sent four miles above Fort Laramie to a camp that had been established on the opposite side of the Laramie River. Lowe wrote that the campsite was lovely,

> green and beautiful as ever—an amphitheater of rugged hills, the pure, clear river with its pebbly bottom running gently by, fringed with willows, orchards of box elders in the bottoms, cedars and pines upon the hills, fragrant flowers on every hand. Any good hunter could bring in a black-tailed deer in a few hours, and the river afforded plenty of fish. All of our party could cook, but McDonald was excellent, Russel made good bread, and O'Meara, well, he was the epicure of the party; the coffee must be browned just so, a certain quantity of ground coffee to a given amount of water; the venison must be seasoned right, whatever that was, and 'twas always good. Everything was clean, tin cups and plates included. We had new forks at every meal; McDonald insisted on that, and O'Meara whittled them out of tough dry willow—straight sharp sticks. We stretched the Major's tent fly for a dining-room, drove down four stakes to lay the endgate of the wagon on, and that was our table; water-buckets and boxes for seats. Russel tore a flour-sack into squares, hemmed them and put one at each man's plate. "Gentlemen," he said, "must use napkins," and he changed them as often as was necessary. Another flour-sack ripped open made a table-cloth. Russel and O'Meara did most of the hunting, and we were seldom without venison. McDonald put out the hooks at night and was almost sure to have nice channel catfish for breakfast. I frequently took down a quarter of venison to the Major. Except reporting to him daily I made it a rule not to be out of sight of camp long at a time. I explored every nook for sev-

Enlisted men at Fort Riley, Kansas, at a drinking party in 1897. (Courtesy Joseph J. Pennell Collection, Kansas Collection, University of Kansas Libraries)

eral miles around and reveled in the pure air, the delicious water and the delightful scenery. We moved a short distance and made a fresh camp every few days for cleanliness and good grass. The Major gave me some papers out of the semi-monthly mail, and we borrowed a few books from G Company.[10]

Many officers, including Colonel Richard Dodge, also preferred life in the field. In 1877 he wrote:

No description of life on the plains can now be given which will be more than a special record of a particular time and place. But a few years ago the journey across the plains was the work of a whole summer. From the time of leaving the Missouri River the party was lost to the world, and lived only in and for itself: no mails, no news, no communication of any kind with civilization . . . each man became a host in himself. To the fascination of a life of perfect freedom from all conventional restraints, of constant adventure, was added that other fascination, far stronger to many natures—the desire to penetrate the unknown.

Enlisted men from Fort Riley, Kansas, swimming near the post in 1897. (Courtesy Joseph J. Pennell Collection, Kansas Collection, University of Kansas Libraries)

Dodge, added, however:

> I confess to being something of a sybarite. I like to have a good tent,
> nice mess-kit, plenty of bedding, and everything to make me comfort-
> able. For six or eight years of his youth a man can manage with a cou-
> ple of blankets for bed, saddle for pillow, hard tack and bacon for
> provender; but after that, these become a little monotonous, and the
> ordinary human longs for something more. Especially in this case in
> the army, where, after some years of hardships, the result many times
> more of bravado than of absolute necessity, one begins to realize that
> this is his life, and that the enjoyment of life is simply the aggregation
> of the enjoyments of each day.[11]

Books provided soldiers with pleasure if other temptations were ignored.
After Percival Lowe returned to Fort Leavenworth in the early 1850s, he
recalled his company commander's decision to establish a library for his unit.
The commander, Major R. H. Chilton, Troop B, First Dragoons,

> had learned the cost of "Harper's Classical and Family Libraries"; a
> pair of book cases, with hinges closing the edges on one side, and two
> locks the edges on the other side, held the library of uniform size and
> binding. When open the title of each book could be read, and when
> closed no book could move or get out of place; the books were all the
> same length and breadth, and an excellent collection. The Major led off
> with a subscription of $25.00. I followed with the same, Peel the same,
> then followed a calculation of what percentage would be due from each
> man in proportion to his pay to make up enough to pay for the whole.
> I took the list with each man's name. The Major spoke to the troop on
> the subject at the retreat roll call, explaining to them the advantages of
> so much good reading matter, and before dismissing the troop I
> requested each man who wanted to subscribe to come to the orderly
> room and sign the list pledging himself to pay the amount opposite his
> name on pay day. Most of the men off duty and at liberty signed
> immediately and the others soon after, and the library was assured with
> scarcely an effort. The Major collected the money at the pay table, and
> the books in their cases came on the first steamboat in February.[12]

Most soldiers, especially the enlisted men, created their own amusements—reading, writing letters, playing cards, horse- and foot-racing, and

The baseball club of Jefferson Barracks (near St. Louis, Missouri), one of the first teams
organized in the U.S. Army, sometime in the 1880s.
(Courtesy Western History Collections, University of Oklahoma Library)

athletic competitions including baseball, a game supposedly invented by Abner Doubleday about 1839. (In fact baseball probably evolved from the English games of cricket and rounders, with the help of American variations. Soldiers undoubtedly brought the game west with them.) In addition, there is at least one account of soldiers enjoying a debate. The debate was recorded by one of the participants, Plympton J. Kelly, who volunteered late in 1855 when George Curry, Washington territorial governor, called in troops to move against hostile Yakima, Walla Walla, and Cayuse Indians, who resented white intrusion on Indian lands. On January 22, 1856, while serving in Company K, Ninth Regiment, Oregon Mounted Volunteers (Rangers), Kelly noted in his diary that "we got up a debate on the question which has done the most to enlighten and civilize the human race, the religion of the Bible or Science."[13]

Independence Day, among other holidays, was usually a special time for organized activities. George A. Armes recalled that on one Fourth of July at Fort Stockton, Texas, the soldiers invited nearby ranchers and cowboys to join them on the post. "My company put up a greased pole, and we had a pig shaved and greased. Got up a wheelbarrow race and sack race, Major excusing his whole command in order that they might enjoy the fun."[14]

Spectators, including Indians, watched this baseball game at Fort Sill, in what is now south-western Oklahoma, in 1892. (Courtesy Western History Collections, University of Oklahoma Libraries)

Many companies held dances for the enlisted men every sixty days or so, and some companies put on minstrel shows and theatricals, but one of the more common forms of pleasure was the practical joke. The diaries, journals, and narratives of nineteenth-century soldiers tell of such amusements. For instance, before army regulations in 1874 forbade the branding and tattooing of deserters, recruits were often initiated into the service by pranks. One First Cavalry soldier painted the raised letters *US* on his army-issue belt buckle with red ink and stamped them on his hip. He then informed new recruits that they would be branded with a hot iron, and to prove it he would drop his trousers and show them his brand. He fooled many recruits.

In another instance some enlisted men at Fort Laramie staged a drumhead court-martial for the benefit of an emigrant found in possession of army horses. Just as the terror-stricken culprit supposed he was about to be hanged, an officer intervened and told him to run for his life, which he did "amidst a volley of balls fired in every other direction but his, and ran for the hills with the speed of a greyhound."[15]

In the field it was not uncommon for a soldier to capture a harmless snake and tuck the reptile into another soldier's sleeping blankets. At other times a snake found its way into a soldier's blankets on its own. Colonel Richard Dodge related one such incident, which occurred along the Nueces River, about twelve miles from Fort Inge in southwest Texas:

> On the long hard trip my friend had abandoned the habit of changing his dress for the night; but, being so near to "white people," he determined to treat himself to a civilized sleep, and to this end arrayed his person in a long night-shirt. He had been asleep some time when he was partially awakened by a cold sensation down his back. Thinking, in his nearly unconscious state, that it was rain, he moved his position and fell asleep. Again he was partially awakened to repeat the process. The third time he was roused more fully. The moon was shining brightly, and he was just wondering where the water could come from, when he felt the cold clammy touch on his back, and a sensation as if a snake was fitting itself against his spine. With a wild yell he sprang to his feet, and rushed from the tent, bursting out the whole front, and was only stopped in his flight by getting his bare feet full of cactus spines. The snake was against the bare skin, and was carried in the folds of the shirt outside the tent, where it fell, and was found and killed by the aroused party. It was a very large "rattler," and appeared stupid, either from cold or fright, and made no attempt at resistance. "Joe" afterwards declared that no money could tempt him again to sleep when in camp in a nightshirt.[16]

The arrival of a paymaster at any post was usually cheered by the soldiers. At distant and isolated posts, however, several months might pass before the troops were paid. While some men saved their pay, many quickly spent their money either in a nearby town or at the sutler's or post trader's store. Sutlers were licensed to travel with specific regiments, but after 1867 roving sutlers were replaced by franchised traders, who set up permanent stores on army posts. These post trader's stores became the center of social activity. Nearly every store had a bar, where at least beer and wine, if not whiskey, were served. The options available to customers depended on the attitude of the post commanding officer. It was here, too, that officers and enlisted men could buy tobacco, soap, combs, and—to find relief from the monotony of army food—canned fruit and meat as well as sugar and other food items.

Many post traders provided a room where the soldiers could play cards and in some instances billiards. At Fort Hays, Kansas, the post trader offered soldiers another kind of entertainment. In 1869 he had come across a buffalo calf whose mother had been killed by hunters. He brought it to the fort and raised it on a bottle. By the time it was two years old, the animal was spoiled rotten. Living just outside the post trader's store, where many a soldier quenched his thirst with a glass of beer after a hot and dusty day on the prairie, the young bison frequently got beer from the troops, sometimes by the bucketful. It acquired a great fondness for the beverage and got drunk easily. On one occasion, after finishing off a bucket of beer in the officers' room at the store, the buffalo charged and mounted a billiard table. It took the soldiers about an hour to dislodge the animal. Another time the buffalo, which had climbed the stairs leading to the second story of the trader's store, was obviously afraid to go back down. The officers blindfolded the animal, and with ropes and planks managed to push it down the stairs. It provided much amusement for the soldiers, and people came from great distances to view the beer-drinking buffalo.[17]

Although army regulations forbade gambling, it usually existed, and although regulations likewise prohibited prostitution and even denounced and deplored its existence, it was not uncommon for post traders to provide this service for soldiers as well. At Fort Union, New Mexico Territory, whiskey sellers and prostitutes set up shop among the caves and rocks over-looking the post during the early 1850s. One of the "soiled doves" was Maria Alvina Chaireses, sometimes called "Jesusitta," but known to soldiers as "Black Sus." Another was Maria Dolores Trujigue y Rivale. They and their cohorts were kept supplied with flour, bacon, coffee, sugar, and even candles by soldiers who visited them. Prostitutes also came onto the post with Mexicans who had been given permission to set up a Mexican market each day. Although the post surgeon complained about the filth and the contamination of the Mexican prostitutes, the post commander did not stop their activities; he only ordered that officers keep a closer watch on them. Later a new post commander took action. He raided the caves and burned down some shanties. The women were whipped, their hair was cut off with scissors, and they were escorted out of the fort.[18]

It was not uncommon for commanders to permit prostitutes to live on posts. Since general orders permitted the hiring of company laundresses, prostitutes often took these jobs and did more than the laundry. Although, according to regulations, "women infected by the venereal disease shall in no case, nor on any pretense, be allowed to remain with the army," many actually were permitted to remain. In 1875 General Tasker Bliss noted that many post surgeons "had nothing to do but to confine laundresses and treat the clap."[19] Three years later Congress decided that laundresses caused too much bother in the army and ceased to provide funding for them.

A bar and canteen at Fort Riley, Kansas, in 1895. Only four soldiers and a few civilians have managed to get away from work for some pleasure on this summer afternoon. (Courtesy Joseph J. Pennell Collection, Kansas Collection, University of Kansas Libraries)

When President Rutherford B. Hayes banned the sale of liquor on military reservations in 1881, the prohibition resulted in the establishment of off-post saloons, sometimes called "hog ranches," where whisky sellers, gamblers, and prostitutes (or "ladies of joy," as soldiers often called them) plied their trade. These ladies were usually not the most attractive. In Kansas, Wyoming, Colorado, Montana, and New Mexico, the cowboys in the cattle towns were willing to pay prostitutes more than were soldiers. The higher-class prostitutes therefore favored the cattle towns, while the less attractive offered their services in towns near military forts. In some instances the prostitutes worked for post traders. The "hog ranches" flourished until 1890, when the post trader or sutler system was abolished and replaced by canteens at the forts offering more healthful amusements for off-duty soldiers. In 1892, the name "canteen" was changed to "post exchange."

The interior of the sutler's store at Fort Dodge, Kansas, as it appeared in the middle 1860s. This illustration appeared in Harper's Weekly, *May 25, 1867. (Author's collection)*

As more and more forts were built in the West to protect transportation on the overland routes—there were about seventy by the late 1850s—the wives and families of officers came west. Although regulations made no provision for them, nearly every post had a few, and the larger forts usually had many. Margaret I. Carrington, wife of Colonel Henry Beebee Carrington, described her life as an officer's wife in the West in her book *Absaraka (Ab-sa-ra-ka) Home of the Crows*, published in 1868, two years before her death in 1870 at the age of thirty-nine. Although she experienced many hardships as an army wife, there were pleasant times, too. She wrote:

> There were real cozy times in tents, houses, or in cabins. The good nature and good sense of Uncle Samuel [i.e., Uncle Sam] had furnished canned provisions, greatly to our personal comfort and pecuniary convenience; but fresh vegetables were most precious and rare. A few potatoes from Bozeman City, sent with the regards of Brevet Lieutenant-Colonel Kinney, were a great treat; and Major Almstedt, paymaster, was good enough to spare a half cabbage and eleven onions, through one of his trips, to astonish the palate and minister to a crav-

Buffalo hunting was a popular sport on the plains of Kansas. The soldier driving the mule-drawn vehicle has escorted the two hunters to the buffalo range from a nearby military post, perhaps Fort Hays. This illustration appeared in Harper's Weekly, *March 21, 1874. (Author's collection)*

ing for something novel from the United States. Ingenuity was tasked to invent new cookery for cove oysters and other savory preserved edibles; and wild plums, gooseberries, currants, grapes, and cherries furnished a preserve basis quite palatable and natural. . . . Evenings had their readings, their games, and quiet quadrilles. Music was a never-failing relief for body and mind; and the interchange of patterns, books, and recipes kept up material for new industry and new themes for deliberation or chit-chat.[20]

A first lieutenant's wife, Lydia Spencer Lane, wrote how she passed the time during the mid-1850s traveling from Fort Duncan on the Rio Grande to Fort Inge near modern Uvalde, Texas, in an ambulance (wagon) that had been provided for her:

The soldiers were on foot, and we had to keep pace with them; hours and hours we were, making the daily distance of ten or fifteen miles between camps. We halted frequently to rest the men and mules, and then the ladies and children would gladly get out of the ambulances, and perhaps walk along the road for a change; but we dared not get

Soldiers from Fort Hays, Kansas, on a buffalo hunt, 1869. One of the riders is believed to be Lieutenant Colonel George Armstrong Custer. The buffalo's raised tail signifies anger. (Courtesy Kansas State Historical Society)

away from the command. It was certain the Indians were never far off, and we kept very close to the soldiers.[21]

For Lydia Lane, though her life at Fort Inge was hardly one of luxury, it was still pleasant enough:

The post was dilapidated; but the surroundings were far more agreeable than at either Fort McIntosh or Fort Duncan. A beautiful little river, the Leona, ran just behind the quarters, which were built of logs, and almost ready to tumble down. We moved into a vacant house of four rooms; the kitchen was behind it, and was in an advanced stage of decay. A high wind might easily have blown it over. Our supply of furniture was not sufficient even for four rooms. We had taken out with us two carpets, and enough pretty chintz for curtains in two rooms; six

Adjacent to Fort Riley, Kansas, is the town of Junction City, which offered soldiers sporting pleasures after prostitution was outlawed on military posts. This 1906 photograph shows Madame Sperber and her girls in one of Junction City's sporting houses. (Courtesy Joseph J. Pennell Collection, Kansas Collection, University of Kansas Libraries)

hard (so hard!) wooden chairs, bought in Corpus Christi, and called "Windsor chairs,"—a bedstead, centre-table, a cooking-stove, which was about the most valuable and highly prized of all our possessions, and a few other articles of the plainest description. We were well provided with good china, glass, house-linen, and silver. We had all we wanted, and were very happy. The pay per month for a first lieutenant of Mounted Rifles was ninety-three dollars!—vast wealth, it seemed to me. More would have been useless, for there was nothing to buy,—no stores nearer than San Antonio,—so that the commissary bill was the only one we owed monthly, except servants' wages and one to the laundress, and we saved money. The commissary furnished only necessary articles of food at that time, such as, coffee, flour, sugar, rice, ham, and pork, which list of eatables did not offer much to tempt the appetite; the day of canned meats, vegetables, and fruits was not yet. Butter, eggs, and chickens were brought to the post sometimes from the ranches, eighteen or twenty miles away, the owners running the risk of being murdered by the Indians every trip they made. Game was very abundant, and almost at our door; deer, turkeys, partridges, and ducks could be found right round the post, while the lovely clear stream that ran just back of the house was filled with magnificent black bass, which were easily caught. Behind the quarters, and extending to the river, was a grove of fine old live-oak trees, and many an hour we passed fishing under their shade, I for minnows to bait the hooks for bass; and in a few minutes I caught enough to supply the fishermen, who only conde-scended to catch the game fish in a scientific manner, with rod and reel. Fine sport they had, the bass taken often weighing six and eight pounds. We became very tired of all the fine game, and would have welcomed a good beef-steak as a luxury. There were so few soldiers at the post that beef was issued only once or twice a month, and was really a treat.[22]

Later, when her husband was stationed at Fort Union in New Mexico, Mrs. Lane ordered a melodeon from Philadelphia, and she had the sender write on the box "to be sent by first *wagon-train* from Fort Riley, Kansas, to Fort Union, New Mexico." As she later recalled:

By some blunder it was sent out on the stage as express matter, and the charges were "fifty-three dollars." The melodeon cost fifty. The plea-sure it gave me more than compensated for the large amount paid for getting it out. There was not then a piano at the post, and, although a melodeon is a mournful grunty, wheezy instrument, a cross between an accordion and an indifferent organ, it was much better than nothing. When we left New Mexico it was bought from us for *one hundred dol-lars,* to be used in a Protestant church in Santa Fe, then struggling for a foothold, which it secured at last, after great perseverance. In it there is now a good organ. What has become of the melodeon since the advent of its more pretentious relation, I never heard.[23]

Parties on western military posts also gave the wives of many officers much pleasure. Frances M. A. Roe, writing to a friend from Fort Lyon, Col-orado Territory, in January 1872, recalled:

Our little party was a grand success, but I am still wondering how it came about that Mrs. Barker and I gave it together, for, although we are all in the same company and next-door neighbors, we have seen very little of each other. She is very quiet, and seldom goes out, even for a walk. It was an easy matter to arrange things so the two houses could, in a way, be connected as they are under the same roof, and the porches divided by a railing only, that was removed for one evening. The dancing was in our house, and the supper was served at the Barkers'. And that supper was a marvel of culinary art, I assure you, even if it was a fraud in one or two things. We were complimented quite graciously by some of the older housekeepers, who pride themselves upon knowing how to make more delicious little dishes out of nothing than anyone else. But this time it was North and South combined, for you will remember that Mrs. Barker is from Virginia.

The chicken salad—and it was delicious—was made of tender veal, but the celery in it was the genuine article, for we sent to Kansas City for that and a few other things. The turkey galantine was perfect, and the product of a resourceful brain from the North, and was composed almost entirely of wild goose! There was no April fool about the delicate Maryland biscuits, however, and other nice things that were set forth. We fixed up cozily the back part of our hall with comfortable chairs and cushions, and there punch was served during the evening. Major Barker and Faye made the punch. The orchestra might have been better, but the two violins and the accordion gave us music that was inspiring, and gave us noise, too, and then Doos, who played the accordion, kept us merry by the ever-pounding down of one government-shod foot.[24]

From the earliest days of military posts in the West, music provided much pleasure for nearly everyone stationed there. For Lambert Bowman Wolf, an enlisted man in Company K, First U.S. Cavalry in Kansas, Nebraska, Colorado, and Indian Territory (now Oklahoma) between 1856 and 1861, music was a favorite pastime, as he wrote in a diary kept during these years. He observed that during 1858 and 1859, a favorite song with the cavalrymen was:

Bucking and Gagging

Come, all Yankee soldiers, give ear to my song;
It is a short ditty, t'will not keep you long;
It's of no use to fret on account of your luck,
We can laugh, drink and sing yet in spite of the buck.

Chorus: Dary down, dary down, &c.

Sergeant, buck him and gag him, our officers cry,
For such trifling offenses they happen to spy;
Till with bucking and gagging of Dick, Tom and Bill,
Faith! the Mexican ranks they have helped to fill.

Chorus.

The treatment they give us, as all of us know,
Is bucking and gagging for whipping the foe;
They buck us and they gag us for malice or for spite,
But they are glad to release us when going to fight.

One of several Christmas dinner settings in 1904 at Fort Riley, Kansas. Such events were major
occurrences on military posts. (Courtesy Joseph J. Pennell Collection, Kansas Collection,
University of Kansas Libraries)

Chorus.

A poor soldier's tied up in the sun or the rain
With a gag in his mouth till he's tortured with pain;
Why, I'm blest! if the eagle we wear on our flag
In its claws shouldn't carry a buck and a gag.

Chorus.[25]

Military bands provided many soldiers with music, but such bands were stationed only at the largest posts, which served as regimental headquarters. Forts Laramie, Riley, Abraham Lincoln, Leavenworth, and Hays were among those that had military bands, and they were important to military and social life. One small post without a band was Fort Duncan, on the Rio Grande at Eagle Pass in Texas. When Lieutenant Orsemus B. Boyd was stationed there during the winter of 1879 and 1880, he and his wife often crossed the Rio Grande to enjoy the sights in Piedras Negras, the Mexican town opposite Fort Duncan. Boyd's wife, Frances Anne Mullen Boyd, later wrote that they attended a bullfight, adding:

> The only delightful features connected with that so-called pastime were the perfect Mexican band and superb drilling of Mexican soldiers, who marched and countermarched for at least an hour without a single order being spoken, they responding merely to a tap of the drum as each new movement was initiated. The band was superb, and the music so sweet and thrilling we could have listened for hours without weariness. On account of exchanging many hospitalities with the Mexican officers, we enjoyed numerous opportunities of hearing it. On one occasion the band was brought over to serenade us, and we listened as in a dream to its rendering of various operas and Mexican national airs, played with such expression that all the sentiments they indicated were aroused. We were invited to all balls given by the Mexican officers, and found them curious affairs. The women's costumes were tawdry in the extreme, and their manner of dancing so slow as to seem most monotonous; yet I have never seen more perfect natural grace anywhere displayed than in those measured Spanish dances. The variety those balls afforded was quite enjoyable until one night a Mexican officer of high rank drew a pistol and fired directly at a man who moved too slowly out of his path to suit the officer's dignity.[26]

Fort Hays, Kansas, served as headquarters for several regiments between 1867 and 1889. The first band to be stationed at Fort Hays was that of the Fifth Infantry, and when Lieutenant Colonel George A. Custer and the Seventh Cavalry returned there following the winter campaign of 1868–69, the band welcomed them with the strains of "Garry Owen in Glory," the regimental march.

Such bands not only performed on the parade fields but for post social events, including balls. A story in the Junction City (Kansas) *Union,* April 4, 1874, provided the following description of a grand ball given by Company C, Sixth Cavalry, at Fort Hays, Kansas:

> Probably no similar event has ever transpired in Western Kansas that can equal it. The ball was given in the company quarters. . . . The quarters were cleared of everything and were transformed into an elaborate ballroom, one hundred feet in length by twenty-five feet in width, the ceilings covered with flags, the dropping ends along the walls caught in graceful festoons, and supported by an endless chain of evergreens extending entirely around the room; the walls were ornamented with pictures, quaint designs in sabres, pistols, and carbines, and occasionally a helmet was displayed midst a profuse ornamentation of rosettes and evergreens, the music stand, an elaborate platform, tastefully decorated with flags and evergreens, from which the Sixth band discoursed elaborate strains of music. Hays City turned out en masse, and, in fact, the crowd was immense, and good will pervaded the entire affair, and not an ill word was spoken nor an intoxicated person seen or known to be around the premises.

Military bands often traveled to give concerts. The Third Infantry Band from Fort Hays, Kansas, went to Denver in late September 1872 and performed a concert at Sigl's Hall. Denver newspapers praised their performance, and the *Rocky Mountain News* (September 27, 1872), listed the band's musical selections as "Grand Paris Entry," "Overture to Poet and Peasant," "The Beautiful Blue Danube," "Cujus Anima from Stabat Mater," "Nightingale Polka," "Selections from Martha," "What is the German Fatherland," "Coronation March from The Prophet," "Jolly Brother (Brother Ludwig) Gallop," and "Louisen Quadrille."[27]

Military bands also provided music for weddings, and in the case of Fort Niobrara in Nebraska, a short distance south of the South Dakota border, it was a twenty-piece string orchestra. Martha Summerhayes, wife of an officer stationed there, remembered that as spring approached one year in the early 1880s, the post began to wake up following a dreary winter:

> Cupid had not been idle. It was observed that Mr. Bingham, our gracious host of the Ninth Cavalry, had fallen in love with Antoinette, the pretty and attractive daughter of Captain Lynch of our own regiment, and the post began to be on the *qui vive* to see how the affair would end, for nobody expects to see the course of true love run smooth. In their case, however, the Fates were kind and in due time the happy engagement was announced. We had an excellent amusement hall, with a fine floor for dancing. The chapel was at one end, and a fairly good stage was at the other. . . . Uncle Sam provided us with a chaplain, and a weekly service was held by the Anglican clergyman—a tall, well-formed man, a scholar and, as we say, a gentleman. He wore the uniform of the army chaplain, and as far as looks went could hold his own with any of the younger officers. And it was a great comfort to the church people to have this weekly service. During the rest of the time, the chapel was concealed by heavy curtains, and the seats turned around facing the stage.[28]

She also remembered that since there were a number of active young bachelors at Fort Niobrara, a series of weekly dances was inaugurated:

> Never did I enjoy dancing more than at this time. Then Mrs. Kautz [wife of the post commander], who was a thorough music lover and had a cultivated taste as well as a trained and exquisite voice, gave several musicales, for which much preparation was made, and which were most delightful. These were given at the quarters of General August V. Kautz, a long, low rambling one-story house, arranged with that artistic taste for which Mrs. Kautz was distinguished. Then came theatricals, all managed by Mrs. Kautz, whose talents were versatile. We charged admission, for we needed some more scenery, and the neighboring frontier town of Valentine came riding and driving over the prairie and across the old bridge of the Niobrara River, to see our plays. We had a well-lighted stage. Our methods were primitive, as there was no gas or electricity there in those days, but the results were good, and the histrionic ability shown by some of our young men and women seemed marvellous to us. And now the summer came on apace. A tennis-court was made, and added greatly to our amusement. We were in the saddle every day, and the country around proved very attractive at this season, both for riding and driving.[29]

. . .

THE INCREASED SETTLEMENT of the West following the Civil War provided more civilized forms of entertainment for soldiers to pursue during
their leisure time, but military discipline still restricted the freedom of the
soldiers, especially the enlisted men. This was noted by Samuel June Barrows, a student at the Harvard Divinity School, who worked as a correspondent for the *New York Tribune* during the summers of 1873 and 1874. The
first summer he accompanied General David S. Stanley's expedition to the
Yellowstone; the next, that of Custer to the Black Hills. Barrows was
impressed by the civilian teamsters who drove mule-drawn wagons loaded
with military supplies. The teamsters were not only paid more than most
enlisted men but enjoyed more freedom than the soldiers during their leisure
time. Barrows wrote:

> The teamster's duties are simple but arduous. He drives his team on the
> march, and in camp sees that they are well cared for. . . . The teamster's
> pastimes are simple, but not always innocent. Wherever there is a sutler,
> a large share of his time and earnings are spent at the bar. An indispens-
> able part of his outfit is a pack of cards. His philosophy of life, his creed,
> his hopes and expectations for the future, are all implied in those fifty-
> two elements. No expedition goes out without three or four profession-
> als, who engage as teamsters. On the Yellowstone expedition there were
> several who reaped a good harvest. The most successful, nicknamed
> "Governor Wise," took some three thousand dollars as the result of four
> months' work. One of his best "hauls," known only to a few, was made
> one night just after we had buried the one unfortunate teamster who was
> killed on the trip. The game lasted all night, and when the bugle sounded
> reveille, Wise had made fifteen hundred dollars. It is only professionals
> who can play such heavy games. The teamster's wages do not admit of
> large stakes; but he will stake all he has. Let a hundred teamsters be paid
> off, and in three or four days nearly the whole amount of money will be
> in the hands of three or four men. Many an expert gambler has graduated
> wealthy from a mule's back. At Fort Bridger, an accomplished teamster
> made sixteen thousand dollars from his comrades in three months. There
> is a man in Leavenworth to-day worth fifty thousand dollars, who made
> it in the same way. But reverses are equally noticeable. A man at "Dobe-
> town," Utah, owned property worth one hundred and seventy-five
> thousand dollars in gold. He lost it all in a single game of poker, and to

keep from starving was obliged to take a black snake and drive a team side by side with the man who told me the story. "But," said old Martin, "it cured him of gambling."[30]

The diaries and journals of soldiers who fought in the Indian wars following the Civil War provide other accounts on how the soldiers sought pleasure even while heading for battle. In 1876 General George Crook led the Powder River and Yellowstone expeditions against the Sioux—a three-pronged attack, with General Crook moving up from the south, General Alfred H. Terry moving in from the east, and (Brevet) Colonel John Gibbon leading troops from Fort Ellis, Montana Territory, in the west. The journal of Lieutenant James H. Bradley, who commanded a detachment of scouts—including a group of Crow Indians, moving east with Gibbon's force—provides a vivid insight into the pleasure-seeking propensities of his men:

Monday, June 5. Soon after the soldiers camped early in the afternoon after advancing nine miles, they routed a bear out of the thicket near their camp. After a short chase Colonel John Gibbon killed it. He caused it to be butchered, and distributed the meat to several of the officer's messes, giving to many their first experience of such fare. It was quite palatable and strongly suggestive of fresh pork. . . . The afternoon was very warm, but by rolling up the sides of the tents and admitting the slight air stirring it was pleasant enough. It looked more like picnicking than going to war, to see officers and men comfortably reclining in the shade reading books and newspapers, writing letters, posting diaries, playing cards, talking or dozing "the happy hours away," according to their individual moods. And the picnic impression was heightened when, later in the afternoon, the supper was made ready on the grass and hungry groups gathered here and there over cups of steaming, savory coffee and other fare. Nor was coffee the only beverage. From the capacious recesses of secure mess chests came forth at odd times nutmeg, lemon, sugar, Angostura bitters [still available today], champagne cider, and *spiritus frumenti,* from which were made tempting "Rosebuds" [probably something like a modern "Shirley Temple"], cocktails, toddies and other harmless compounds. When each member of the charmed circle had been duly supplied, the master of ceremonies would briefly announce, "Here's How!" and, with a chorus of "Hows" from his co-laborers, the exhilarating compounds were gently put where they would do the most good.

In the dusk of evening, when most of the officers were gathered in front of some of the tents, a chorus of cavalrymen not far away burst forth with a round of merry camp songs, that came pleasantly to the ear and suspended for a time the conversation upon battles we haven't fought and victories we haven't won. And when "taps" imposed silence upon the enlisted men, the officers, who enjoyed larger liberties, took up the suspended harmony and woke the night air with many a song of sentiment and jollity. We have a number of very sweet singers in our command, and the music at times is of a delicious sort. But rest is needful for the march of tomorrow and after a time the group of singers and listeners broke up with a mutual "good night," tents are sought, sleep settles upon the camp, and all is quiet upon the Yellowstone. Not even a sentinel is visible, for, disposed in groups of three around us for some distance from the camp, they are all lying flat upon the ground with nothing to mark their locality. It is hard to realize when about the camp that we are an invading army, liable at any moment to be engaged in deadly conflict with a cruel foe.[31]

Soldiers on bivouac at Fort Riley, Kansas, in 1897, enjoying a friendly card game. (Courtesy Joseph J. Pennell Collection, Kansas Collection, University of Kansas Libraries)

These two soldiers, identified only as Richmond and Noak, apparently found pleasure in posing for the photographer in 1904. (Courtesy Joseph J. Pennell Collection, Kansas Collection, University of Kansas Libraries)

For the soldier in the Old West, life left much to be desired, yet there were pleasant times, especially for the officers who brought their wives with them. Martha Summerhayes perhaps summed up the feelings of many soldiers when she wrote: "My early experiences were unusually rough. None of us seek such experiences, but possibly they bring with them a sort of recompense, in that simple comforts afterwards seem, by contrast, to be the greatest luxuries."[32] Other Americans in the nineteenth-century American West probably had similar thoughts, including the men and women associated with the growing cattle trade.

CHAPTER VII

In Cow
🐂 Country

All work and no play isn't much better than all play and no work.
—Anonymous

I F ONE WERE TO BELIEVE old Hollywood Westerns, the only place where the nineteenth-century cowboy found pleasure was in the dusty cattle-town saloon, where he could drink, gamble, and enjoy the company of a beautiful dancing girl. Certainly some cowboys did indulge in such activities following the Civil War, especially, say, after driving large herds of longhorn cattle north from Texas to the railhead towns in Kansas and Nebraska, or to ranches in Colorado, Wyoming, Montana, or the Dakotas. The cowboy, however, also had many other forms of pleasure at his disposal, spanning all of the nineteenth century and earlier times as well. Even today, remnants of cowboy pleasure still exist and have even been embellished.

The customs of American cowboys are rooted in those of the Mexican *vaqueros,* who, during the eighteenth century, brought cattle into portions of what are now New Mexico, Arizona, Texas, and especially California. Private cattle ranchos, or ranches, developed there in the late 1830s after Mexico gained independence from Spain and the Spanish mission system collapsed. Life on the ranchos was primitive and each was generally self-sufficient, except for luxuries obtained from Yankee trading ships stopping along the coast. The climate was favorable for cattle ranching, and during most years there were good pastures and an abundant supply of water. Life itself was a pleasure for the *vaqueros,* as the following contemporary description so vividly paints:

The *rancho* lay beyond the mountain range and extended over rolling hills and little valleys. A creek flowed through it, and on the banks were many sycamores. Shaded by oaks was the long, low adobe house, with its red tiled roof and wide veranda. Behind the fence of chaparral was the orchard and the melon patch, and beyond the orchard was the meadow, golden with buttercups in the early spring. In the open fields, dotted with oaks, the rich alfilerilla [alfalfa] grew, and on the hillsides were the wild grasses which waved like billows as the breezes from the distant ocean blew across them. The sameness of recurring events of each succeeding year seemed monotonous, but brought repose, contentment and peace. When the dew was still on the grass, we would mount our horses and herd the cattle. . . . In the wooded cañons where the cool brooks flowed, and where the wild blackberries grew, we ate our noon day meal and rested. And as the hills began to glow with the light of the setting sun we journeyed homeward. When the long days of summer came, we ate our evening meal beneath the oaks, and in the twilight we listened to the guitar and the songs of our people. In the autumn we harvested the corn and gathered the olives and the grapes.[1]

Still, California *vaqueros* were apparently not entirely content to lead quiet lives in what must have seemed like the Garden of Eden, and were known to seek out more tangible forms of pleasure. Zenas Leonard, a fur trapper and trader, who joined Joseph Walker's expedition to California during the early 1830s, described how the Spanish cowboys found pleasure in "bull-baiting." This sport had been brought to America from England during the seventeenth century, but California bullbaiting was something new to Leonard, who was born and raised in Pennsylvania. Bullbaiting as he knew it used a dog to tease a bull, making it mad, pleasure being taken in the animal's reaction. But in California during the 1830s, it involved roping the animal, much as American cowboys rope cattle today. Leonard told how the sporting *vaqueros* would ride the ranges until they came across a large herd. They would then make bets on who would be the first to rope and catch one of the animals: "The one that gets the rope round the animal's horn or neck first claims the assistance of the rest to throw the animal to the ground— which ends the chase for this time," he recalled.[2]

California *vaqueros* also found pleasure in capturing grizzly bears and then letting them fight domestic bulls. Leonard recalled:

Taking a bear is a much more dangerous piece of work, than any other animal, owing to their enormous strength. . . . In taking a bear, their object is to noose him round one of the hind legs, in order to keep him from biting the cord, which they are very apt to do if fast round the neck. A single hunter can do but little with a large bear, and they are

California vaqueros *found enjoyment in bullbaiting, roping a bull around the horn or neck and throwing the animal to the ground. (Courtesy California Historical Society Library)*

seldom attacked single handed, or without the certainty of assistance from some of their comrades. When overtaken by the foremost rider, the bear stops running and prepares for war. This man will then engage the attention of the bear by teasing him, whilst another hunter will come up in the rear of the excited animal and noose him by the hind foot; when the cord is securely fastened to the hind foot, he is generally considered safe. It is then that their sport begins in good earnest, and the feats that are sometimes performed by the men, bear, and horses, would be incredible to any person who has never seen any sport of this kind. After the bear finds himself secure and has become pretty well worried, he seats himself sullenly on the ground and lets the horse pull at the cord, stretching his leg out until the pain becomes too severe, when he will draw up his leg, horse and all, with as much apparent ease as a horse would a sleigh. I have been told that some of the largest bears have been known to drag two horses a considerable distance in a fit of rage, in spite of all the exertions of the horses and riders to the contrary. After the bear is pretty well worried in this way, another noose is fastened round one of the fore feet or neck, when the bear will commence beating the ground with his feet and manifesting the most intense rage and anger imaginable—and in this manner they drag, whip, and coax him along to the pen where the bull is confined.

Leonard continued:

When the bear has arrived at the bull pen, their bets on taking him and all disputes are settled, refreshments taken, and preparations made for another scene, which is by far the most pleasing to the Spaniards. They begin to enrage a bull by pricking him with a nail fixed in the end of a stick, and when his anger has rose to the war pitch, the bear is let into the pen with the bull. The men now bet all they are worth on which will be the conqueror, and everything manifests the greatest possible excitement. Sometimes the animals refuse to fight until they are forced to it by being tormented with the sharpened sticks, but when one receives a blow from the other, nothing can part them until one or the other falls. These fights last sometimes half an hour without relax-ation. The bear is much the strongest, but it has no chances of avoiding the thrusts of the bull, in consequence of the smallness of the pen; but in an open field, a grizzly bear will conquer a bull in a few moments. When the fight is over the conquered animal is taken out and the bets are again settled. If it is the bear that is whipt, the game is continued and the bets renewed on some person who will offer to go into the pen with the enraged bull, lay his hand on some part of his body, and escape untouched. This is by far the most dangerous part of the whole play, and many lives have been lost at it; but so fond are the Spaniards of gambling, that in play a life is of but little consequence.[3]

Although Spaniards first brought cattle into Texas, it was the "Texians," as the first emigrants to Texas from the United States were called, who capi-talized on cattle raising, though not until after the Civil War. Texans returning home from the battlefields found that their cattle had multiplied on the open ranges. They began hiring more young men to take care of their cattle and to round up and drive the longhorns to market. The men who owned the cattle became known as "cowmen" and, in time, "cattlemen." It was then that the label "cowboy" became firmly attached to the hired man on horseback, who soon found ways to pass his leisure time as he drove cattle to railhead markets in Kansas and Nebraska. The recollections of many old-time cowboys pro-vide insights into how they found simple pleasure in what was a rough life.

When Texan John Young drove cattle up the Chisholm Trail to Kansas, he remembered that in camp after supper "the boys not on herd would tell yarns, sing songs, wrestle, and act generally like a bunch of kids, which most we were. Like many of the outfits, ours had a fiddle, and while some artist in spurs 'made it talk,' we often put the end gate of the chuck wagon on the ground and then took turns dancing jigs upon it. Or maybe some lad would take the fiddle out to the herd with him and 'agitate the catgut' to the tune of 'Billy in the Low Ground,' 'Dinah Had a Wooden Leg,' 'Hell Among the Yearlin's,' 'Old Rosin the Bow,' 'Cotton-Eyed Joe,' 'Saddle Ole Spike,' 'Sally Gooden,' 'The Devil's Dream,' or some other such favorite. Many a night I have led Lake Porter's horse around the herd while he made the longhorns snore to music." Young continued:

> Some people say that the reason cowboys sang to the cattle was to prevent their being frightened by any sudden or irregular noise. There is something in that, but I am sure that the music of the fiddle was appreciated by some of the old time longhorns—whatever may be the taste of modern whitefaces. One lazy old brindle steer that always stayed in

Texas cowboys enjoying their meal next to a chuckwagon. (Author's collection)

the drag by day and slept on the south edge of the herd at night seemed particularly fond of "One Evening in May"—a waltz tune. More than once Lake Porter and I stopped to see him wriggle his ears and kind of blow in an appreciative manner. Pleasant it was on a warm, clear night to circle slowly around a herd of cattle that were bedded down quiet and breathing deep and out there to catch the strains of song or fiddle coming from camp, where the fire was like a dim star. But it was pleasanter to be in camp and, while just catching now and then a note from singer or fiddler on herd, to be dropping off to sleep. As long as a cowboy heard music he knew that all was well.[4]

Another Texas cowboy with similar experiences was Young's friend Lake Porter, who drove longhorns north to Kansas during the early 1870s. Porter remembered:

When I was growing up I learned to play the fiddle, but there were only two tunes that I could play to perfection, one of which was "Seesaw," and the other was "Sawsee." Often I have taken my old fiddle on herd at night when on the trail, and while some of my companions would lead my horse around the herd I agitated the catguts, reeling off such old-time selections as "Black Jack Grove," "Dinah Had a Wooden Leg," "Shake That Wooden Leg, Dolly Oh," "Give the Fiddler a Dram," "Arkansaw Traveler," and "The Unfortunate Pup." And say, brothers, those old long-horned Texas steers actually enjoyed the old-time music. I still have the old music box which I used to play in those care-free, happy-days.[5]

Young remembered a cowboy named Sam in his outfit, who played the banjo, but one night someone accidentally stepped on it and demolished it. The boys chipped in and bought Sam a fiddle, "and whenever he got a chance Sam would pick 'Green corn, green corn, bring along the demijohn,' on this fiddle." Among other selections, Young recalled that Sam had a kind of chant called "Dog" that the boys often called on him to give. The words were:

There was a man who had a dog, a bob-tailed ornery cuss,
And this here dog got this here man in many an ugly muss.

The man was on his muscle, and the dog was on his bite;
To touch that bobtail son-of-a-gun you were sure to start a fight.

These Wyoming cowboys seem to be enjoying themselves singing around the chuckwagon and cook fire about 1900. (Courtesy Belden Collection, Wyoming State Museum)

There was a woman who had a cat that fit a fifteen pounds;
The other cats got up and slid when this here cat came 'round.

The man and dog came along one day by where this woman did dwell;
The cat he growled fe-ro-cious-ly and made for the dog like—rip.

The man he cussed and ripped and swore and picked up a big brickbat;
He swore he'd be damned eternally if he didn't kill that cat.

The woman she said she'd be darned if he did and picked up a big shot-gun;
She whaled away and shot him in the back with birdshot number one.

They carried him home on a cellar door and the doctors healed him up;
He's never since been known to tackle a cat or own a terrier pup.

Some folks may turn up their nose at this, but I don't give a darn for that,
For it goes to show that a man may tackle the wrong old Thomas cat.[6]

It seems likely that some *vaquero* in what is now Mexico may have been the first singing cowboy in this hemisphere as early as the sixteenth century, but Spanish and Mexican documents make little mention of the *vaquero*'s day-to-day life, perhaps because he was at the lower end of the social ladder in New Spain. The singing cowboy, as we know him, was a product of the open range in Texas beginning in the 1850s. Most early Texas cowboys had a strong sense of rhythm, often set by their ponies' gait. But as one old-timer said, "Many of the cowboys I knew couldn't carry a tune less'n they pack it over their shoulders in a gunny-sack. They'd just say it or speak it off."

There were two types of songs sung by nineteenth-century Texas cowboys. One was loud and vigorous and was often used to prod the slower-moving cattle along the trail. The other was soft—something like a lullaby—to keep the cattle quiet after they were bedded down for the night. Both types probably started as yelling or talking to cattle, which gradually gave way to singing. It appears that cowboys sang to keep cattle from being startled. If a cowboy did not make any noise while on watch, moving slowly around a herd, his horse might still step on one of the sleeping steers; the animal might wake, jump up, frighten other cattle, and cause a stampede. To eliminate this problem, cowboys riding around herds sang or whistled softly. This tended to wake up the steers nearest to them in a lazy way, so they would go back to sleep after the cowboys passed.

Apparently a cowboy's ability to sing to cattle became an important skill. Some trail bosses refused to hire a cowboy unless he could sing. And those who could sing often helped to pass the time by thinking up new verses to songs as they trailed their longhorns to market. One Texas cattleman, J. M. Grigsby, recalled that his cowboys would consider it a dull day's drive if they did not add at least one verse to a song. And on dark nights, trail bosses looked with high regard on the cowboy—often called the "bell-wether"—who could keep up the most racket by singing.

The singing also served another purpose: It kept the other cowboys awake.

Many of the songs sung by cowboys on the early trail drives from Texas northward to Kansas and Nebraska were songs they had learned back home—"Green Grow the Lilacs," "When You and I Were Young, Maggie," and hymns, especially Methodist hymns, plus a few old-fashioned Negro minstrel songs. But by 1870 authentic cowboy songs began to develop as more and more Texans drove cattle north. In many cases the cowboys made up their own lyrics to existing melodies. The words reflected the human condition of frontier life and revealed the changing character of the West, especially the shifting frontier, where laws and eastern institutions and traditions were either not effective or nonexistent. Such songs were simple and reflected the cowboy's work, his likes and dislikes, his experiences and dreams. They were free from self-consciousness and reflected a sense of what was real and appropriate. They provided the cowboy much pleasure.

Most of the old and really authentic cowboy songs were slow, often mournful, and had something of a pacifying quality. Such songs included the night-herding songs sung like lullabies. These included "Doney Gal," a waltz; "Good-Bye Old Paint"; and "The Old Chisholm Trail," a song actually reshaped from Stephen Foster's minstrel tune titled "Old Uncle Ned." The song is very simple, one to which anyone could add a stanza or two if he or she could make a simple rhyme and perceive the rhythms of a couplet. The melody of an Irish ballad, "The Forsaken Girl," was the basis for "The Cowboy's Stroll" and its variant, called "Jack O'Diamonds." Another old Irish song provided many of the ingredients for the well-known ballad "Git Along, Little Dogies." The still-popular "Red River Valley" was adapted from a song titled "The Bright Sherman Valley," which in turn was taken from an upstate New York song, "The Bright Mohawk Valley." "Cowboy's Life Is a Dreary, Dreary Life" was adapted from a song popular among lumberjacks in Michigan and northern New England. And the song "The Gal I Left Behind Me" has been traced back to the eighteenth century. By the early nineteenth century it was popular in eastern music halls, before it found its way west to be sung by cowboys. The melody of what many people have considered a cowboy classic, "Bury Me Not on the Lone Prairie," was actually taken from the sentimental parlor ballad "The Ocean Burial," popular during the 1870s.[7]

Whenever a cowboy from another outfit drifted into camp, he was expected to sing any new song he knew or additional stanzas for an old one. Otherwise, to pass their time, cowboys often made up chants or stories based on their own experiences. Young recalled one such occasion in the late nineteenth century when he and some other cowboys had delivered a herd of cattle to Denver, Colorado. After disposing of the cattle, they took in the sights and went to a theater to see a stage show. As Young recalled:

> We were waiting uneasily for the curtain to go up when the manager came out on the platform and apologetically announced: "The leading lady has lost her tights. There'll be no show tonight." I supposed the announcement was part of the program; but while the audience was sitting perfectly still, not knowing exactly how to take it, a fat Irish

woman, who sat on one side of me, exploded with such a laugh that the whole house went laughter wild and actually we had no show. Laughter is catching, and when the audience dispersed, still uproariously laughing, the people in the streets joined in. That night Denver laughed itself to sleep. The next day as we rode down toward Las Animas one of the cowboys in our outfit made up a song that he entitled "There'll Be No Show Tonight." It was not a printable song, but it got itself adopted into the repertoire of the trail men, and within a year or two it was being sung from the Gulf of Mexico to the Canadian Rockies.[8]

Other cowboys found pleasure in telling stories about themselves. One such was Jack Potter, who recalled with a smile the time he got lost from his Texas outfit somewhere in Kansas. In the distance he saw a dugout, a cabin dug into a ridge—a sure sign of homesteaders. Potter rode over to it and told the "granger" (farmer) that he was lost. The granger said Potter was welcome to stay, although their accommodations were very limited. The granger fed Potter's horse and then invited him down into the dugout, which consisted of one room about sixteen feet square, but as neat as could be. In this room there were a clean bed, one table, four chairs, a stove, cooking utensils, the man, his wife, and two small boys. The wife soon prepared a good supper for Potter, and after they had eaten they stayed up and talked for quite a while. During this time the little boys fell asleep on the bed. Finally, the mother picked up the two boys and sat them in a corner, leaning them, still asleep, against the wall. She then informed Jack that he could occupy the bed, and she and her husband went outside. Potter turned in and was soon asleep, and slept soundly all night long, but when he awoke the next morning he found himself sitting in the corner with the two little boys, and the man and his wife were occupying the bed. After breakfast he gave them five dollars, but they protested, saying that fifty cents was quite enough for the poor accommodations he had received. Jack informed them that what he had seen and learned was worth five dollars to him.[9]

During the 1870s and 1880s, the games of monte and poker were "as popular on the range as bridge now is among women," recalled John Young early in this century. "The men who carried decks of cards with them were few, and consequently monte rather than poker or some other game was often played in camp so as to allow all hands to enter. Any number of people can with one deck of cards pike monte. The monte banker, whether in camp or in a big gambling house, always set a limit to the 'pikers.' Among us cow hands the limit was generally a dime. Unless the banker did set a limit he would, provided he played an honest game, 'go broke,' " recalled Young.[10]

These cowhands of the Three Circle Ranch in Texas are playing "hearts," a favorite card game of many cowboys. (Courtesy Erwin E. Smith Collection of Range-Life Photographs, Library of Congress)

By the late nineteenth century another popular pastime for cowboys was dominoes, which originated during the eighteenth century in Italy, or perhaps in the coffeehouses of Paris, from where it spread to Germany and later to America. In the last century, before plastic was invented, dominoes were made of ivory or bone, generally with ebony backs. On the face of each piece are two compartments. Each compartment is either blank or contains one or more pits—one, two, three, four, five, or six pits—representing numbers. They are shuffled on the table with their backs up, and each player draws at random the number that a given game requires. Several games can be played with dominoes, each with two to four players. There is Block and Draw, in which each player draws seven pieces; Muggins, where each player draws five; and Bergen, where each player draws six. In Block and Draw, the player with the highest-numbered double places the piece on the table, blanket, or some other flat surface. Each player leads alternately until the end of the game. If a player cannot play, it is the next player's turn. To play a piece, the number of pits in either compartment must match the number at the end of a piece that does not join any other. If no player can play, it is said that the "set is blocked," and the players count the number of spots on the pieces each still holds. Whoever has the lowest number of spots adds to his count the number held by his opponents. If anyone is able to play his last piece while his opponents hold theirs, he cries "Domino," and wins the round, adding to his count the number of spots the rest hold. The number required to win the game is one hundred, but it may be made less by agreement.[11]

Still another activity enjoyed by some cowboys was a shooting match. One Texas cowboy, J. L. McCaleb, remembered the time in the late 1860s that he found a five-dollar bill while he and some other cowboys were waiting to drive a herd of longhorns across the Red River into Indian Territory (now Oklahoma). It was the first five-dollar bill McCaleb had ever seen. The cook with McCaleb's outfit bet a two-year-old heifer against the five dollars that he could beat McCaleb in a shooting match. McCaleb knew the cook was a pretty good shot, but agreed to the bet. As McCaleb recalled:

> One of the boys got a little piece of a board, took a coal out of the campfire, made a black spot about the size of a twenty-five-cent piece, stepped off fifteen steps (about 45 feet) and yelled, "All ready, shoot." I jerked my old cap and ball Navy out and just about one second before I pulled the trigger I saw the heads of six Indians just over a little rise in the ground coming toward the camp. This excited me so that I did not hit the spot, only about one-half of my bullet touched the board just to the right of the target. I yelled to the cook, "Shoot quick! Look at the Indians!" By that time we could see them plainly on top of the rise. The cook fired, but never touched the board. So six big Osage Indians saved me my valuable find—the five-dollar bill.[12]

When the trail herds reached their destinations, the railhead cattle towns of Kansas and Nebraska, the cowboys were primed for pleasure. After weeks on the trail with lanky long-horned bovines, the cowboys were happy to turn them over to cattle buyers, receive their wages for the drive, and head for the business district. While some cowboys might bathe in a nearby river, creek, or pond, others might head for a local barbershop where for two bits they could use a tub with hot water in the back of the shop. A shave and a

A friendly game of cards among cowboys on a Wyoming ranch, ca. 1915.
(Courtesy Belden Collection, Wyoming State Museum)

haircut usually followed, and then the purchase of some new clothes to replace the frayed, dirty, and smelly ones worn on the trail, and sometimes a new pair of boots as well. Some cowboys on their first trail drive might decide to sample what the cattle town had to offer, including gambling, drinking, and women.

There were twice as many saloons as other businesses in most cattle towns. Only a few were of the Hollywood variety, with ornate bars, brass mountings, imposing mirrors, and paintings of nude women relaxed in beauty prostrate. Most were nothing more than long, narrow rooms, darkly lit, containing small and not very fancy bars and a few tables and chairs. About the only shiny objects were cuspidors and perhaps a bartender's balding head. At night kerosene lamps provided yellowish light. Everything was dirty and smelly. The blend of tobacco, liquor, straw, horses, kerosene, and human sweat in the summer and sometimes the sizzling spit of tobacco juice on a hot stove in the fall or early spring produced an unforgettable odor, one that many cowboys probably looked forward to on the long trail drive, but

Probably in anticipation of going to town, one cowboy
gives another a shave in camp on the Wyoming cattle
range, about 1903. (Courtesy American Heritage
Center, University of Wyoming)

one they often tried to forget after they had drunk or gambled away their
wages and were headed back to Texas, pockets empty and heads aching.

J. L. McCaleb, the young cowboy who found the five-dollar bill, experienced this "rake's progress" at firsthand during the late 1860s at Abilene,
Kansas. Late in life McCaleb recalled:

We bedded out our cattle for the last time near Abilene. . . . The boss
let myself and another boy go to the city one day. As it had been a long
time since we had seen a house or a woman, they were good to look at.
I wore a black plush hat which had a row of small stars around the rim,
with buck-skin strings to tie and hold on my head. We went into town,
tied our ponies, and the first place we visited was a saloon and dance
hall. We ordered toddies like we had seen older men do, and drank
them down, for we were dry, very dry, as it had been a long ways
between drinks. I quit my partner, as he had a girl to talk to, so I went

During the early days when Abilene, Kansas, was a cattle town, one Texas cowboy is said to have ridden into a combination saloon and billiard parlor and mounted a billiard table on his horse. The story inspired this drawing by an unidentified artist. (Author's collection)

out and in a very short time I went into another store and saloon. I got another toddy, my hat began to stiffen up, but I pushed it up in front, moved my pistol to where it would be handy, then sat down on a box in the saloon and picked up a newspaper and thought I would read a few lines, but my two toddies were at war, so I could not very well understand what I read. I got up and left for more sights—you have seen them in Abilene, Dodge City and any other place those days. I walked around for perhaps an hour. The two toddies were making me feel different to what I had felt for months, and I thought it was about time for another, so I headed for a place across the street, where I could hear a fiddle. It was a saloon, gambling and dance hall. Here I saw an old long-haired fellow dealing monte. I went to the bar and called for a toddy, and as I was drinking it a girl came up and put her little hand under my chin, and looked me square in the face and said, "Oh, you pretty Texas boy, give me a drink." I asked her what she wanted and she said anything I took, so I called for two toddies. My, I was getting rich fast—a pretty girl and plenty of whiskey. My old hat was now away back on my head. My boss had given me four dollars spending money and I had my five-dollar bill, so I told the girl that she could make herself easy; that I was going to break the monte game, buy out the saloon, and keep her to run it for me when I went back to Texas for my other herd of cattle. Well, I went to the old long-haired dealer, and as he was making a new layout I put my five on the first card (a king) and about the third pull I won. I now had ten dollars and I thought I had better go and get another toddy before I played again. As I was getting rich so fast, I put the two bills on the tray and won. Had now twenty dollars, so I moved my hat back as far as it would go and went to get a drink—another toddy, but my girl was gone. I wanted to show her that I was not joking about buying out the saloon after I broke the bank. After this drink things did not look so good. I went back and it seemed to me that I did not care whether I broke him or not. I soon lost all I had won and my old original five. When I quit him my hat was becoming more settled, getting down in front, and I went out, found my partner and left for camp. The next morning, in place of owning a saloon and going back to Texas after my other herds, I felt—oh! what's the use!¹³

Whiskey was the principal drink served in most cattle town saloons. A few of the better-known "bitters"—by 1870 the generic term for liquors— were Squirrel, Old Crow, and McBryan, a very popular brand. Texas cowboys often called whiskey "Kansas sheep-dip," not to be confused with the real thing, which was advertised as "the only certain cure for Scab and its Prevention" in sheep.

WOMEN AND DANCING also provided entertainment for the cowboys in cattle towns. The cowboys' dancing partners were usually prostitutes, known by a variety of names including "sporting women," "calico queens," "girls of the night," "painted cats," "sports," "*nymphes du prairie*," and "soiled doves." Some cowboys undoubtedly did more with them than just dance in the saloons and dance halls, and the fact that nearly all cattle towns had one or more brothels suggests a demand for such establishments to provide pleasure not only for the cowboys and drovers but for some local residents. Some researchers believe the term "red-light district" originated in Dodge City, Kansas, supposedly from a sporting house called the "Red

This late-nineteenth-century photo supposedly captures four cowboys playing cards with their six-shooters handy. In all likelihood, the scene was staged in a photographer's studio, perhaps in Cheyenne or Laramie, Wyoming. (Courtesy American Heritage Center, University of Wyoming)

Light" because of the blood-red glass in the front door, through which the light shone at night. Another tradition holds that the phrase came from the practice of trainmen leaving their railroad signal lanterns in front of a prostitute's place of business while availing themselves of her services.

While many of the girls used their real names, others did not. They chose names that appealed to their mostly Texas customers, southern names like Annie, Fanny, Jenny, Katie, Minnie, Hattie, and Mattie. One girl in Wichita, Kansas, was called Tit Bit, while in Dodge City there were Hambone Jane, Dutch Jake, and Cuttin' Lil Slasher. Other Kansas cattle towns had girls with such names as Peg-Leg, Lost Chicken, Lady Jane Gray, the Galloping Cow, Cotton Tail, and Sweet Annie.[14]

Teddy Blue, another early cowboy, who was reared in Nebraska, told of the time he and two friends visited the girls in one cattle town. As he recalled, "Three of us was in the parlor of Maggie Burn's house giving a song number called 'The Texas Ranger.' John Bowen was playing the piano, and he could play the piano, and Johnny Stringfellow was there sawing on a fiddle and he

This "soiled dove," called Squirrel Tooth Alice, resided in Dodge City,
Kansas, during its cattle-town days. She took much pride in her pet squirrel.
(Courtesy Kansas State Historical Society)

couldn't play the fiddle, and I was singing, and between the three of us we
was raising the roof. And Maggie—the redheaded, fighting son of a gun—
got hopping mad and says: 'If you leather-legged sons of bitches want to give
a concert, why don't you hire a hall? You're ruining my piano.' " It was also
Teddy Blue who said of Connie the Cowboy Queen and her $250 dress:

Sadie, a calico queen in Dodge City, Kansas,
during its cattle-town days.
(Courtesy Kansas State Historical Society)

"They said there wasn't an outfit from the Yellowstone down to the Platte, and over in the Dakotas too, that couldn't find its brand on that dress."[15]

Many cowboys apparently gambled in the cattle-town saloons and gambling halls. In addition to such card games as monte and poker, they indulged in a few dice games, including keno (which was something like bingo) and what we call chuck-a-luck today. In the post–Civil War period it was known as chucker luck or sweat, because an unlucky player would "sweat more than the law allows." The game is played with dice upon a piece of cloth on which the numbers one through six have been printed. "The money bet is deposited upon these numbers, according to the choice or fancy of the player. The bets being made, the 'dicer' [banker] puts three dice into a cup, shakes them up, and throws them upon the table; the numbers thrown win for the player, while the bank takes all the money not upon the fortunate numbers."[16]

After weeks of driving herds of longhorns up the trail from Texas and sleeping under the stars, cowboys found clean beds and good food in the Dodge House, and amusement in the adjacent billiard hall, at Dodge City, Kansas. (Courtesy Kansas State Historical Society)

As for the cattlemen who raised and owned the cattle, many became wealthy, especially those in Texas, and they found pleasure in using their wealth to buy material things they had previously been unable to afford, and to travel with their families. Most cattlemen in Texas and the Southwest were more careful with their money than the eastern and foreign ranchers on the northern plains. Many, including Charles Goodnight, who pioneered cattle raising in the Texas Panhandle beginning in 1876, did not gamble. In one instance, Goodnight told three cowboys he had hired that he never allowed gambling—that he didn't think it best. The three men agreed not to gamble and started out on a trail drive. As Goodnight recalled:

> All went well that day and night, but on the first graze with the herd next day, they got down, went to gambling, and left me with the cattle to herd. I worked around to them as soon as I could, and told them they had agreed not to gamble, and they must mount and get back around the cattle, which they did. We drifted on, and the next day at noon they got down under a pinon tree and again went to playing cards on a saddle blanket. I got around to them as before, and tried to talk with them

Cowboys from the LS Ranch in the Texas Panhandle disporting themselves at the bar in a Tascosa, Texas, saloon. (Courtesy Erwin E. Smith Collection of Range-Life Photographs, Library of Congress)

reasonably, but the fighter of the bunch, thinking he had me in a hole, looked up and said, "Well, by God, what're you gonna do about it?"

"One thing I can do; I can pay you off."

"What'll you do with your cattle?"

"Listen here . . . that's none of your business. They're my cattle and I paid for them. See that trail. Get your horse and get on it damned quick." I happened to have plenty of silver in my pocket, and just pitched their wages down to them without getting off my horse, made them saddle their own, and saw that they took the back-trail then and there.[17]

Most Texas cowboys working for cattlemen who opposed gambling found other ways to pass their leisure time, including reading, pitching horseshoes, chasing jackrabbits on horseback, racing horses, or having foot-races. Playing pranks on other cowboys (like the soldiers putting harmless snakes in bunks or bedrolls) was also popular, and, as we have already seen, singing or telling stories. Philip Ashton Rollins, a native of New Hampshire, who as a teenager rode twice with trail herds from Texas to Montana, later recalled:

Another form of amusement which might from time to time be conducted for a few minutes at table or about a camp-fire was a competitive
reciting of the inscriptions upon the labels of the cans of condensed
milk and other foodstuffs habitually used at the ranch. Partly for recre-
ative nonsense and partly out of loneliness when solitary in camp, every
cowboy sooner or later committed to memory the entire texts upon
these labels and could repeat them verbatim. With a penalty of five
cents for each mistake in punctuation, of ten cents for each error in a
word, the competitive recitals offered a sporting possibility.[18]

After the arrival of barbed wire and the end of the open range, cattlemen began acquiring their own ranches and fencing them. Soon towns were
established in ranching country, with schools, businesses, churches, law and
order, and other eastern institutions, and such communities provided cowboys with places to go to spend their money or simply sit and watch other
people. Most such communities in cattle country did not offer the earlier
pleasures of the railhead towns in Kansas, Nebraska, and elsewhere, but
they did provide opportunities for people to gather and hold dances. Dances
were big occasions for the cowboys, and they looked forward to shaving,
putting on clean shirts, and going to a dance. Dancing was so popular among
cowboys around Springer, New Mexico, that for many years they held
annual balls. By their fourth year they sent out eight hundred invitations—
not only to people in the region around Springer but abroad. One invitation
contained the following verse, actually a square dance call:

> *Caller, let no echo slumber,*
> *Fiddler sweatin' like a steer,*
> *Huffs a-poundin' at the lumber,*
> *Makin' music the stars could hear;*
> *Hug the gals up when we swing 'em,*
> *Raise them plum off their feet,*
> *Balance, all ye saddle warmers,*
> *Rag a little, shake your feet,*
> *On to next 'un, and repeat it,*
> *Balance to the next in waitin',*
> *Promenade, and off you go,*
> *Seat your pards, and let 'em blow.*[19]

There were cattlemen in Texas and the Southwest, of course, who did
find pleasure in gambling, sometimes for high stakes. What was described in

A turn-of-the-century horse race between two cowboys, with other cowboys and some towns-people of Tonkawa, Oklahoma, looking on. (Courtesy Western History Collections, University of Oklahoma Library)

its day as the world's biggest poker match took place between Isaac Jackson, a Colorado City, Texas, cattleman, and John Dougherty, a well-known Arizona gambler. The game was played in Bowen's Saloon in Santa Fe, New Mexico, in the spring of 1889. According to the traditional account, Dougherty raised the ante of the no-limit game until there was more than a hundred thousand dollars in the pot. Jackson, out of cash, met Dougherty by writing out a deed to his ranch along with ten thousand head of cattle. Dougherty, by then also out of cash, wrote something on a piece of paper, rose from his chair, and walked up to L. Bradford Price, the territorial governor, who happened to be watching the game. Dougherty drew his gun and demanded that the governor sign the paper. Price did, and Dougherty tossed it into the pot, announcing that the governor had just deeded him the Territory of New Mexico, and he was meeting Jackson's raise. At that, Jackson is said to have thrown his cards on the table in disgust. The gambler promptly returned the deed to New Mexico Territory to the governor and bought drinks for the three hundred or so people who were looking on.[20]

As the cattle industry spread onto the northern plains during the 1870s, many wealthy easterners and foreigners were attracted to cattle raising. Something of a new ranching aristocracy developed on the northern plains,

These Oklahoma cowboys, one playing a banjo, were apparently trying to find some pleasure when this photo was made late in the nineteenth century in front of a bunkhouse on the ranch they worked for. (Courtesy Western History Collections, University of Oklahoma Library)

and their idea of pleasure reflected the growing sophistication of the East. Perhaps most noteworthy was the Cactus Club, formed in Cheyenne, Wyoming, in June 1880 by twelve eastern-bred cattlemen, all members of the Wyoming Stock Growers' Association, who found Cheyenne's three major hotels—the Railroad House, the Inter-Ocean, and Tim Dyer's—lacking in the creature comforts they desired. By the summer of 1881, members of the Cactus Club had constructed a three-story, mansard-roofed brick-and-wood building, with hardwood floors and thick carpets, at a cost of $25,000. It became known as the Cheyenne Club.

The facilities included a dining room, where members often dressed in tuxedos for dinner, and a reading room and a billiard room on the first floor, six sleeping rooms upstairs, and a kitchen and a wine room in the basement. Trained servants were brought from the East to wait on the members. The best liquors money could buy were shipped by train to Cheyenne, along with all sorts of delicacies to please the tastes of the wealthy cattlemen. The racks in the reading room contained the latest copies of *Harper's Weekly* and major eastern newspapers, including the New York *Tribune* and the Boston *Herald-Traveler*. Here and there were copies of livestock journals, including the latest issue of *Breeder's Gazette,* published in Chicago.

John Lane, a well-known old-time country fiddler, who provided pleasure at many a cowboy dance in Texas. (Courtesy Western History Collections, University of Oklahoma Library)

The walls of the Cheyenne Club were decorated with fine paintings by such well-known artists as Albert Bierstadt and Paul Potter, a seventeenth-century Dutch artist. The paintings reflected the tastes and upbringing of the members, as did the club rules, which were not really in keeping with the rough nature of cattle ranching. Profanity or obscenity was prohibited, as was cheating at cards or any game in the clubhouse, and no games were to be played for a "money stake." But tradition has it that some of the wealthy cattlemen would bet on anything at any time, including the weather, the number of pages in a book, or the speed of a horse. Thousands of dollars supposedly changed hands in card games in the members' rooms at night.[21]

In 1885 a number of Wyoming cattlemen, including a few members of the Cheyenne Club, started a similar club in Laramie, about sixty miles northwest of Cheyenne. Other exclusive clubs for cattlemen and their pleasures included the Denver Club, housed in a large brownstone building on

The riders of these horses tied to the hitching posts were undoubtedly inside the Castillo Saloon. (Courtesy American Heritage Center, University of Wyoming)

Seventeenth Street in Denver, and another formed in Helena, Montana, during the middle 1880s. These clubs reflected a more gracious style of living for cattlemen on the northern plains. Their wealth enabled them to hire managers to administer their ranching operations for them, so that they had more time to enjoy the creature comforts, including city life. Many established homes in Cheyenne, Helena, Kansas City, Denver, and Fort Worth, though some preferred ranch life.

The Englishman Moreton Frewen was one Wyoming rancher who wanted his pleasures in his home. During the late 1870s he built a spacious two-story, thirty-six-room log ranch house on the high ground above a bend in the Middle Fork of the Powder River (east of modern-day Kaycee, Wyoming). Having decided that his home should have a piano, he ordered one from the East. When the piano arrived by rail at Rock Creek station, more than two hundred miles from his ranch, it had to be freighted overland by wagon to his house. This was in 1879, not quite two years before Frewen went to New York City to marry Miss Clara Jerome, sister of Jennie Jerome, who became Lady Randolph Churchill, mother of Sir Winston.[22]

Certainly the wealthy cattlemen, especially those in Texas who had worked hard for their money, found pleasure in buying things that had once been beyond their means, and in traveling. Captain Richard King enjoyed traveling from his huge ranch in south Texas to San Antonio, where he and his family would enjoy the luxury of the Menger Hotel and the city. On one visit Captain King arrived just ahead of his family and headed for the bar to have a drink. When he went upstairs, Mrs. King complained that she had ordered water for the pitcher on her washstand, and the water had not been delivered. King picked up the pitcher, walked to the balcony overlooking the lobby, and hurled the pitcher to the marble floor below, where it smashed into many pieces. He then called out to the desk clerk: "If we can't get any water up here, we don't need a pitcher." Moments later several pitchers of cool water were sent to the King rooms.[23]

The Cheyenne Club was a pleasure palace for Wyoming ranchers, but its rules were strict. Constructed in 1881, the club offered the best liquors and delicacies but prohibited obscenity, profanity, and gambling for a "money stake." (Courtesy American Heritage Center, University of Wyoming)

Another Texas cattleman who found pleasure in traveling was Abel Head "Shanghai" Pierce, who once arrived at a hotel in Hot Springs, Arkansas, without a reservation. After being told several times that there was no room available, Pierce, bellowing in his out-of-doors voice, asked the manager if the hotel was for sale. The manager said he owned a half-interest and would sell it for fifteen thousand dollars. Without batting an eye, Pierce wrote out a check for that amount and went upstairs to one of *his* rooms.[24]

Of all the cattlemen in the West who found pleasure in ranching, perhaps Theodore Roosevelt is best known. In 1884, Roosevelt established two ranches in the Badlands of Dakota Territory. The future president of the United States intended to make ranching his regular business, although his coming west was something of a retreat from painful memories and political defeat in the East. Roosevelt's political hopes had vanished with the presidential nomination of James G. Blaine, a man Roosevelt bitterly opposed, and only a few months before he headed west, Roosevelt's wife of four years had died in childbirth. Within hours his mother died too. Still, he found pleasure in the West. Years later he wrote:

While Wyoming cattlemen enjoyed the pleasures provided by the Cheyenne Club, these cowboys found their own pleasure shooting craps. (Courtesy American Heritage Center, University of Wyoming)

No life can be pleasanter than life during the months of fall on a ranch in the northern cattle country. The weather is cool; in the evenings and on the rare rainy days we are glad to sit by the great fireplace, with its roaring cottonwood logs. But on most days not a cloud dims the serene splendor of the sky; and the fresh pure air is clear with the wonderful clearness of the high plains. We are in the saddle from morning to night. The long, low, roomy ranch-house, of clean hewed logs, is as comfortable as it is bare and plain. We fare simply but well; for the wife of my foreman makes excellent bread and cake, and there are plenty of potatoes grown in the forlorn little garden-patch on the bottom. We also have jellies and jams, made from wild plums and buffalo berries; and all the milk we can drink. For meat, we depend on our rifles; and, with an occasional interlude of ducks or prairie chickens, the mainstay of each meal is venison—roast, broiled, or fried.[25]

Roosevelt's neighbors included the Eaton brothers—Howard, Alden, and Willis—who had left their native Pennsylvania to settle in the West. About two years before Roosevelt established his ranches in Dakota Territory, Bert Rumsey of Buffalo, New York, had visited the Eaton ranch. Because he found ranch life very pleasant, he remained longer than planned and soon insisted on paying for his keep. Reluctant at first, the Eatons agreed to take his money, and the dude ranch business was born. According to tradition, it was the Eatons who first applied the term "dude" to a paying eastern visitor. Custer Trail, as the Eatons called their ranch, was located at a spot where General George Custer had once camped, near what is now Medora, North Dakota. Visitors paid about twenty-five dollars a month to stay on their ranch and eat bacon or sowbelly, beans, potatoes, and meat from wild game. Many of the paying guests helped with the cattle and other ranch work. Accommodations were rather primitive, with the visitors staying in sod-roofed log cabins or in tents, but the Eatons' business continued to grow until the winter of 1886–87, when vicious winter storms swept the plains, killing thousands of cattle, including nearly all the Eatons' stock. That same winter their ranch house burned to the ground.

Why the Eaton brothers decided to move to Wyoming is unclear, but by 1904 they were operating their dude ranch under the shadow of the Big Horn Mountains, near modern Sheridan. Not only did easterners come to experience and find pleasure in daily western ranch life, but even westerners, including Charlie Russell, the cowboy artist; Will James, a cowboy turned artist and author; and Will Rogers, the Oklahoma humorist, stayed at the Eaton Dude Ranch, where guests could go horseback-riding, help with ranch chores, and find pleasure in the out-of-doors. While countless other dude ranches have since been established in many western states, the seven-thousand-acre Eaton Dude Ranch, adjoining the Big Horn National Forest, continues to operate, managed today by the fourth generation of the family. However, the Eatons no longer put on an annual rodeo for guests and the public. It simply became too much of a chore.[26]

THE WORD "RODEO" comes from the Spanish word *rodear,* meaning "to go around" or "to surround or encircle." To the Spanish in New Spain, or what is now Mexico, as early as the 1550s, *rodear* simply meant to round up the cattle. It was not until the nineteenth century that the foundation of the modern rodeo was laid. After the annual cattle roundup, cowhands might make a contest out of breaking a particularly wild bronco, or they might hold a competition to determine which cowboy was the best roper. Eventually these contests became better organized and became the foundation for the modern rodeo. Rodeos developed as celebrations. Perhaps the earliest one was held on July 4, 1869, at Deer Trail, Colorado. Cheyenne, Wyoming, held such a celebration in 1872, the forerunner of "Cheyenne Frontier Days" that began in 1897, but the 1872 event was nothing like the weeklong celebration now held in Cheyenne. Some Texas cowboys had arrived in Cheyenne and decided to celebrate the Fourth with an exhibition of steer riding. The following year Cheyenne residents watched as some cowboys celebrated Independence Day by breaking horses—broncobusting—on Sixteenth Street. The event was nothing like bronc riding in rodeos today; in 1873 the horse was ridden until it or the rider gave out, a process that could last fifteen or twenty minutes. Today there are two forms of bronc busting in rodeos, one in which the rider using a saddle, stirrups, and a braided rope tries to stay on a bucking horse for ten seconds. The other is bareback bronc riding, which came into its own in rodeos during the 1920s. The rider has no saddle, but a ten-inch-wide piece of leather with a handhold is cinched around the horse, in back of the withers. The rider has no reins to aid him in trying to control the horse and no stirrups to aid his balance. Only one hand is allowed for handhold, and the rider may not switch hands. Both forms of bronc riding are judged by two persons who watch for infractions of the rodeo rules.

The label "rodeo" for such events was apparently first used in 1882 by W. F. "Buffalo Bill" Cody, who is generally accepted as the originator of the

Wild West show as a form of entertainment. Cody used the term "rodeo" to describe an Independence Day celebration in North Platte, Nebraska, on July 4, 1882. Cody's rodeo, also labeled an "Old Glory Blow-Out," included roping, riding, and bronc busting. Perhaps a thousand cowboys competed for prizes.

Soon cowboys were referring to their celebrations as rodeos, and what became the grand finale of the modern rodeo was the judged event of bull riding. While any bull might be used in this event during the early days, Brahma bulls are generally used today, along with some Herefords, Angus, and Brangus—an Angus-Brahma cross. Under today's rules a rider must remain on the bull for eight seconds to qualify. Bull riding involves more than just the rider: There is a flank man whose job is to buckle onto the bull a broad leather flank strap that makes the bull buck. Sometimes a manila rope, fashioned with a honda, or slipknot, that can be pulled tight around the bull by the rider, is used. On a signal someone opens the gate to the chute where the bull and rider are waiting. Once the bull and rider are in the arena, the rodeo clown goes to work to distract the bull from attacking the rider, should he fall off. Nearby are the pickup men on horseback, ready to lift a fallen rider and head to safety since an angry bull, unlike a bucking horse, will often try to gore or trample a cowboy or horse. The experienced bull rider knows that every bull has something of a pattern in his bucking. For instance, some bulls create a whiplash effect with their hindquarters, throwing the rider forward, where the bull may toss his head back and hook the rider with his horns. Such a bull is often described as a "hooker." Another type rapidly bucks in a tight circle until the cowboy loses his equilibrium. This type of bull is usually called a "spinner."

In addition to the judged events of saddle and bareback bronc busting and bull riding, there are several timed events, including steer wrestling, in which a cowboy races his horse after a steer and hurtles from the saddle onto a running six- or seven-hundred-pound animal. The cowboy tries to get the steer off balance and throw him to the ground before he recovers.

Another timed event is calf roping, in which a cowboy on a good horse races after a calf, trying to rope it; if he succeeds, the horse takes over as the cowboy jumps to the ground. The horse is trained to keep the rope taut while the cowboy runs to the calf, tries to flip it to the ground, and with a piggin' string—a short piece of rope—carried in his teeth, ties the calf's two hind legs and a foreleg in a half hitch. When this is done the calf is said to be "hog-tied." The cowboy raises his arms in the air to signal he is done, and the calf then has five seconds to get free. If it does not, the cowboy qualifies. Really good calf ropers perform the task in less than ten seconds, reflecting tremendous coordination between man and horse.

Team roping is another timed event of modern rodeos that dates back to the nineteenth century, when two mounted *vaqueros* or cowboys raced after a steer until one had successfully roped the animal's head and the other its

These three young men found pleasure in dressing in cattle-range gear and posing for a Wyoming photographer, perhaps in Cheyenne, late in the nineteenth century. Whether they were real cowboys is not known. (Courtesy American Heritage Center, University of Wyoming)

heels. While their horses hold the lariats taut, the riders throw the steer to the ground and tie its legs. In rodeo competition today the cowboys must use either a square knot or a granny, both considered legal ties, and they must be below the hocks and above the dewclaw.

During the late-nineteenth and early-twentieth centuries, steer roping was another popular event in rodeos. It evolved from the open-range era, when cowboys often had to rope a steer that was sick or simply needed to be separated from the herd. By the 1920s, however, steer roping began to fade as an event because the cattle industry had changed and range cattle had all but disappeared. Calf roping simply replaced steer roping as a major rodeo event.[27]

By the 1890s celebrations that included rodeos were commonplace throughout the cattle-raising regions of the West, including the Oklahoma Panhandle. There the year's most popular family entertainment was the annual three-day Fourth of July celebration at McDermott's Grove on Frisco Creek, a few miles west of the D.C. Ranch headquarters. The picnic ground was owned by Myra McDermott, whose 160-acre claim included a beautiful cottonwood grove. Myra came from Liberal, Kansas, where her father owned a hotel. Families would begin arriving in the grove on July 3, camp there, and not leave until July 5. Steers were butchered and barbecued. Ice was hauled in by wagon. The central event was a competition (later called a rodeo) featuring local stock and local cowboys. A historian friend, Don Green, who knows the region well, noted that some local residents set up and operated concessions. One, run by Tommy McQuillen, consisted of a little glass case, mounted on a pedestal, enclosing a model racetrack with seven metal horses. McQuillen, cattlemen, and cowboys crowded around the little glass dome. McQuillen then provided a description of the race much as a broadcaster would do today, heightening the excitement of the miniature race.[28]

CHAPTER VIII

On the
🐑 Homestead

Though my bill of fare is always rather tame,
But I'm as happy as a clam
On this land of Uncle Sam's,
In my little old sod shanty on my claim.

—Unknown

I T MAY BE DIFFICULT for some readers to believe that the men, women, and children who homesteaded in the West had any leisure time or found any pleasure in their lives. "Proving up" on a claim was hard work, and each member of a family did his or her share to realize the dream, dangling on the horizon, of owning their own land. Those who did lived in simplicity, reared their children in simplicity, and found their pleasures in simple things.

Before Congress passed the Homestead Act in 1862, people who settled in the West had to pay $1.25 an acre for unimproved government land. Speculators also offered unimproved land for sale, but to make a profit they charged more than the government. For most settlers, buying such land was a burden. They often had to go into debt to do so, and even deeper into debt to buy livestock, tools, farm implements, household goods, and a supply of food to last a year, until they could raise enough to become self-sustaining.

After the westward movement gained momentum during the early part of the nineteenth century, there were calls for the federal government to provide free land for settlers. Congress passed a watered-down Homestead Bill in 1860, but President James Buchanan vetoed it. He was under heavy obligation to the proslavery Southerners, who wanted to slow westward growth, thereby maintaining a balance in the number of slave and free states. Buchanan's veto, however, divided the Democratic party and contributed to the election of Lincoln, whose Republican party strongly supported homestead legislation. After the Southerners withdrew from the Union, Congress passed a strong free land measure that authorized any citizen or intending citizen to select any surveyed but unclaimed tract of public land, up to 160 acres. If a citizen made prescribed improvements, paid a modest fee, and resided on the claim for five years, it was his land.[1]

Unfortunately, much of the land in the humid sections of the Middle West had already been sold or granted to railroads by the time President Lincoln signed the Homestead Act in 1862. As a result many settlers were forced to push farther west into the more arid and more isolated sections of the generally treeless Great Plains, where they built their homes of sod and fueled their fires with buffalo chips.

The barrenness and the isolation of the Great Plains combined to create countless human hardships, and homesteaders quickly learned to make do or do without. During the first three decades following the passage of the Homestead Act, it was not uncommon for homesteaders to take claims thirty or forty miles from the nearest town where staples and other supplies could be purchased. Everyone learned to improvise, salvage, and substitute one thing for another. Apple pies were sometimes made out of soda crackers, and people learned to stretch their existing supply of coffee by adding barley or rye that had been parched in the oven and ground in a coffee mill. When cream was added the coffee had a pleasing taste. When sugar was not available, sorghum molasses was the common sweetener, and sorghum taffy, popped milo, and corn were favorite refreshments, especially when neighbors came calling. Homesteaders learned to gauge the heat of burning buffalo or cow chips or corncobs to such a fine point that they could turn out as fine an angel food cake as can be made in the most elaborate contemporary oven. One Nebraska pioneer, Myrtle Oxford Hersh, recalled:

> I can't call up adjectives to describe the super quality of [corn] bread when eaten with "cow butter" or ham gravy, with a glass or two of rich milk or buttermilk made in the old wooden churn. It was simply "out of this world," as the youngsters today would say. So while we did not have frosted cakes, pies with two inches of meringue, and many other musts of today, we had food which met the needs of growing healthy bodies and we did not have to keep a bottle of vitamins from A to Z to keep us in good health. After a night of sound sleep we would be awakened in the morning to the tune of the coffee mill grinding the coffee for breakfast, or Mother sharpening her butcher knife on the stove pipe or a stoneware crock as she prepared to slice ham, bacon, or venison for

This couple apparently found a little pleasure when they stopped for a meal while crossing Greer County, Kansas, perhaps en route to a homestead claim late in the nineteenth century. Once such emigrants staked a claim, they probably lived in their wagon until they completed the construction of their sod house. (Courtesy Kansas State Historical Society)

breakfast as an accompaniment to hot butter-milk biscuits, potatoes, or fried mush, which made a real meal on which to start a strenuous day.[2]

In all likelihood, if the early homesteaders had not had a few social contacts, few settlers would have remained to suffer the drudgery and toil of frontier life. The narratives, recollections, and diaries of many early homesteaders, who lived in dugouts or built the walls of their homes out of slabs of sod cut from the prairie, leave little doubt that they took advantage of every opportunity to meet other people, to come together for a visit, a meal, and to sing, dance, laugh, and join in social games. Such social ties bound the homesteaders together. They found pleasure in the simple things, and they adapted to conditions, often making fun of their hardships. Humor enabled them to endure. In the Sand Hills of Nebraska there was a standing joke among some homesteaders. When a visitor would ask a homesteader how his family was, he would reply that the children were doing all right, but he hardly knew about his wife since theirs "was a passing acquaintance." When the visitor asked what the homesteader meant, he replied he only saw his wife when she was going out with a pan of ashes and he was coming in with a bucket of cow chips for the fire to keep from freezing in their soddy. With all that hustle and bustle, there was no time for idle conversation.[3]

Evan Jefferson Jenkins, who worked as receiver in the U.S. Land Office at Concordia, Kansas, during the 1870s, wrote that while the life of a home-

The musicians on the roof of this Logan County, Kansas, sod house may have selected the location to catch the breeze. This late-nineteenth-century photo was made on the Anderson homestead. (Courtesy Kansas State Historical Society)

steader entailed hardships and a wild appearance, "it also had its attractions and picturesque beauties. The fertile soil awaiting development, covered with nutritious grass and beautiful wild flowers; the whirring of the prairie-chickens or grouse as they arose out of the tall grass and sailed away with their free flight to an adjacent ridge; the shrill whistle of the curlew and plover; the gobble of the wild-turkeys in the timber skirting the streams; the familiar notes of the lark, robin, jay, and other of nature's songsters, possessed attractions for every member of the family. The prospect of a home unburdened with rent and unincumbered with debt and mortgage; the future prospect of schools and churches, and the noble impulse to establish the nucleus of a civilization unsullied by human slavery, in which the healthful breeze would fan the brows of a free people, served to dispel the otherwise gloomy outlook." Jenkins added:

> The conveniences and comforts of life being necessarily limited, induced the sanction of those social and neighborly customs adopted by the first settlers of the Middle and Western States. . . . Their limited means would not permit social entertainments on the scale of the Knickerbockers, in former times, on the shores of the Hudson; but the traditional friendship and unrestrained hilarity that prevailed in the log cabins of fifty years ago, in the then frontier settlements, were fostered and encouraged by the first settlers of Northern Kansas. The cold rules and artificial lines of polite society were ignored. Visiting among the women and spontaneous gatherings of the men were pleasant occasions, at which their wild surroundings and future prospects were discussed, serving the two-fold purpose of affording mutual aid and confidence, and of banishing any lingering regrets at leaving their homes in the East.[4]

Most homesteaders used any excuse to visit their neighbors, and most would welcome any visitor who might pass their way. Anne Bingham, who with her husband went west from New York State in 1869 to make a home in Kansas, remembered that "I had to be ready always for company, for some one from town or from the neighborhood came unexpectedly, and always for the day, staying for dinner. I kept fruit cake or cookies on hand all the time, and in the winter I usually made several mince pies and had them frozen to keep. With our fresh meats in winter, our home-cured ones in summer, chickens and eggs always plenty and fresh, I had no difficulty in getting up a meal. Before our fruit trees came to bearing, the wild grapes and plums were made into jelly for the year."[5]

During the warm months picnics were popular, especially on Independence Day and at the end of harvest. These picnics included not only food but races, games, speakers, a dance, and other amusements. During the 1880s and early 1890s, L. L. Scott of Ness County, Kansas, would take his homemade merry-go-round to picnics throughout the area. Scott recalled that his brightly painted red-white-and-blue merry-go-round was always a big hit, especially among the children. Scott remembered that people

> would come from miles around in lumber wagons, spring wagons, two-wheeled carts, horseback and afoot. I have known them to come 25 to 30 miles in a hayrack with 15 or 20 passengers. They would bring their

grub box and bedding with them and camp out on the picnic ground, for it would take them one day to get there and another day to get back home. There would always be a basket dinner at noon when the ladies would spread their tablecloths down on the ground in a low row, get out their knives, forks and spoons (no silverware), tin cups to drink from, tin pie pans to eat off of. Then there would be roast chicken, dried buffalo meat, ginger bread and they would trade enough butter to the country merchant for sugar, and they all had their milk and eggs and with sugar we always had custard pie and other edibles until the ground fairly groaned with the weight of it all. After dinner there would be speaking of some kind, a ball game, horse racing, greased pig catching and other sports for the older people and with a platform dance, both day and night and the men would put up rope swings for the children to play on. Everything was free. Just enough money to pay the fiddler was all that was needed.[6]

Social gatherings called bees saw neighbors and friends come together to help each other with major household chores such as apple paring, house or barn raising, quilting, and cornhusking. Since corn was often the staple of the homesteader's diet, and many families subsisted almost entirely on corn cakes, corn mush, corn dumplings, corn gruel, and corn on the cob for many months each year, the drudgery of husking all the corn was shared. A cornhusking bee turned otherwise tiresome work into a festive occasion. Most cornhusking bees were held during October, when the labor of harvest was almost over. Such bees were usually turned into contests where teams of young people would attack large piles of corn at the same time, stripping off the leaves and tossing the ears into waiting bins. The lucky young man who found an uncommon red ear was sometimes rewarded with a kiss from the girl of his choice. The first team to complete the shucking of its pile of corn would be declared the winner. When all the corn was shucked in this manner, everyone would sit down to dinner. Sometimes it might be potluck, where everyone brought a dish, or the meal might be prepared on the spot with each dish made from corn. After dinner there might be a square dance in a barn decorated with bunches of cornstalks or maize.

During the fall and early winter months quilting bees gave women the opportunity to gather socially to visit and to produce patchwork quilts needed for warmth on their beds during the winter months. Quilting bees might also include husbands who gathered to visit and children who played games while the women stitched together the top, bottom, and stuffing, which might consist of old blankets, pieces of rags, cotton batting, or even dried leaves.

Patchwork quilting in America dates back to colonial times, when newly arrived residents discovered that the quilted coverlets brought with them from England did not provide sufficient warmth. Since fabric was scarce, women stitched together whatever scraps of cloth they could find to create larger pieces of cloth. The first patchwork quilts were probably sewn randomly, in the style that came to be known as crazy quilt, but as fabric became more plentiful, simple geometric designs were developed, and patchwork quilting began to evolve into a genuine American art form with certain popular designs becoming widely known. One such design was called the Mourning Quilt, made from bits and pieces of a departed person's clothing. Other popular designs were the Album and Friendship quilts containing the favorite pattern blocks and the signatures of those sewing it. When the westward movement occurred, the pastime and the popular designs moved west with the settlers.

Another form of social gathering was a public sale, when a homesteader would decide to sell out and move to greener pastures to start life anew, or move back to where his own or his wife's parents lived, or to move to town. The homesteader selling out might serve a free lunch at noon on the day of the sale, or if he was hard up the neighbors would get together and bring food. All of the neighbors would come, including the women and children, and they would spend the whole day. The homesteader's goods would be sold, but for those attending the sale this was not that important. Most of them came for the social contact and the pleasure such a gathering provided.

Novelist and short-story writer Hamlin Garland, who lived in Dakota Territory during the 1880s, wrote:

> Haying was a delightful season to us, for the scythes of the men occasionally tossed up clusters of beautiful strawberries, which we joyfully gathered. I remember with especial pleasure the delicious shortcakes which my mother made of the wild fruit which we picked in the warm odorous grass along the edge of the meadow. Harvest time also brought a pleasing excitement (something unwonted, something like entertaining visitors) which compensated for the extra work demanded of us. The neighbors usually came in to help and life was a feast.[7]

Receiving letters and packages from back home nearly always brought pleasure to the homesteaders. When one man received a letter from his parents in the East asking what his children most wanted or needed for Christmas, he wrote his answer but lacked the two-cent stamp, or the money to buy one, to send it off. He asked a neighbor a couple of miles away for a stamp, but he had none. The neighbor, however, told the homesteader to go to the creek, where some traps had been set. The neighbor said the man might find a skunk, and skunk skins were worth from eight to ten cents each. The homesteader checked the traps, got his skunk, and skinned it. He then walked several miles to the nearest town to sell it, but the buyer refused because it was too fresh. The homesteader eventually sold it to another buyer in another town and received in payment a two-cent stamp, with which he mailed his reply to his parents. Several days before Christmas the homesteader received a package from his parents containing presents for their grandchildren.[8]

Christmas was usually a time of festivity, with parents planning weeks in advance to make the celebration special. The presents exchanged were often as simple as a pair of handmade mittens or wristlets or an apple or a little candy. Since there were few evergreens on the Great Plains, another tree or simply a branch from a tree sometimes found miles from the homestead was festooned with strings of popcorn and other homemade decorations. While some families preferred to spend Christmas Day alone, others might invite neighbors to join them and even hold a dance. Evan Jenkins recalled an incident early one Christmas Day when a farmer fired a shot from his gun outside the bedroom window of his lazy, late-sleeping neighbor. It was a signal "for bringing forth the 'little brown jug,' with the repetition of the adage, 'It is the early bird that catches the worm,' or the more patriotic expression, 'Eternal vigilance is the price of'—a Christmas dram!"[9]

Music was important to many homesteaders. Hamlin Garland remembered:

Our home was a place of song, notwithstanding the severe toil which was demanded of every hand, for often of an evening, especially in winter time, father took his seat beside the fire, invited us to his knees, and called on mother to sing. These moods were very sweet to us, and we usually insisted upon his singing for us. True, he hardly knew one tune from another, but he had a hearty resounding chant which delighted us, and one of the ballads which we especially liked to hear him repeat was called "Down the Ohio." Only one verse survives in my memory:

> *The river is up, the channel is deep,*
> *The winds blow high and strong.*
> *The flash of the oars, the stroke we keep,*
> *As we row the old boat along,*
> *Down the O-hi-o.*

When girls tired of outside games, they could turn to dolls. This photo was taken in Kansas about 1900. (Courtesy Kansas State Historical Society)

Mother, on the contrary, was gifted with a voice of great range and sweetness, and from her we always demanded Nellie Wildwood, Lily Dale, Lorena or some of Root's stirring war songs. We loved her noble, musical tone, and yet we always enjoyed our father's tuneless roar. There was something dramatic and moving in each of his ballads. He made the words mean so much.[10]

It seems to have been something of an unwritten rule that when a house raising was held, those who helped to build the house had the right to hold a dedication dance before the new settlers moved in. A square dance or "breakdown" was a popular form of home entertainment and pleasure. The services of a local fiddler and someone with experience as a "prompter," or caller, were obtained. Seated or standing on a raised platform, the fiddler would begin to play and the caller would give instructions. To such tunes as "Arkansas Traveler," "Turkey in the Straw," "Wagoner," and other melodies of equal flavor, the prompter called the figures either standing next to the fiddler or sometimes while dancing. One favorite call went like this:

This family orchestra made its own music in the parlor early in this century. (Courtesy Kansas State Historical Society)

Choose your partner, form a ring,
Figure eight, and double L swing.

First swing six, then swing eight,
Swing 'em like swinging on a gate.

Ducks in the river, going to the ford,
Coffee in a little rag, sugar in a gourd.

Swing 'em once and let 'em go,
All hands left and do-ce-do.

You swing me, and I'll swing you,
And we'll all go to heaven, in the same old shoe.

Chase the possum, chase the coon,
Chase that pretty girl 'round the room.

How will you swap, and how'll you trade
This pretty girl, for the old maid?

Wave the ocean, wave the sea,
Wave that pretty girl back to me.

Swing your partners, once in a while,
Swing them all in Indian style.

Rope the cow, and kill the calf,
Swing your partner, a round and a half.

Swing your partner before you trade,
Grab 'em back and promenade.

Grab your partner and sail away,
Hurry up, it's breaking day.

Swing 'em round, and round an' round
Pockets full of rocks to weigh 'em down.

There comes a girl I used to know,
Swing her once and let her go.

When you meet your partner, pat her on the head,
If she don't like coffee, give her corn bread.

Three little sisters, all in a row,
Swing 'em once and let them go.

Old shoe sole is about worn out,
Grab a girl and walk about.

Swing 'em east and swing 'em west,
Swing the girl that you like best.[11]

    In Nebraska and elsewhere on the Great Plains, dances would be held in a homesteader's house with a board floor, but if that was not available, a dirt floor would do. In the latter case, the music sometimes had to be stopped to sprinkle the dirt with a little water to keep down the dust. Dancers without boots often borrowed a pair or simply danced barefoot. When space was at a premium, dancers would take turns. If there was no fiddler around, the music would be provided by the player of some other instrument—a mouth organ (harmonica), accordion, or Jew's harp. The whole family attended the dances. When the younger children got sleepy they were placed in a row on a bed, where they slept through the music and noise until the dance ended.

    Dancing, however, was not universally accepted by homesteaders, especially after the churches and organized religion gained a foothold. In some areas of the Great Plains, strongly religious settlers disliked dancing because they believed the "waist-swing" was indecent. Also, dances often attracted the worst characters in the neighborhood, people who drank too much, and many a dance came to an abrupt end with a drunken brawl. Some church members tended to rank dancing on a moral scale with fishing and gambling on Sunday. Certain denominations forbade dancing outright. Even if a girl danced alone to the music of a fiddle, the act was deemed sinful and the girl was considered a fit subject for reconversion. On the other hand, a boy and girl might dance together to their own singing, even if they did so into the wee hours of the morning. This was not considered dancing, only playing.

To satisfy their elders' objections, young people established what they called the "play-party." These gatherings were held by invitation in a private home, usually in the front room with all of the furniture removed. During warm weather the play-party was often held outside in the front yard. Parents frequently accompanied their young people to the parties to chaperone their activities, but at dark they usually moved inside the house to visit, the men gathering in one room, the women in another, leaving the young people alone outside.

Such play-parties usually began about dusk and continued until about eleven o'clock or midnight. There were refreshments such as apples, pies, cakes, and cider, but no fiddler or square dance caller. Instead all the young people sang songs and played games, which required the players to walk, march, swing, skip, run, circle, hold hands, advance and retreat in rows, and otherwise dance to what were usually considered square dance songs, such as "Choose Your Mate," "Old Joe Clark," "Miller Boy," and "Skip-to-my-Lou"—

> *Lost your partner,*
> *What'll you do?*
> *Lost your partner,*
> *What'll you do?*
> *Lost your partner,*
> *What'll you do?*
> *Skip-to-my-Lou, my darling.*

Then, when a boy would take some other young man's partner and swing her around, he would sing:

> *I'll get another one,*
> *Better one, too.*

I'll get another one,
Better one, too.
I'll get another one,
Better one, too.
Skip-to-my-Lou, my darling.

Another favorite was "Jim Along Jo":

Cat's in the cream jar,
Run, girls, run!
Fire in the mountains,
Fun, boys, fun!

Chorus:
Hey, Jim along, Jim along, Josie!
Hey, Jim along, Jim along, Jo!

First to the courthouse,
Then to the jail,
Hang my hat on a
Rusty nail.[12]

The tunes used with such crude rhymes were often familiar airs handed down from colonial times. It was not uncommon for the words to be repeated over and over until someone felt the need of a change, perhaps to play a game. Popular running games included Forfeits; Ring-around-the-Rosy; Drop-the-Handkerchief; Run, Sheepie, Run; and Flying Dutchman. Often used with these games was the popular stanza:

Moses had an overcoat,
Hung it on the wall.
Some one stole that overcoat
And Moses had to bawl.
Down the river, oh, down the river,
Down the river we go.
Down the river, oh, down the river,
Down the O-hi-o.[13]

Another game popular at many play-parties was Old Mother Wobble Gobble. Old Mother Wobble Gobble began with the participants seated in a circle around the young person presiding, who began to recite a rhyme:

Old Mother Wobble Gobble, pray pity you;
Old Mother Wobble Gobble, do as I do.

At that point he or she would make a face or do a headstand or some other ridiculous thing. All the players were expected to imitate the person in the center of the ring. If they failed to do so, they had to forfeit some personal belonging such as a ribbon, necktie, handkerchief, ring, or shoe. To redeem the object, someone would hold the item over the owner's head and say, "Heavy, heavy hangs over your head; what shall the owner do to redeem it?" Another person, acting as a judge and sitting in the center of the circle, would ask, "Fine or superfine?" The person holding the object would answer "Fine" if the owner was a man, or "Superfine" if the object belonged to a woman. The judge would then pronounce the penalty. A popular penalty for young ladies was for each of the young men to "pick three cherries," which meant each gentleman would kiss her three times.[14]

Another of the more than a hundred play-party games known to have been popular was called "Clap-in, Clap-out," and it was usually played indoors. The young men would go out of the room, leaving the young ladies alone. A girl would then name a boy as her choice of partner. The named young man would be called into the room to guess who had chosen him. To make his selection, he would sit next to the girl. If he guessed correctly, the girls kept silent and the game was repeated with another boy. If, however, the first boy made a mistake, all the girls clapped their hands, and the boy had to leave the room to be called back later. This was kept up till all the girls had partners.[15]

Blind-Man's-Buff was another popular game. The 1864 edition of *The American Boy's Book of Sports and Games*, published in New York City, described the game as consisting of one person "having a handkerchief bound over his eyes so as to completely blind him, and thus blindfolded trying to chase the other players, either by the sound of their footsteps, or their subdued merriment, as they scramble away in all directions, endeavoring to avoid being caught by him; when he can manage to catch one, the player caught must in turn be blinded, and the game be begun again. In some places it is customary for one of the players to inquire of Buff (before the game begins), 'How many horses has your father got?' to which inquiry he responds, 'Three.' 'What colors are they?' 'Black, white, and gray.' The questioner then desires Buff to 'turn round three times, and catch whom you may,' which request he complies with, and then tries to capture one of the players. It is often played by merely turning the blindfolded hero round and round without questioning him, and then beginning. The handkerchief must be tied on fairly, so as to allow no little holes for Buffy to see through."

Another variation of Blind-Man's-Buff was called Boston. The players were numbered and all were seated in a circle, with the exception of one, who stood blindfolded in the ring. When he called two numbers, the persons answering to them had to change places, and if in doing so one of them was caught by the Blind Man, or if the Blind Man slipped into one of the vacant seats, the one who was caught or left without a seat then became the Blind Man. Whenever the Blind Man called "Boston!" all changed seats, giving him a chance to secure one for himself.[16]

Still another variant of the game was "Quack." One player was blindfolded, and the rest formed a revolving ring around him or her. The blindfolded person ordered a halt by tapping on the floor with a cane. The person to whom he or she pointed cried, "Quack, Quack!" in a disguised voice. The first person whose voice was recognized took the blindfolded person's place.[17]

While the descriptions of games and activities at play-parties suggest that they were often noisy and merry, they were not rough or risqué. Even kissing games were frowned upon by most young people and their elders. Girls who engaged in such games often lost the respect of others. Play-parties were conducted in a spirit of decency and order, but then, in the homesteaders' setting, nearly everything a person did was open to the public eye. There were well-established bounds of conduct beyond which one could not go with impunity. When a young man reached courting age, in his late teens, it became customary for him to procure a buggy, a sure sign that he was interested in some young lady. If she was of marriageable age, usually also the late teens, and was interested in matrimony, the courtship was usually brief, and a wedding date quickly set. Weddings were often festive occasions at which friends and neighbors came together, sometimes more for the food and merriment than to witness the nuptial ceremony. Afterward the couple often went to the bride's home for a wedding feast. Extended honeymoons usually were not possible, and the couple might spend their first night in the home of the bride's or groom's parents. Though the couple would generally try to keep their plans for the first night secret, the news often leaked out and their friends would come calling just after dark to serenade the newlyweds with drums, horns, tin pans, sleigh bells, and other noisemakers. This became known as a chivaree. The gathering did not disperse until the newlyweds made an appearance and gave the visitors a treat.

During the 1870s Evan Jenkins was invited to the wedding of a homesteader's daughter at her dugout home, which was surrounded by a beautiful grove of trees a few miles from Concordia, Kansas. He later wrote:

As I approached the dwelling my friend was issuing his commands to the playful children, while caring for the teams that had arrived; while his wife and a couple of neighbor ladies were dextrously plucking the feathers from the body of a large turkey and other fowls, and the prospective bride, blushing and happy, was receiving her lady friends. Beneath the branches of the grove was a sward of blue-grass, sown and cultivated by the settler. After caring for the teams, he showed me his farm, his fields and his improvements, closing his conversation by avowing his determination to build a more substantial residence in the near future. The hilarity of the guests upon arrival, evidenced that they were thorough partakers of the genuine enjoyment of witnessing a wedding on the frontier. The whole scene was one of happiness and pleasure. A number of the neighbors and friends of the parties had arrived, conspicuous among whom was the officiating clergyman, the Rev. Romulus Pintus Westlake, with the conventional plug-hat shading his manly brow, his bland countenance wreathed in happy smiles. . . . The neat calico dresses and sun-shade hats of the ladies, and the cheap but durable raiment of the gentlemen, were in harmony with the times, and with the plain domestic spirit that prevailed in the homestead region. The hour having arrived for the ceremony, the "dug-out" being found inadequate to accommodate the assembly, an adjournment to the grove was carried unanimously. The Rev. Romulus appeared to be in his natural element, supremely happy, prefacing the ceremony with a flow of eloquence, and an elaborate allusion to the happy union about to be consummated beneath the canopy of heaven, according to the institutions and laws of God and man. After he had pronounced the parties man and wife, he proceeded, in an impressive manner, to give them some gratuitous advice as to their marital obligations, throwing in some camp-meeting phrases concerning their duty to lead Christian lives, such as, "Train up your children, while young, in the way they should go, and when they become old they will not depart from it," and kindred benevolent injunctions! Good advice, I thought, but rather premature. . . . In due time the tables were spread in the grove, and dinner announced. Such a dinner! It seemed the culinary skill had been taxed to the utmost to prepare the bountiful repast spread before the assembly—roast turkey, pyramids of cake, columns of pumpkin pies, superb coffee, goblets of sweet milk, neatly indented rolls of choice butter, &c., &c. . . . Dinner over, the fiddler took a position on a bench under the shade of the trees, and the young people quickly formed for the customary dance. A number of middle-aged men and women joined in the quadrille, and seemed to have renewed their youth as they tripped lightly to the inspiring music. . . . The whole scene was one of enjoyment. The music, borne by the breeze to every part of the grove, and interrupted only by the clarion voice of the prompter, created a marked sensation of pleasure. A group of elderly ladies gossiped as they watched the agile movements of the young men, and graceful, modest promenading of the young ladies. A stalwart settler, leaning against a tree, declared to a neighbor that, "no new got-up cotillion could compare with the 'old Virginia reel,' when he and the old woman were young. The healthful, blushing faces of the ladies, and sun-tanned features of the gentlemen, when dancing, were radiant indices of genuine pleasure and happiness."[18]

As the lives of homesteaders became organized and the institutions of the East were set in place on the Great Plains, lodges were organized by the menfolk who had been members of the Masons, Knights of Pythias, Independent Order of Odd Fellows, Sons of Malta, Good Templars, Sons of Temperance, and other fraternal and benevolent societies back East or wherever they came from. And there was the Order of Patrons of Husbandry, better known as "the Grange," whose members—male and female—were called "Grangers." Many social affairs in each rural community were connected with the Grange, founded in 1867 by Oliver Hudson Kelley, a clerk in the agricultural department in Washington, D.C. Kelley, a Mason, copied Masonic methods in organizing the agrarian group. The first local Grange was established at Hiawatha, Kansas, in 1872, the same year Montgomery Ward and Company of Chicago was founded as the original wholesale Grange supply house, providing members with cooperative buying and in turn saving members as much as 20 percent of the retail price. By April 1874 there were twelve hundred local Granges in Kansas, Nebraska, Dakota, Iowa, Minnesota, Missouri, and Indiana, and a national membership of more than thirty thousand. The Grange promoted social relaxation and pleasure through association as legitimate human needs.[19]

While many emigrants settling on the Great Plains joined the Grange, some organized their own groups. Soon after a group of Bohemian emigrants settled in central Kansas during the late 1870s, they organized a union of Bohemian American settlers which they called "Blahobyt." Francis J. Swehla, who called the first organizational meeting, later remembered:

The object of the union was mutual aid in sickness and distress caused by misfortune; the cultivation of a fraternal feeling; mutual up-lift;

mental, moral and physical cooperation; and the burial of dead members. There being no public hall, no schoolhouse or church building, the society adjourned its meetings from the home of one member to that of another, generally upon invitation. The meetings were held regularly each month, a special meeting being called by the secretary only upon urgent necessity and at the request of some members. Dues were twenty-five cents per month, but in case of emergency a collection was made at a meeting. This union did a great good while it lasted, and it was active five or six years. Perfect harmony prevailed in its meetings, as all religious propaganda was forbidden by the constitution. We aimed at temporal welfare only, leaving freedom of conscience to all.

Later, after a hall was constructed in the rural neighborhood for meetings, another society was organized. Swehla wrote that the second society had "a different object, a library or reading club with a dramatic and athletic branch. . . . We began collecting money for the library by charging membership fees at the time of joining, and by monthly dues. Also we made donations of books. I started this by donating my *History of the Jesuits,* and others followed the example. However, we were all poor in the supply of books that could be spared."[20]

In many areas on the Great Plains, settlers organized "literaries," or discussions of literature, politics, and other issues of interest. In one neighborhood the farmers organized a Lyceum and met every Thursday evening to discuss the topics of the day. In many areas libraries were established within a year or two of the arrival of settlers, sometimes in rural schoolhouses that often were nothing more than dugouts. (Most homesteaders were anxious to provide schooling for their children even before school districts were formed and before any taxes were available for that purpose.) Such hurriedly constructed schoolhouses were often crude, but they served the purpose and provided satisfaction to the homesteaders. The settlers would simply take up a collection to buy windows, window frames, and doors and then hold a school raising to erect the building or construct a dugout.

On many homesteads, as elsewhere in the West, people found pleasure in laughing at themselves, though usually after the fact. In one instance a homesteader and his wife went to bed one winter night only to hear a commotion in their chicken house. The homesteader, who slept in his long underwear, jumped out of bed, pulled on his boots, grabbed a shotgun, and ran out the kitchen door. The buttonholes that held up the flap on his long johns got torn, and now the flap was hanging open. The homesteader stopped in front of the chicken-house door and demanded that whoever was inside come out. At that moment the family's old hound dog slipped around the corner of the house and sniffed at the homesteader from behind. Surprised by the dog's cold nose on his bottom, the homesteader accidentally fired his shotgun. His wife later recalled with a smile, "We spent the rest of the night picking chickens. He killed thirteen."[21]

The lives of homesteaders were simple. So were their pleasures. But as the newcomers proved up on their claims and rural areas began maturing, trading centers developed. In these growing towns the institutions of the civilized East took hold, offering homesteaders and townspeople alike the opportunity to find new pleasures.

CHAPTER IX

In the Prairie ~ Towns

The high prize of life, the crowning fortune of a man is to be born with a
bias to some pursuit, which finds him in employment and happiness.
                                        —*Ralph Waldo Emerson*

OPPORTUNITIES TO FIND pleasure on the western prairies and
plains increased as small rural towns developed during the latter
half of the nineteenth century. The establishing of towns was a
natural occurrence, since homesteaders had to have someplace to sell what
they produced on their farms, and to buy goods and merchandise they could
not. Then, too, not everyone who came west wanted to till the soil. Certainly
this pattern of town development was not unique to the West. It had also
occurred east of the Mississippi, although in the West, towns were often laid
out and named even before houses or commercial buildings were constructed. Commenting on western towns when he crossed Kansas Territory
to the goldfields of what is now Colorado in 1859, Horace Greeley
observed: "It takes three log houses to make a city in Kansas, but they begin
calling it a city as soon as they have staked out the lots."[1]

As they grew, most towns on the prairies and plains were nothing more
than villages, but the pride felt by their residents dictated that they be called
cities. Although each community hoped its settlement would grow into the
metropolis the word "city" suggested, most did not, as the number of ghost
towns in the West attests. But many new towns did grow to become cities,
and in turn, places where people sought pleasure.

Many people still remember what life was like in the small towns on the
western plains and prairies before the arrival of radio, television, videos,
compact discs, and other forms of modern canned entertainment. They
recall how they enjoyed simple pleasures, and how they used every excuse
imaginable to celebrate. A national holiday, house or barn raising, birthday,

graduation, visit by a relative, anniversary, or a wedding was excuse enough to come together to eat, drink, relax, and celebrate.

Early settlers on the prairies and plains made their own music whenever possible. This couple in Comanche County, Kansas, entertained themselves in the sitting room of their home at the dawn of the twentieth century. (Courtesy Kansas State Historical Society)

Weddings were something special, and chivarees followed almost every wedding. While no two chivarees were exactly alike, most followed the pattern established in homesteading times. Members of the chivaree party, both men and women, would march to the home where the newlyweds were staying, to the sound of banging drums, ringing cowbells, and rattling pots and pans. The party would usually try to arrive just after the couple had gone to bed and begin to beat on the door demanding entrance so that they could celebrate the wedding or drink to the bride's health. Sometimes the husband would give the leader of the party money to celebrate somewhere else, perhaps at a local saloon or someone's home. But should the new husband ignore the demands of the visitors, he might be dragged off into the night. Such was the case in September 1857 at White Cloud, Kansas Territory, a town of perhaps two hundred people located on the Missouri River. The local newspaper reported what happened:

The first "hocht zeit," as the Dutch would say, came off last Sunday, and was a rich affair. The wedding party started from the "Jug Tavern" or "Globe Hotel," in a two-horse wagon, in the morning to proceed two miles below town, where the ceremony was to be performed. Upon their departure they were saluted with yelling, screaming, and hammering on all manner of tin pans and buckets. In the night a crowd proceeded to the house where the happy young pair was roosting, after they had stowed themselves away for the night. They entered the house, seized the bridegroom, and dragged him out amid the firing of guns and the yelling of the crowd. They were taking him in chemise to a creek nearby to duck him, but were bought off by the promise of a treat on the morrow. Matrimony is no small undertaking in White Cloud.[2]

About three years later, in 1860, the editor of the same newspaper reported: "We believe the practice of belling, and fussing generally, upon wedding occasions, prevails in all parts of the country, but our Western people have a way of their own to do these things. We are informed that a wedding came off somewhere in the Missouri bottom, a short time ago, and in the evening a crowd went to the place for a spree. They performed such tricks as shooting bullets through the windows, breaking down the door, dragging the couple out of bed, and tumbling them about on the floor, cutting open the feather beds, tearing up the floor, and indulging in other equally innocent tricks. It requires backbone to get married out this way."[3]

The yellowing pages of nineteenth-century western newspapers contain countless reports on weddings, dances, and other local activities of pleasure in towns on the plains and prairies. The newspapers—nearly all of them were weeklies—were necessary institutions if a town was to grow and survive. For a town to have a weekly newspaper was a sign of growth and prosperity, and it helped to promote the town. A newspaper also provided a sense of community for its readers, since it provided them with news and information of local interest and a sense of belonging. If the paper had an active editor who combed the town for gossip and amusing incidents, readers found much pleasure in reading the news. Here is a sampling of such items from nineteenth-century western papers:

The other morning a young man thought he felt a bug on his neck, and brushed away at it for five minutes before he discovered it was a chunk of chewing gum on his collar, deposited there by his girl the night previous, just before business hours.[4]

The Ladies Sewing Circle at Osborne, Kansas, late in the nineteenth century. (Courtesy Kansas State Historical Society)

Dr. H———— tells a good story at the expense of our worthy ex-city marshal. While the latter was endeavoring to rescue the team which broke through the ice on election day, he broke through himself, and came very near drowning. As the ice was giving way, and he about going down, he exclaimed, at the top of his voice, "I have not voted—I have not voted!" Of course he was rescued, as candidates could be found within the hearing of every man's voice.[5]

The Methodist folks have tacked cards on the walls of their church calling attention to the fact that you are not expected to spit on the walls of the building or throw nut hulls around promiscuously. They intend to break up this practice if it takes all winter.[6]

In an obscure corner of this county (if any place in the county can be obscure) lives a young man troubled with a ring, too tight for his finger. To remove it he adopted the original plan of shooting it off with his revolver. He made a perfect success of it, but the probabilities are that the doctor will have to finish the job of taking off the finger.[7]

These men in Hays, Kansas, posed for a photographer while playing duplicate whist. (Courtesy Kansas State Historical Society)

A couple came from Ohio, arriving in Leavenworth a few days since, and were married about noon. At 8 o'clock in the evening a bouncing boy weighing ten and a half pounds, was born to the blooming bride of less than ten hours. This is only another evidence of the fertility of Kansas, and a proof that the drought is not so general and fatal in its effects as some of our eastern friends suppose.[8]

The citizens of Winfield turned out en masse lately headed by a band of music and fought grasshoppers all day. The account says: "As the people drove clouds of these pests before them, the band discoursed sweet music, and made the war a very amusing and interesting one. The army of citizens fought them all day long, and returned at night in good order."[9]

Music provided townspeople on the plains and prairie with much pleasure. As the towns grew in population, brass bands were organized as soon as a community had enough musicians. Most of the bands had eight to fifteen members, and by the end of the nineteenth century they were as common in Kansas and Nebraska as the town well on Main Street or the hitching posts in front of the post office and the blacksmith's shop. It did not take much to get a bandsman to don his uniform, get his cornet or bass drum, and march down Main Street. At the first sound of band music, the townspeople turned out and other activities ceased.

The local band also usually played at the county fair. As farming became more diversified in rural areas surrounding the towns, merchants in the county seats organized fairs. "It was even more glorious than the Grange Picnic, was indeed second only to the fourth of July, and we looked forward to it all through the autumn," wrote Hamlin Garland.

Garland remembered the fair in a town near his father's farm. The fair, he wrote, "came late in September and always lasted three days. We all went on the second day, (which was considered the best day) and mother, by cooking all the afternoon before our outing, provided us a dinner of cold chicken and cake and pie which we ate while sitting on the grass beside our

The town band in Wakefield, Kansas, had its own bandwagon in 1899. (Courtesy Kansas State Historical Society)

This late-nineteenth-century town band was in Arkansas City, Kansas. (Courtesy Kansas State Historical Society)

wagon just off the race-track while the horses munched hay and oats from the box. All around us other families were grouped, picnicking in the same fashion, and a cordial interchange of jellies and pies made the meal a delightful function. However, we boys never lingered over it,—we were afraid of missing something of the program.

"Our interest in the race was especially keen, for one of the citizens of our town owned a fine little trotting horse called 'Huckleberry' whose honest friendly striving made him a general favorite. Our survey of fat sheep, broad-backed bulls and shining colts was a duty, out to cheer Huckleberry at the home stretch was a privilege.

"To us from the farm the crowds were the most absorbing show of all. We met our chums and their sisters with a curious sense of strangeness, of discovery. Our playmates seemed alien somehow—especially the girls in their best dresses walking about two and two, impersonal and haughty of glance," recalled Garland.[10]

Many residents of towns located along or near creeks or rivers found relaxation not only in catching fish but in eating their catches, especially very large catfish. This was particularly true in Nebraska and Kansas. At

These two children apparently found pleasure using turkeys to pull their wagon near Nortonville, Kansas, around the turn of the century. (Courtesy Kansas State Historical Society)

Topeka, Kansas, during the summer of 1859, the largest catfish caught in the Kansas River weighed 160 pounds. In 1865, near Junction City, Kansas, fishermen using a seine pulled in seven fish weighing between 40 and 105 pounds. Trying to catch the big fish was sometimes dangerous. Harry Pipher went fishing in the Kansas River, near Manhattan, in April 1871. After a few minutes he had a bite. It was a big catfish, weighing 40 pounds, and it was all Pipher could do to pull it to shore—he weighed 56 pounds. Another Kansas fisherman, Abe Burns, was not so lucky. One day he went fishing below the dam and mill on the Kansas River in Lawrence. He attached a grabhook to his wrist, waded into the river, and swam under the mill in an effort to hook a big catfish. According to tradition, Burns apparently hooked a big cat he could not handle. He fought to take the fish, lost, and probably drowned.[11]

True stories of fishing apparently were the basis for embellished tales often reported by editors of local newspapers for the pleasure of their readers. In one such story a fisherman supposedly caught two large catfish in a net. According to the editor, the fisherman treated the fish so well that they became friendly. The fisherman then rigged a harness on them, which he attached to the bottom of his small boat. The catfish happily pulled it along the river as he checked his trout lines and fishnets. Another fish story related

This early settler made full use of his leisure time fishing. This photo probably was taken during the late nineteenth century on Walnut Creek in Rush County, Kansas. (Courtesy Kansas State Historical Society)

how catfish had grown sacks under their chins in which to carry water should the stream dry up during a drought.

Such hyperbole, as reported by local newspapers, provided considerable pleasure to readers. In this vein, the editor of the *Lakin* (Kansas) *Eagle*, wrote in the May 20, 1879, issue:

As a truth and no fabrication, Kansas is not a windy country. We have here during twelve months of the year an imperceptible circulation of air from the south, west, north and east (varied to suit one's taste and incon-

*Fishing gave many people pleasure. Avid Kansas fishermen Abe Burns (left) and Jake
Washington caught these blue catfish (sometimes called Mississippi channel catfish) in the
Kansas River late in the nineteenth century. The fish on the left weighed 90 pounds, the one
on the right 110. Abe Burns later lost his life trying to hook another large catfish.
(Author's collection)*

venience) that in other states as in Colorado, Illinois and Nebraska,
might be called high wind, but here it is considered nothing but a gentle
zephyr. In some states they have high winds but never in Kansas. A two
gallon funnel turned flaring end windward and gimlet end downward
will collect enough of Kansas zephyrs in seven hours to drill a hole in
solid sand rock one hundred and eight feet deep. Condensed air does the
work most successfully. . . . The men here are all pigeon-toed and bow-
legged. This is caused from an unceasing effort to stick the toes into the
earth and trying to keep a strong foothold on terra firma.

The gentlemen carry a pound of shot in each breaches [*sic*] leg to
keep them (the gentlemen) right side out.

Such tall tales reflected readers' interest in storytelling and their desire
to be entertained. Without the numerous forms of packaged entertainment
found today, people sought amusement in stories, and if they were not good
at telling them, they listened. Nearly every town on the plains and prairies
had at least one good storyteller, whose tall tales were enjoyed (although
rarely believed) by many. One often-repeated tale made the rounds, during
wet years, from southwest Kansas northward into South Dakota. Farmers
visiting nearby towns would claim their crops were so good that when they
climbed to the top of their tallest cornstalk and looked west, they could see
the Rocky Mountains.

A master yarn spinner of the plains, F. J. Cloud, claimed he had the most
intelligent toad ever born. Cloud told how the toad knew every member of
the Cloud family on sight and would follow them around like a pet dog. At
night, when the toad had had his fill of insects, it would pester some member of the family until that person turned off the light that was attracting the
insects. When the toad was happy about something, it would perform acro-
batic stunts, including handsprings. Cloud said he never learned where the
toad hibernated during the winter months, but it turned up regularly every
spring for many years.[13]

On the western plains and prairies the extremes in climate—vicious
thunderstorms and tornadoes in the spring, extreme heat in the summer,
and arctic cold and blizzards in the winter—provided good material for tall
tales. After a tornado passed through one county during the 1890s, a
farmer came to town and claimed the tornado had helped him. The storm,
he said, came as he was plowing one of his fields. The tornado took his
plow and spun it around till the land he had laid out was plowed up as well
as if he had done it himself. Abe Peters, a western Kansas storyteller,
recalled:

> I have seen some hard winters out in western Kansas. There are some
> things that an old resident learns out there from observation and expe-
> rience. One is that when you are facing a hard wind to keep your mouth
> shut.
>
> One day I was traveling with a tenderfoot from the East. He was a
> long, slender man about 6 feet 3 inches long and about 6 inches wide.
> He had no more meat on his bones than a fork handle and was about the
> most emaciated looking person I ever saw.

As I was saying, one day we started to ride across the prairie when the wind came up in our faces, blowing at the rate of a hundred miles an hour or so. The tenderfoot opened his mouth to say something to me. I heard him make a curious noise and looked around to see what was the matter and saw that he had inadvertently swallowed about six or seven barrels of wind. He looked like an inflated air cushion and seemed to be about four times the size he was naturally. It seemed to set him sort of crazy and he jumped out of the buggy. When he lit on the ground he bounced into the air like a rubber ball and then went bounding across the prairie like a tumbleweed before the wind. At the end of three miles he fell into a canyon where the wind couldn't hit him and stopped, but it was a week before he was back to his normal size.[13]

As photographers settled in the towns on the plains and prairie during the late nineteenth century, they did their share in contributing to the tall-tale version of the West through pictures. Photographers produced exaggerated prints that depicted everything from giant ears of corn to wagons loaded with outsize produce. These illustrations, created by using double negatives and other tricks of the trade, were sold as postcards, which townspeople found pleasure in mailing to their friends and relatives in the East.

While weekly newspaper editors frequently reprinted the better tall tales heard in their communities, they also entertained their readers with fiction, poetry, and other material similar to that found in modern magazines. Sometimes editors reprinted such material from eastern publications, but they were not averse to printing the works of local writers and poets. One poem that eventually gained national attention was "Western Home," by a local physician, Brewster Higley. In 1873, the *Smith County Pioneer*, a weekly newspaper at Smith Center in north central Kansas, published Higley's poem. Higley received so much praise for the poem, he asked Dan Kelley, a local musician, to set the words to music. Kelley then asked two other musicians, John C. Harlan and his younger brother, Eugene, to help, and they spent many hours until they composed a tune to fit the words. The Harlan brothers—John played the guitar and Eugene the violin—played the song along with others when performing at dances, reunions, parties, and celebrations in Smith Center and other communities in Smith County. The song became very popular, and it was passed along from memory and by word of mouth.

Through the years the song spread across much of the West, and the names of those responsible for the words and music were forgotten until

A photographer made it appear that giant cabbages were grown on the plains. (Courtesy Kansas State Historical Society)

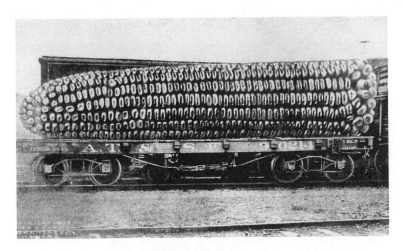

A load of Kansas corn produced by a photographer having a little fun. (Courtesy Kansas State Historical Society)

(Left) Dan Kelley, the man who wrote the music to "Home on the Range." (Courtesy Kansas State Historical Society). (Right) Dr. Brewster Higley, who wrote the words to "Home on the Range." (Courtesy Kansas State Historical Society)

John Lomax, a professor at the University of Texas in Austin, compiled a book called *Cowboy Songs and Other Frontier Ballads,* which was published in 1910. The song became even more popular during the years that followed, but it was not until 1933 that the song became the vogue—thanks to President Franklin Roosevelt. According to one account, a group of newspaper reporters sang the song on Roosevelt's doorstep in New York City the night he was first elected president. When Roosevelt heard them he asked them to sing it again. Then he supposedly said, "That's my favorite song." By then the song was known as "Home on the Range," and its words, as first printed by the *Smith County Pioneer* in 1873, were:

> *Oh, give me a home where the buffalo roam,*
> *Where the deer and the antelope play,*
> *Where never is heard a discouraging word*
> *And the sky is not clouded all day.*
>
> *Chorus:*
> *A home, a home, where the deer and the antelope play,*
> *Where never is heard a discouraging word*
> *And the sky is not clouded all day.*

Oh, give me the gale of the Solomon vale
Where life streams with buoyancy flow,
On the banks of the Beaver, where seldom if ever
Any poisonous herbage doth grow.

Oh, give me the land where the bright diamond sand
Throws light from the glittering stream,
Where glideth along the graceful white swan,
Like a maid in her heavenly dream.

I love the wild flowers in this bright land of ours,
I love, too, the curlew's wild scream,
The bluffs of white rocks and the antelope flocks
That graze on our hillsides so green.

How often at night, when the heavens are bright
By the light of the glittering stars,
Have I stood there amazed and asked as I gazed,
If their beauty exceeds this of ours.

The air is so pure, the breezes so light,
The zephyrs so balmy at night,
I would not exchange my home here to range
Forever in azure so bright.[14]

Another Kansas newspaper that accepted poetry and prose from its readers was the *Fort Scott Monitor*. One contributor was Eugene Fitch Ware, a young man from Iowa who had homesteaded near Fort Scott during the late 1860s. The editor was so pleased with Ware's material that he was hired in 1870 to work full-time for the paper. Two years later Ware himself became the editor, but after only a short tenure in that post he resigned early in 1873 to read law and become an attorney. However, he continued to entertain local readers with his poems in the paper, written under the pen name Ironquill. Even men enjoyed his verse, which soon was published by other newspapers in Kansas and elsewhere.

One of his poems is "A Sea-Rious Story":

From Panama to San Francisco bay,
An overcrowded steamship sailed away.

The third day out, a husky miner came
Up to the clerk, and calling him by name,

He said: "Your ship is crowded, sir, a heap
Too much for me; find me a place to sleep."

The clerk responded, with a stately smile:
"Sleep where you've been a sleeping all the while."

"It kaynt be did," the miner answered quick.
"I slept upon a deck hand who was sick;

"He's convalessed, and now since he is stronger,
He swears he won't endure it any longer."

The clerk was pleased to hear the miner's mirth,
And fixed him with a "snifter" and a berth.[15]

The outspoken views of some western newspaper editors also provided entertainment for their readers. Many early frontier editors were highly individualistic and idiosyncratic, and their papers reflected their personalities in a way that is nearly lost in today's corporate journalism. Many country editors were self-educated printers, but others were former lawyers, teachers, preachers, and storekeepers who did not hesitate to speak their minds. Most of them did not have polished educations, but as residents of their communities they were usually strong advocates of schools, lecture programs, libraries, and the like, which would not only educate but entertain their readers. Through the printing of excerpts from books like Sir Walter Scott's *The Lady of the Lake,* many editors helped to make contemporary English literature popular. Some newspaper offices also sold stationery goods, including books, many by such British authors as Scott, Byron, and Burns. Printed by eastern U.S. publishers, these books began to flood the West during the latter half of the nineteenth century, providing westerners with much pleasure. For a time James Fenimore Cooper was acclaimed in the West as a rival of Scott, but—though he did influence western fiction to some degree—he never achieved Scott's prestige. Books by British authors were plentiful because they could be published at little cost. There were no international copyright laws, and they were reprinted without the authors' permission and without any kind of payment to the authors or their English publishers.

Oscar Wilde learned this firsthand while traveling by train from Salt Lake City to Denver. A noisy young man came down the aisle of Wilde's car shouting: "Oscar Wilde's poems for ten cents!" Wilde supposedly stopped the young man, grabbed a copy of the book (printed on cheap paper), and accused the seller of infringing on the rights of an author. The seller reportedly responded: "Do you suppose the feller that rit the book cares a damn? Why, he won't know it." Wilde replied, "I'm the author of those poems." The bookseller did not believe Wilde, but after another passenger told him that Wilde was in fact who he claimed to be, the young man took Wilde some oranges as a gift.[16]

Charles Dickens also resented the loss of royalties from the piracy of his works in the United States—one reason for the sour commentary on the United States in his book, *The American Notes*. Until 1891 American publishers could reprint any British writer without paying a cent for the privilege. In turn, British publishers were not enthusiastic about U.S. authors who demanded royalties.

Civil and criminal trials provided another form of entertainment for residents lucky enough to live in county seats. Courthouses were frequently packed by townspeople and farmers from nearby rural areas, especially if a trial involved someone prominent in the community or a well-publicized crime. The same was true in newly established county seats where courthouses had not yet been built. Louis Kossuth Pratt, who settled at Norton in northwest Kansas in 1877 to practice law, recalled such a situation during his first courtroom case:

> Dr. Simmons was plaintiff and Mr. McGuire was defendant. It was one of those justly celebrated corn stalk and buffalo grass cases. The whole country there was at the trial, including quite a delegation from Nebraska. . . . This very important suit took three days to dispose of and resulted in a verdict of $5 or $6 for Dr. Simmons. It was tried before a jury, and an audience of, I should say, twenty or thirty men. Some of them traveled quite a distance to hear it. . . . It rained continuously, night and day, for about three days and ended in a snow storm. At that time there was nothing but sod roofs on any building in the country and they all leaked like sieves after the rain had lasted for perhaps a day. The trial was opened in Squire Ellis' house, but it leaked so badly that we adjourned to the school house, and the result was not quite so bad for a while. Every once in a while the solemnity of the trial would be broken by the fall of a bucketfull of mud and water coming down through the roof and alighting on the table or somebody's head or lap. . . . We had a great time dodging to keep out of the way of the water and mud when expounding the law to the justice.[17]

In many towns, schoolhouses were built before courthouses. By the 1870s settlers in many areas of Kansas and Nebraska were beginning to substitute a faith in popular education for religious zeal, and they lost no time in establishing schools and, in time, colleges. Schoolhouses were often used for the play-parties that replaced more conventional dances. They usually followed a school program, and the whole evening was sometimes called "school entertainment" to distinguish it from polite society balls and eastern sophistication. Schoolhouses were also used for political meetings, debates, literary societies, and other forms of entertainment during evenings and on weekends. In some communities rudimentary public libraries were first established in schoolhouses.

Traveling lecturers, including professors, would often present programs for townspeople in the local schoolhouse. In addition, "spelling schools," or spelling bees, were frequently held during the winter months, especially in the late 1860s and 1870s. Parents and children attended and sides were chosen. The schoolteacher or some other educated person of prominence in the community was selected to call the words. Two systems were used. One was called "spell down," in which the word caller alternated between two lines of standing spellers. When one person missed a word he or she was "spelled down" and took a seat. The side that stood the longest had "spelled down" the other side and won the contest. The other system was called "chase the fox." It was built on the principle of head marks awarded for spelling each word correctly. When a speller received a head mark it registered a point for his or her side. The side with the most points at the end was the winner.[18]

Occasionally spelling contests were followed by a dance. Because dancing was so popular, merchants often sponsored them to help promote their businesses. When C. W. Bell, a businessman and fiddler in Ness County, Kansas, purchased the St. James Hotel during the early 1880s, he celebrated its reopening by holding a ball. His wife played the organ, supplementing her husband's fiddling.[19]

During the spring of 1879, T. A. McNeal, who later became a well-known Kansas newspaperman, witnessed his first town dance. The dance was organized by a local businessman to dedicate a new building constructed to house his store. McNeal recalled:

> There was room for three "sets" of four couples each to dance at once and the musician and caller was Dume Evans. Just what "Dume" was a contraction of I never knew. His music didn't appeal much to even my unpracticed ear, but his unique and poetic improvisation as he "called" to his own fiddling impressed me more than the movements of the dancers. When the "sets" were full Dume's fiddle and also his voice

Recess was usually a pleasure-filled time for schoolchildren. This recess took place in Montgomery County, Kansas, in 1892. (Courtesy Kansas State Historical Society)

came into action. He always sang in a droning monotone, keeping time also with his foot. The opening was always the same.

"S'lute yer pardners."

"Jine hands and circle to th' left."

"Right hand to yer pardner an' gran' right and left." By this time his eyes were closed and his voice had risen to a sort of rhythmic wail as he sang:

"First couple lead to the couple on the right."

"Lady in the center an' three hands round; min' yer feet fellers, don't tromp on her gown."

"First lady swing out and second lady in, three jine hands and circle ag'in."

"On to the next couple, hoe it down; jine hands three and caper aroun'."

"Third lady to center; give your honey a whirl, lead to the next with your best girl."

"Grab your honies, don't let 'em fall, shake your hoofs and balance all."

To attract attention and to be seen by townspeople, this medicine show barker climbed to the roof of a general store at Bazine, Ness County, Kansas, in 1908. Most residents of small towns found amusement when such barkers arrived in their communities. (Courtesy Kansas State Historical Society)

"Ringtailed coons in the trees at play; grab yer pardners and all run away."[20]

Soon after organized religion arrived and churches were built in the towns, camp meetings were often held during the summer months. A large tent might be erected near a church. People would gather, camp on the grounds, picnic, listen to a preacher, and pray inside the tent. The Chautauqua had its roots in a camp-meeting course for Sunday school teachers in New York State about 1874. In time the Chautauqua developed and spread west. It was, as one early participant noted, something of a cross between a camp meeting and a country fair. Chautauqua was cultural and educational. "When a meet was held . . . it would be attended by hundreds of neighboring farmers as well as townspeople. They would camp on grounds made available near the auditorium or lecture tents, and for a solid week enjoy an astounding succession of learned and inspirational talks interlarded with the

*Small western towns filled with excitement and anticipated
pleasure when a circus came to town. This photo of a circus
parade was made in Manhattan, Kansas, in the 1890s.
(Courtesy Kansas State Historical Society)*

performances of xylophone orchestras, Swiss yodelers, jugglers and magicians, college-girl octettes, boy whistlers, dramatic monologists, and jubilee singers. Sports also were encouraged in the afternoon, with croquet for the ladies and baseball for the men. . . . The atmosphere of Chautauqua was highly moral. There could be no drinking or smoking: the Sabbath was rigidly observed. A Methodist Dining Tent or Christian Endeavor Ice Cream Tent supplied all refreshments. Since Chautauqua derived its chief support from the churches and ladies-aid societies, the emphasis was always placed on the importance of 'the Work.' As entertainment inevitably proved the more potent drawing-card, it had to be given all possible protective coloring. The prominent singer 'lectured' on 'The Road to Mandalay'; the monologist 'gave a reading' rather than a dramatic performance. When in

Chautauqua's later days a musical company staged *Carmen,* it was considered necessary to have the heroine work in a dairy rather than in a cigarette factory."[21]

The mostly out-of-doors nature of the Chautauqua was in keeping with a growing trend in activities not only in the West but throughout the United States. Beginning just after the Civil War, several eastern magazines began publishing numerous articles on out-of-doors activities. It was as though eastern writers had rediscovered nature. In 1869 one magazine, *Appleton's Journal,* carried an article entitled "Picnic Excursions." The author wrote: "We find fascination in carrying back our civilization to the wilderness. The eagerness with which we enter upon picnics, the keenness with which we relish them, are proof of the supremacy of the out of doors. Nature is still dear to us, notwithstanding all the veneering of civilization; and it is pleasant to reflect how, at this moment, on the sides of innumerable hills, on mountain tops, in wooded valleys, by many a lake and rivulet, on little wooded islands, in the far off prairies, in southern savannas, are countless picnic parties, all of which, let us hope, are finding full realization of the true ideal of a picnic." The ideal was to eat, drink, lie, sit, walk, or talk "with something of the unconstraint of primitive life." It was a social

People traveled many miles to pitch their tents and attend this Chautauqua, held at Emporia, Kansas, in 1912. (Courtesy Kansas State Historical Society)

device to snatch a brief spell of freedom from the binding conventions of urban existence.[22]

The first countywide Fourth of July picnic in Ness County, located in west-central Kansas, was held in Young's Grove at Ness Center (now Ness City), the county seat, soon after the county was first settled in 1874. About 150 people attended and, as one newspaper reported, "made the old eagle screech again. Every appointment was perfect; and one of the most pleasant occasions was enjoyed by all. A long table was spread in the grove and it was loaded down with farmer's fare; to us it appeared a most sumptuous dinner. When the fragments were gathered together, enough was found to feed a regiment of soldiers." There were speeches, instrumental music, and everyone joined in singing of "the grand old national hymns." That evening the people "gathered together and for many a gleeful hour, heeled and toed it to the inspiring strains of music."[23]

More sedate picnics also became a common form of entertainment in and around many western towns on the plains and prairie. Food preparation by the women took time, as did the travel to a picnic site, often a grove of trees

Croquet became a popular outdoor game in the West during the late nineteenth century and early in the twentieth century. This photograph was made just after 1900 at Sycamore Springs near Sabetha, Kansas. (Courtesy Kansas State Historical Society)

Tennis became a popular form of pleasure in some western communities during the late nineteenth century. The young ladies in this photo belonged to a tennis club in Lawrence, Kansas. (Courtesy Watkins Community Museum, Lawrence, Kansas)

offering shade along a cool creek or river. For well-read residents, picnics became the thing to do after sampling Ralph Waldo Emerson's 1844 essay "Nature," in which he wrote that human beings needed nature—the sight of the fields and the stars and the distant horizons—as they needed food and drink. Nature was medicinal and healing. Nature, he wrote, was "the circumstance, and judges like a god all men that come to her. We have crept out of our close and crowded houses into the night and morning, and we see what majestic beauties daily wrap us in their bosoms. How willingly we would escape the barriers which render them comparatively impotent, escape the sophistication and second thought, and suffer nature to entrance us."[24]

In most small western towns, the local young men kept their eyes open for visitors from the East. When they found such a newcomer, one of them might brag about bagging dozens of plump, fat snipe the night before and how delicious they were. If the easterner seemed interested, the locals would string him along with more palaver. One of them might say he had just spotted a big flock of snipe somewhere on the outskirts of town. The locals immediately made plans to go out that evening and bag some. The

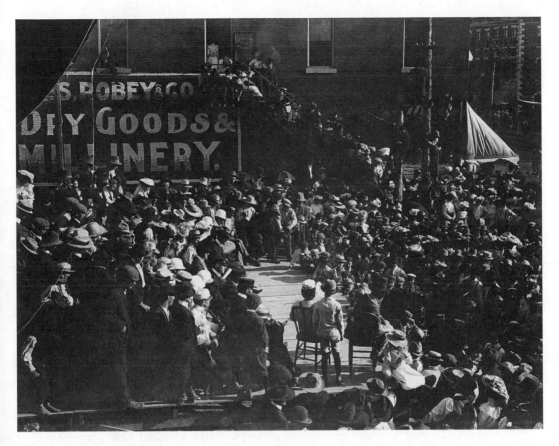

Residents of Junction City, Kansas, turned out on July 4, 1902, to hear the town band and patriotic speeches. (Courtesy Joseph J. Pennell Collection, Kansas Collection, University of Kansas Libraries)

easterner was, of course, invited to go along. One writer described what happened next:

> So about eight or nine P.M. the hunters would gather at a given starting point and depart in a bunch for the hunting grounds. Some of the creek dwellers would post themselves around in different locations and give occasional snipe calls as the bunch of hunters approached. The methods of "circling" and "driving" and "guarding the bag" were discussed as they went to the place where the snipe "used," and, as the new man was not onto the methods of circling, driving, or calling, it would be unanimously agreed that he be given the best and easiest job, that of guarding the bag. If the night was rather cool, he was told to discard his hat and coat; and if it was a warm night, he was provided with an extra overcoat and mittens, and told to keep on his hat, or preferably a

heavy cap, with ear-flaps, the reason being that snipe were very sensitive to scent and the heavy clothing would keep in the "man scent." If it was a cool night the "man scent" could be dispelled by the discarding of as much as possible of his clothing.

A large sack, with mouth propped open, was set in what the manager declared was a good "snipe run" and the guard [easterner] was secreted beside it, being instructed how to suddenly close it when the first flock had been driven in. The snipe would come in a long string, one behind the other, generally from one to two dozen in a string. Like sheep, they would all follow the leader.

Being all set, the drivers and circlers would fade away in the darkness, uttering occasional snipe calls from different points of the compass. But principally they would all be making tracks for town as fast as possible to assemble at Allen's drug store, Zutavern's stable, or Old Rome, to enjoy themselves with story and song and speculation on how long their Eastern friend would wait for those snipe to come into the fold.[25]

Another popular sport in small towns was badger-baiting. A badger fight, with a different twist, appears in Will E. Stoke's little book *Episodes of Early Days,* which he had printed toward the end of his life at Great Bend, Kansas. During the late-nineteenth century, Stoke recalled that "prairie dogs, jack rabbits, cotton tails, skunks, raccoons, opossums, bob cats, coyotes, an occasional grey wolf and a scattering of antelope" could be seen in or near Great Bend in central Kansas. But the badger, he wrote, "got more attention from the town sportsmen than all the other animals combined."

Of the badger, Stoke wrote:

This animal is a fighting scamp. In full growth the badger in size is about half way between a bob cat and a coyote; has a broad, flat body, short legs and jaws like a steel trap. When dug or dragged out of his hole he will put up a winning fight against 'most any kind of a dog, and will often hold a whole pack of dogs at bay for hours, so that a badger fight was classed as among the best sports of the day, and the boys in town always arranged to have a fierce badger in captivity, so that any newcomer with sportsmanlike intentions could be accommodated 'most any time.

The badger was generally kept at Bill Zutavern's livery stable, or in the rear of Henry Moss' store, or down by Heiko Feldkamp's bakery, where the crowd had to go to see the fight pulled off. The local sports

The residents of Junction City, Kansas, turned out for the firemen's parade in 1905. A military band on horseback from nearby Fort Riley, Kansas, leads the parade. (Courtesy Joseph J. Pennell Collection, Kansas Collection, University of Kansas Libraries)

would generally divide on picking the winner, some placing their bets on the badger and some on the dog—which was generally a big and scrappy looking bull dog. After all the preliminaries were arranged— the dog under leash by his master, the badger in an overturned wash tub or box, the question came up: "Who would pull the badger out from under the box and let the dog go at him?"

Some backers of the dog would offer to pull him out, as would also some who were backing the badger, both sides jockeying to get some supposed advantage for his animal.

Finally a compromise would be reached, and all would agree that the stranger, or visiting sport, should turn the badger loose and let the dog at him.

So all would be set, a ring formed of from ten to a hundred or more men standing a safe distance from the center to avoid casualties, the man told to pull him out quickly at the word "go," then jump back out of the danger zone, while some other man was placed to yank the box or tub out of the way.

At the word "go" the puller would generally give a husky yank, and out from under the box would come—what in those days we called a "thundermug"—you know what I mean; one of those things we used to conceal under the bed in the daytime, before we had sewers and such—and the laugh would be on the man who pulled the badger.

And you could generally hear that laugh from one end of town to the other. And the victim would generally keep the joke to himself, and would try to steer some other traveling man or sojourner up against the Great Bend bunch for another "badger fight."[26]

If a town was lucky enough to be on a stage or rail line, going to meet the stagecoach or passenger train was another form of entertainment. Many townspeople were curious to see if someone from their old home state might be arriving, or to watch the drummers selling their goods, or perhaps to get

Sitting on the front porch and enjoying a summer breeze was one form of pleasure enjoyed by many. This photo shows the W. W. Hurley family on the porch of their home in Junction City, Kansas, in 1900. (Courtesy Joseph J. Pennell Collection, Kansas Collection, University of Kansas Libraries)

acquainted with a new settler or to learn the latest news from wherever the stage or train had arrived. In towns without stage or rail service, it was not uncommon to find chairs or benches in front of stores, the livery stable, and the blacksmith's shop. During the daylight hours patient men with little else to do occupied these positions and amused themselves by watching and listening for any news, gossip, or local scandal.

While brothels and red-light districts did exist in the cattle towns on the plains and prairie, they were not plentiful in the quieter farming communities. Certainly such towns did have their share of loose ladies, but they usually provided services discreetly in their homes or perhaps in the back room of a hotel. Saloons, however, were found in most towns until the arrival of Prohibition. After the Women's Christian Temperance Union (WCTU) was founded in 1874 at Cleveland, Ohio, and the movement spread westward, temperance crusaders like Carry Nation provided a form of entertainment for the residents of many towns as they wrecked saloons and other

The bartenders and customers posed for this photograph in the Horseshoe Saloon, Junction City, Kansas, just after the turn of the century. (Courtesy Joseph J. Pennell Collection, Kansas Collection, University of Kansas Libraries)

Drugstore soda fountains provided much enjoyment for residents of towns. This 1899 photo shows the fountain in the Miller and Shoemaker Drug Store, Junction City, Kansas. (Courtesy Joseph J. Pennell Collection, Kansas Collection, University of Kansas Libraries)

establishments selling whiskey. Those who sold whiskey were the only ones who did not find much enjoyment in the visits of Carry Nation.

During the late-nineteenth century, the isolation of life on the plains and prairies gave nearby small towns an almost magnetic appeal. There rural residents found schools, churches, and the amenities of civilized life, especially social activities. Yet, though these towns provided many forms of pleasure, life there was dull compared to that in the mining towns of the West.

CHAPTER X

In the Mining ♟ Regions

What is the worth of anything,
But for the happiness 'twill bring?
                    —*Richard Owen Cambridge*

HERE IS STILL MAGIC in the words "gold rush." The words conjure up a feeling of excitement, and for some they paint a mental picture of long-haired men with weather-beaten faces and unkempt beards, wearing flannel shirts, shapeless pants, high boots, and an old hat, panning or digging for gold or gambling and drinking in a dirty saloon. Early drawings and photographs and countless Hollywood motion pictures have helped to create these images of men with visions of wealth with which to buy the good life.

Far from their homes, the fortune seekers were responsible for the booms. Wherever there was a rumor of a strike and a hole in the ground, they jerry-built a camp. And if there was gold or silver or both, and the diggings did not play out, a boomtown soon appeared. Except for a few settlements in the Appalachian goldfields of Georgia early in the nineteenth century, such mining boomtowns were a phenomenon unique to the American West. They sprang up in California, Nevada, Wyoming, Idaho, far-western Kansas Territory (now Colorado) and anywhere gold or silver was discovered. The mine-rush era in the American West lasted more than fifty years, beginning in California early in 1848 when gold was discovered near John A. Sutter's mill at Coloma, on the south fork of the American River. Mining camps soon sprang up along nearby streams, where men pitched their tents and panned or dug for gold.

The first gold seekers in California were mostly single men. The lack of affordable housing, the hostile environment, the high cost of travel, and the expense of living in a boomtown prevented men from bringing their wives and families or sweethearts to join them. Most of the married men who did come planned to strike it rich and return home to enjoy a life of leisure. As such they had little feeling of permanence or belonging to the community they helped to create. It is a paradox that while most of these men wanted quick wealth with which to buy leisure time and to find pleasure, few actually acquired any. Many of those who did lost it to gamblers, prostitutes, and saloonkeepers, who could make a thousand dollars a day selling shots of whiskey for two dollars each.

Seeking gold was hard work, but at dusk the miners would leave their picks where they had last dug and return to their camps with their pans. They considered their pans to be more valuable than their picks, since they could be used not only for washing gold but washing clothes, mixing flour cakes, feeding a mule, or holding the pot in a game of poker.

Leonard Kip, a young man who went from his home in Albany, New York, to California in 1849, left a word picture of how some miners sought pleasure during their evening hours. He wrote:

> The camp fires are lighted, supper prepared, and then a long evening is ahead, which must be occupied in some way. As to books there are comparatively none at the mines, and indeed they are seldom thought of, for candles being a dollar apiece, their use would be "a pursuit of knowledge under difficulties" to which few Californians are prone. But in lieu of such entertainment, the more sedate and sober miners, gather around their fires, and beguile the evening with conversation, and jest and songs. Whatever is there sung, has generally some reference to the home which all have left behind them. The song wherein an enterprising traveler states that California is the land for him, and announces his intention of proceeding there "with his washbowl on his knee," I never heard at the mines; but that wherein an aged Negro wishes to be carried back to old Virginia, is an especial favorite. Evening after evening it was brought forward, party after party joined in the chorus, and the melody would come pealing round odd corners and from distant tents, in heartfelt strains.[1]

The two songs alluded to by Leonard Kip were "Carry Me Back to Old Virginny" and "Oh! Susanna," both popular in the goldfields. Unlike the cowboys, whose rather monotonous work was conducive to reflection and the slow creation of a personal music, the miners' work was hard, tense, and exciting. Most did not have the time to create their own music. Instead, they sang the ballads they had learned back home, wherever that was, or they sang or recited parodies of such songs. One parody was penned by John Nichols in 1848 aboard a sailing ship heading for California. He borrowed the tune of "Oh! Susanna," by Stephen Foster, penned new words, and called it "Oh, California." The words to the first stanza and chorus were:

> *I came from Salem City,*
> *With my washbowl on my knee,*
> *I'm going to California,*
> *The gold dust for to see.*
> *It rained all night the day I left,*
> *The weather it was dry,*
> *The sun so hot I froze to death,*
> *Oh, brothers, don't you cry!*
>
> *Oh, California,*
> *That's the land for me!*
> *I'm bound for San Francisco*
> *With my washbowl on my knee.*[2]

Certainly not all miners sat around their campfires each night singing and talking. Leonard Kip wrote that there was another class of miners who took little pleasure in such relaxations and cared little "for songs of home; perhaps because many of them never had any. These can invariably be known at a glance, by their long beards, red sashes, and clattering spurs. As soon as evening comes on, these men leave their tents or the trees beneath which their blankets lie, and repair to the village, there to spend the earnings of the day in maddening riot."[3]

Many of the villages referred to by Kip sprang from camps where miners had found gold—usually near streams or the timbered divides they had followed in their search. Many of the sites were given names like Angel's Camp, Big Bar, Carson's Creek, Coloma, Gold Bluffs, Hildreth's Diggings, Long Bar, and Mormon Island. If the gold did not give out, a village of sorts took shape, providing miners with a convenient place to buy supplies and occasionally indulge in champagne, wine, and tinned oysters, if they had saved sufficient pinches of gold dust. Kip's description of such a village not only is vivid, but echoes descriptions of similar settlements found in diaries and other accounts recorded by miners:

A drinking saloon in early San Francisco. (Author's collection)

The village, as one might call it, generally consists of two rows of stores, forming a short street between. The stores are mainly tents, before each of which extends a *rustic arbor,* composed of dead boughs and twigs. The effect is certainly rather pretty by candle light, for then all the impurities and dirt of the place are thrown into the shade, and the varied costumes of the occupants are softened down so as to have a somewhat picturesque effect; but in the daytime, all this is lost, and the broad glare which penetrates every corner, reveals a spot which few would care to choose for their permanent residence.

Within the borders of this street, the miners throng. Wines and brandy flow freely, dice are brought out and particularly monte enchains eager groups around the different tables; lotteries are in full blast; occasional fights arise; and, on all sides, commences a scene of riot drunkenness and wrangling.

So it is also Sunday, except that many then leave the village and go out hunting, or bet high on target shooting. But still, whatever the occupation, strong drink flows freely, and oaths and coarse songs hold a large place in the revels.[4]

A gambling hall somewhere in the West. This illustration appeared in Frank Leslie's Illustrated, *November 3, 1877. (Author's collection)*

In 1850 Franklin Langworthy, another gold seeker, left his wife in Illinois and traveled overland to California. A Universalist minister, Langworthy was especially offended by how the miners spent their leisure time. He wrote: "Packs of cards are kept in nearly every house, tent, and cabin, and are generally in use either for amusement or gambling. Checkers and chess are seldom played, these games requiring the player to exercise some little thought and reflection. Mental labor of every kind is altogether avoided, and looked upon with contempt by the great mass of Californians. Tippling and profane swearing are all but universal."

Langworthy also observed that there were many preachers in California. Some of them held religious services and preached in meeting houses in the larger mining boomtowns, but few miners attended the services. Langworthy wrote that many of the ministers who came to California did so for one "grand motive, viz: to make their 'piles.' Not a few, it is said, who professed to preach the Gospel at home, have since their arrival here, concluded to follow one Apostolic example, in becoming all things to all men, and are now actively engaged at the roulette-table, or in dealing monte."[5]

As the mining boomtowns appeared, so did the women, many from San Francisco and elsewhere. Prostitution gave the miners more variety in how to spend their gold dust and leisure time. Although some accounts suggest that only 8 percent of the California population was women by the start of 1850, there were so many at Hangtown (Placerville) that two dances were held. About then someone borrowed the tune of "New York Gals" and gave it new words and the title "Hangtown Gals." The first stanza and chorus are:

> *Hangtown gals are plump and rosy,*
> *Hair in ringlets mighty cozy;*
> *Painted cheeks and gassy bonnets;*
> *Touch them and they'll sting like hornets.*
>
> *Hangtown gals are lovely creatures,*
> *Think they'll marry Mormon preachers;*
> *Heads thrown back to show their features;*
> *Ha, ha, ha! Hangtown gals.*[6]

Early in 1850 the winter weather around Hangtown was so bad that most miners were forced to remain indoors, and many of those who could afford to do so continued to indulge in gambling and drinking. Miners who did not want to gamble or drink could play tenpins at the Eldorado Hotel. Although bowling can be traced as far back as the sixth millennium B.C., the game

A scene in a San Francisco melodeon called Bella Union, where ballet girls undressed most extravagantly. It was said that at the Bella Union the worship of the calf—padded, not golden—prevailed to such an extent that Moses would have fairly pulverized the stone tablets had he witnessed it. Illustration from J. H. Beadle's The Undeveloped West; or Five Years in the Territories . . . , *published in 1873.*

arrived in America with early British and Dutch settlers. By the early nineteenth century, bowling was played with nine pins. Although it was banned in Connecticut in 1841 because it was thought to be evil, an ingenious Yankee added a tenth pin to circumvent the law, and by 1850, when the game arrived in California, it was gaining respectability and becoming popular.

When miners tired of playing tenpins at the Eldorado Hotel, they could take their pleasure in the hotel dining room, whose menu listed "Roast Beef, wild-$1.50," "Beef, tame, from Arkansas-$1.50," "Sauer Kraut-$1.00," "Jackass Rabbit (whole)-$1.00," "Hash, low grade-$.75," "Hash, 18 carats-$1.00." If a miner wanted a full meal including rice pudding for dessert, it cost $3.00, payable in advance.[7]

For a time in the early 1850s, Placerville was perhaps the most prominent mining boomtown in northern California. Founded in 1848 and first called Old Dry Diggings, the town was renamed Hangtown after residents hanged three men accused of robbery. As the town grew, however, some residents resented the name, and in 1851 renamed it Placerville. By then the

In mining communities where women were not plentiful, miners might dance with each other. As the above illustration shows, miners playing the female role tied handkerchiefs around their arms. The illustration is credited to A. Castaigne and is titled "Miner's Ball." (Author's collection)

miner's pack-mule trails, which followed the courses of the streams and gulches and the contours of the surrounding hills, had become the streets of Placerville, and they had been lined with hurriedly constructed wooden buildings.[8]

In one of those new buildings was a theater, which opened in the spring of 1852. Frank (or Francis) S. Chanfrau, a handsome young actor in his twenties, appeared in its first dramatic performance. The name of the play is not known, but a year later *Hamlet* was presented in the same theater for three or four nights. As one historian of early California theater wrote, "To any overcritical patron of the drama, the choice of *Hamlet* of all things, for a cast headed by two or three amateurs, may have seemed tragic indeed—unless it represented the attainment of the ludicrous in its most convulsing form."[9]

VIGILANTE BANDS, which sprang up during the town's early years to dispense law and order, occasionally provided what many miners considered entertainment. When Dr. J. B. Crane, a schoolteacher, in 1854 killed one of his pupils, Miss Susan Newham, after she refused to marry him, Crane immediately gave himself up to the authorities at Placerville. Vigilantes soon learned what had happened and took Crane away from the constable. They appointed their own judge and jury, tried Dr. Crane, found him guilty, and sentenced him to be hanged. Another man, Mickey Free, convicted of the murder of a Chinese, was to hang on the same day. Miners came from all directions to Placerville. Men and even women, some sitting in buggies and wagons, were waiting at the appointed time. Dr. Crane asked to sing a song he had composed. He stood up in the back of a wagon, the rope around his neck and its other end thrown over a tree limb above him, and sang his song. Apparently intoned to the tune of "Flow Gently, Sweet Afton," the words were:

> Come friends and relations, I bid you adieu,
> The grave is now open to welcome me through.
> No valley of shadows I see on my road,
> But angels are waiting to take me to God.
>
> I killed Susan Newham as you have heard tell,
> I killed her because that I loved her too well.
> Now Susan and I will soon meet at the throne,
> And be united forever in the life to come.
>
> Don't weep for me, friends, but dry up your tears,
> For I have no sorrows and I have no fears.
> I am eager to go to that far, happy land,
> And take my dear Susan again by the hand.

When he finished, the driver whipped the team, and Crane was heard to say, "Here I come, Susan!"

Next came Mickey Free. Not to be outdone by Crane, Free asked permission to dance a jig. The vigilantes, apparently enjoying the spectacle, agreed. Free danced and the wagon box rattled as his feet tapped. When he finished, the driver whipped the team. Some witnesses claimed that Mickey Free continued to dance, hanging from the tree.[10]

Wrestling matches, prizefighting, bare knuckle contests, badger fights, hunting coyotes on horseback, drinking and rifle-shooting contests, and bearbaiting were other forms of entertainment for miners, and circuses began to visit the larger mining towns during the late 1850s. Joseph Andrew Rowe's Pioneer Circus played Placerville for two days in April 1857, with one performance a day. Advertising pamphlets for the circus suggest its performers included Miss Mary Ann Whittaker, described as "the First Female Equestrian Artist in America," William Franklin, "the Greatest Equestrian Artist in the World," and Hiram Franklin, a clown and trapeze artist. During its first performance in Placerville the circus took in $718, but in its second, the following day, only $331.25 was earned.[11]

Auctions often became festive occasions for the company-starved miners, who would bid on boots or blankets or mining equipment or anything anyone wanted to sell. Still another type of entertainment was the practical joke, and some were elaborate. During the winter of 1851–52, there was a large canvas building in Placerville devoted, according to one account, "to all the wickedness and cussedness that could be originated or imported from any land. Twenty or thirty gambling tables were kept constantly running—music, rum, and the necessary glitter.

"Near the centre of the large room was a long sheet-iron box stove—for in those early days there was no cast-iron about—around which were common benches for the habitues to sit on, and warm themselves during the damp and cold winter evenings.

"One dark and rainy night, when the room was packed, a man dressed entirely in buckskin came in; he was well known—known too, as a brave, fearless backwoodsman; he always carried his rifle and powder horn, and moved and looked like a revolving arsenal. But this evening, an unusual thing for him, he appeared to be drunk; his clear, strong voice would occasionally rise above the murmured din and clink of coin, so that even the sitters around the stove seemed inclined to give him all the room he wanted.

"At length, in a loud voice, he called for a drink, which was given him; and then he as loudly said: 'Boys, I have lived long enough.'

"From his powder horn he poured a lot of powder into his hand saying, 'that is all right,' and touched it off—the dull puff and whirl of smoke filled the air, and it seemed as if every eye was turned toward him. Then, apparently becoming furious over some imagined trouble, he tore the large powder horn from his side, advanced to the box stove, filled with blazing wood, and threw it in, crying in a loud and stentorian voice: 'Now, let every man wait!' But there was no waiting—through the windows, out of the doors, even through the side of the house, over the tables, players, gamblers, lookers-on, all stampeded! There was never such a hurried wreck of a house before!

"But as no explosion took place, those who had left large sums of money gradually crept back; for everywhere gold was scattered, and, of course, much was found that never went on the tables again.

"The backwoodsman meantime had quietly stepped out the back-way, mounted his horse, and rode away in the gloom. And it was well he did so, for the gamblers hunted him for a week afterward. But eventually everybody laughed at the joke, and he became known as "Black Sand Jack," for of course his powder horn was filled with sand, except the little he turned into his own hand as an experiment—but that little experiment bewildered the boys."[12]

Most miners in California continued to find pleasure in music. Between 1852 and 1861, at least twelve songbooks were published and sold, especially to miners, in California.[13]

The first gold rush song actually written in California was David G. Robinson's "Seeing the Elephant," which told about conditions in the goldfield. Robinson, a New England road-show performer, established one of the earliest (1850) theatrical houses in San Francisco. In the spring of that year, he presented his first play, *Seeing the Elephant*, which included his song "Seeing the Elephant," sung to the tune of "De Boatman Dance." The song, with at least seventeen stanzas, tells how a miner sold everything he owned to go in search of gold, how he crossed the continent to reach California, and what he found in the goldfields. The words of the chorus and last stanza read:

> *When the elephant I had seen,*
> *I'm damned if I thought I was green;*
> *And others say, both night and morn,*
> *They saw him coming round the Horn.*
>
> *If I should make another raise,*
> *In New York sure I'll spend my days;*
> *I'll be a merchant, buy a saw,*
> *So good-bye, mines and Panama.*
> *Oh no, lots of dust,*
> *I'm going to the city to get on a "bust."*[14]

The phrase "seeing the elephant" was perhaps best defined by Amos Kendall in his two-volume work *The Santa Fe Expedition*, published in 1844. Kendall wrote: "When a man is disappointed in anything he undertakes, when he has seen enough, when he gets sick and tired of any job he may have set himself about, he has seen the elephant."[15]

.   .   .

BY THE LATE 1850S, the character of the California mining towns that survived the boom was changing. The placer mining camps, where miners relied on picks and shovels, prospecting pans, sluices, and other simple tools, were in decline, and mining as an enterprise was shifting from individual to corporate ownership and more complex methods of finding gold. A new social structure developed, similar to that of industrial cities in the East. At the top of the pecking order were the mine owners, managers, engineers, and supervisors. Next came the leading merchants, lawyers, doctors, newspaper editors, and ministers. The core of each community continued to be the miners, including Cornish, Irish, Welsh, German, Italian, and Serbo-Croatian immigrants. The desire for respectability was strong in many of these communities, and the elite and genteel found pleasure in patronizing the local opera house or theater, where they enjoyed musicals, lectures, comedies, or dramas. Drinking, prostitution, and gambling still existed, but not at the level of the boom period.

When silver was discovered during the summer of 1859 in the Washoe Valley of Nevada Territory, many, including men who had not struck it rich in California, hurried to what became Virginia City to make their fortune. In excitement and lifestyle, the new boom duplicated that of the early California mining camps and boomtowns. Within three years, however, corporate ownership dominated, and the community got down to the business of mining. Many miners chose to become employees and earned a few dollars a day working in underground shafts and galleries in what, for a few years, was the most productive mining district the world has ever known.

Many writers, including Mark Twain (Samuel Langhorne Clemens), told what life was like in Virginia City during its heyday. Twain was an enthusiastic though unsuccessful prospector when he went to Nevada Territory in 1861 as confidential secretary to his brother Orion, the newly appointed territorial secretary. Twain gave up prospecting in 1862 and went to work for the *Territorial Enterprise*, a Virginia City newspaper. He found Virginia City "the livest town, for its age and population, that America had ever produced." Fascinated by its carefree, gambling spirit, and by all of its color and movement, Twain wrote: "There were military companies, fire companies, brass bands, hotels, theatres, 'hurdy-gurdy houses,' wide-open gambling places, political pow-wows, civic processions, street fights, murders, inquests, riots, a whisky mill every fifteen steps . . . and some talk of building a church!"[16]

After their long, backbreaking shifts in the mines, the miners sought pleasure, and more than a hundred saloons served them. The most pretentious were the "two-bit" houses, where every kind of drink cost a quarter.

Girls, whiskey, and music, popular pleasures in Virginia City, Nevada, were also found in Virginia City, Montana. Here, a hurdy-gurdy house in the latter, soon after gold was discovered in nearby Alder Gulch in 1863. (Author's collection)

These were the fancy saloons, with long mahogany bars, chandeliers, showy pictures in heavy gilded frames, and a bright facade of mirrors. Games of chance included faro, roulette, monte, and poker. After one gambling house experimented by having "a real living, pretty, modest-looking young girl, in a close-fitting black silk dress" deal cards, the custom spread, and other gambling houses hired attractive female croupiers and dealers.[17]

Other sources of pleasure in and around Virginia City included what was called the Virginia Alkali and Sagebrush Sporting Club, whose members chased coyotes with their greyhounds on Forty-Mile Desert. There were also wrestling matches, Sunday horse races, rifle- and pistol-shooting contests, and prizefighting, all supplemented by betting and drinking. It may have been Mark Twain who reported in the *Territorial Enterprise* that disputed decisions often found the miners hauling out their guns. The paper usually added that the referee "failed to be killed."[18]

The editor of Virginia City's *Gold Hill News* wrote in late 1876:

The Comstock is an improving place to live on. . . . Both Gold Hill and Virginia are well supplied with schools, and there is no lack of churches. We have more saloons than any place in the country. Every Sunday when there is a show in town we have a matinee and an evening

A Virginia City, Nevada, gambling hall. Illustration by W. L. Dodge appeared in Harper's Weekly, *above the caption "The Faro Players."*

performance. On the Sabbath, also, we are entertained with a horse-race or a fight between a bulldog and a wildcat. Every month or so the prize-fighters favor us with a mill, which we all go to see and then indict the fighters, as a sort of concession to the Puritanical element. . . . Every Saturday night small boys parade up and down the principal street of Virginia, carrying transparencies which inform our sport-loving people where cockfighting may be enjoyed. Faro, keno, chuck-a-luck and roulette may be found in every second saloon, and a special policeman, wearing his star, frequently conducts the game. Taking everything into consideration, there are few pleasanter places to live than on the Comstock.[19]

Another writer, J. N. Flint, who recorded his reminiscences of life in Virginia City, provided more details when he wrote: "The men who worked in the mines, the majority of them Cornishmen, were a happy-go-easy set of fellows, fond of good living, and not particularly interested in religious affairs. There were four church organizations in Virginia City—Catholic, Episcopal, Methodist and Presbyterian—but, with a single exception, the churches exercised but slight influence upon the male population of the town. A flourishing commandery of Knights Templar attended the Episcopal Church regularly once a year, on St. John's day, in full regalia. That duty performed, they felt that nothing further was required of them in the line of church-going. The miners who belonged to the Catholic denomination attended mass on Sabbath morning and participated in a target excursion during the afternoon. As regarded deportment, everyone was a law unto himself. Perhaps one reason for the laxity in the observance of the Sabbath was the fact that work in the mines went on uninterruptedly during the whole 365 days of the year. Another demoralizing circumstance was that most of the men employed in the mines were unmarried and enjoyed none of the refining, humanizing influences of home life. They boarded at a restaurant, slept in a lodging-house, and, as a general rule, spent their leisure time on the street or at the gambling-tables. During the flush times as many as twenty-five faro games were in full blast night and day. When sporting men . . . sat down of an evening to a friendly game of poker it was no uncommon occurrence for five or six thousand dollars to change hands at a single sitting. Some idea of the amount of money in circulation may be inferred from the fact that every working-man's wages amounted to at least 120 dollars per month. From what has already been written there is no desire to convey the impression that a low standard of morality was the rule in the Comstock mining district. Men quarreled at times and firearms were discharged with but slight provocation. Nevertheless they all had an acute instinct of right and wrong, a high sense of honor, and a chivalrous feeling of respect for the gentler sex. A woman unattended could pass along the streets of Virginia and Gold Hill without the slightest danger of insult or annoyance."[20]

From Virginia City's beginning, prostitution was legal and generally viewed as simply another business enterprise. It was an accepted part of life because men greatly outnumbered women, single or married, and when they visited a house of prostitution, they did not always do so to have sexual intercourse. Many men simply sought and found female attention, and they enjoyed the music, singing, drinking, and companionship they found in brothels. These gave them relief from their loneliness and from the tension caused by the dangers of working in the mines. Then, too, there was little for miners to do during their leisure hours other than drink or gamble.

Beginning in the 1860s, lanterns with blue glass hung next to outside doors marked the entrances to many brothels. (Why the color blue is not known.) The use of a red light was adopted in the middle 1870s at Virginia City, after it had become something of a universal symbol, at least in the

United States, for houses of prostitution. Later the city fathers of Virginia City sought to confine prostitution to an area along D Street, the route followed daily by miners to and from the mines, and what was called the Barbary Coast district on C Street, which had combination saloon-brothels. Another red-light district developed in Virginia City's "Chinatown," where young Chinese girls, some undoubtedly forced into prostitution, plied their trade. A few madams ignored the city fathers' plan, however, and kept their businesses in residential areas.

Virginia City actually had four classes of houses of prostitution. The most respectable were the parlor houses, offering the most beautiful girls, best liquor, nicest surroundings, and highest prices. Prominent businessmen and politicians are known to have been silent partners with the madams who operated the parlor houses. Next came a lower-quality house, operated by a madam who had two or more girls. Next came the cribs—one- or two-room shacks—where a prostitute lived and worked alone, often soliciting customers by flirting and calling to passersby or exhibiting themselves in their doorways or windows. Those of lowest class were the dives in the Barbary Coast district, where prostitutes drank with customers and had sex with them in tiny bedrooms in the back of the saloon. While prostitution was legal, neither the prostitutes nor the brothels were licensed or taxed. The operators paid off police and city officials and generally paid higher-than-usual rents.

One prominent Virginia City madam was a widow known as Cad Thompson. Her real name was Sarah Hagan, and she had been born in Ireland in 1827. Between the early 1860s and 1892, she ran several houses of prostitution in Virginia City, including a three-story brick parlor house on D Street known simply as the "Brick House." For a time it was the most popular parlor house in Virginia City. When she reached sixty-five, Thompson sold out in Virginia City and apparently retired to San Francisco. By then Virginia City's mines had played out, many miners had lost their jobs, and the community was declining. Prostitution, however, remained legal in Virginia City until 1947—long after the boom had burst.[21]

THE YEAR the Comstock Lode was discovered in Nevada, 1859, another gold rush was already under way eight hundred miles to the east on the other side of the Rocky Mountains. It was called the Pikes Peak gold rush, although Pikes Peak—named for explorer Zebulon Montgomery Pike—was actually located sixty-five miles south of where gold was discovered on the site of modern Denver, Colorado. Nearly a year earlier, William Green Russell and George Hicks, an attorney and a prominent Cherokee Indian, found gold near where Cherry Creek flows into the South Platte River. Word spread quickly, and by early 1859 fortune seekers were arriving from the East and from California.

The first gold seekers found very little gold because the Russell-Hicks strike had been grossly exaggerated, but they soon found pleasure in gambling and liquor. The first saloon on the site of modern Denver was the Western Saloon operated by "Uncle" Dick Wooton, a fur trapper and Indian fighter. On hearing of the Russell-Hicks strike, Wooten and his wife rushed to Cherry Creek from New Mexico, arriving on Christmas morning, 1858. Among the goods they brought with them were ten barrels of Taos Lightning, a pale white whiskey made from wheat, and a large tent. Wooton erected the tent, moved all but one barrel inside it, and opened for business. By then nearly two hundred men, who were camped nearby, had gathered around the tent. Wooton asked his wife to distribute tin cups from their supplies, which she did. Then "Uncle Dick" punched the top of the barrel located outside the tent and announced free drinks for everyone in honor of Christmas and his arrival. It is said that everyone in the settlement had a hangover the following morning. Within a month Wooton constructed a one-and-a-half-story wooden building. On the first floor was a long room, about 30 feet deep and 20 feet wide, which was the saloon. He had a dark wood bar freighted west from St. Joseph, Missouri, and placed along one side. He then filled the remainder of the room with straight-backed chairs and gambling tables. The second floor had a large meeting room.

By the time Wooton's Western Saloon was completed and in operation, other permanent structures were being built to house saloons. One of the earliest was Denver Hall, soon renamed Denver House. It was a one-story structure, 130 by 36 feet, with log walls and windows and roof of white canvas. It was constructed as a hotel, but the owners saw more profit in converting it into a gambling hall and offered most of the games then popular. Libeus Barney, later a part-owner of the Apollo, visited Denver Hall in the spring of 1859 and wrote:

> Upon the first table as we entered, "Lasconette" was the game under consideration; on the next two *Rouge-et-Noire*, or "Red and Black," was being played; "Spanish Monte" occupied the next three; "French Monte" drew its worshippers around the seventh table; "Over and Under Seven" occupied two; "Chuck-a-Luck," three; "High Dice,"

Young ladies dealt faro in Ed West's gaming rooms located on Larimer Street in Denver.
(Author's collection)

one; "Van Tuama," three; "Roulette," one; and "Kansas Lottery," the balance. The tables rent from three to five dollars a night, and seldom a night passes but all are engaged.[22]

Gold dust was the standard medium of exchange since paper money was viewed with suspicion.

Later in 1859 Albert Richardson, a newspaperman from the East, visited Denver House and wrote that the floor of earth "was well sprinkled to keep down the dust. The room was always crowded with swarthy men armed and in rough costumes. The bar sold enormous quantities of cigars and liquors. At half a dozen tables the gamblers were always busy day and evening. One in woolen shirt and jockey cap drove a thriving business at three-card monte, which netted him about one hundred dollars per day. Like all men who gain money easily, they were openhanded and charitable. I never saw a place where more dollars could be obtained in less time for a helpless woman or orphan than among those gaming tables. I saw the probate judge of the county lose thirty Denver lots in less than ten minutes, at cards, in the Denver House on Sunday morning, and afterward observed the county sheriff pawning his revolver for twenty dollars to spend in betting at faro. There were no women and children; and hence none of that public opinion without which few men can stand alone."[23]

Other permanent structures were soon completed, including the Apollo, which had a saloon, gambling hall, and restaurant on the first floor, and a long hall with a stage on the second. "Apollo Hall," as the upstairs became known, was dedicated with a dance on Thursday, September 15, 1859, and three weeks later the first legitimate theater opened, giving gold seekers something different. Colonel Charles R. Thorne and Company performed *Cross of Gold*, a tragedy, followed by a popular song and favorite dance, and concluded with a farce titled *Two Gregories*.[24]

Another saloon was the Eldorado, operated by J. G. Sims, a wealthy black man from Cincinnati. And then there was the House That Jack Built, operated by Jack O'Neal, a native of Troy, New York, who had more female employees and boarders than any other saloon in town. Women began arriving with some regularity when the Leavenworth and Pike's Peak Express Company started regular stagecoach service to and from the East, but men still generally outnumbered women ten to one. Men were willing to pay well for female companionship. Denver's first saloon–dance hall, operated by Hi Dingwall in the back of the Windsor Hotel, charged fifty cents a drink and a dollar a dance. The music for each dance never lasted long.

By the early 1860s other mining camps along the eastern slopes of the Colorado Rockies were becoming boomtowns, each offering its various diversions for miners. There were Hamburg Gulch, McNulty, California Gulch, Gulch Tarryall, Georgia Gulch, Delaware Flats, Parkville, Fairplay, Buckskin Joe, Laurette, Gold Run, and Central City, where John Gregory made a very rich strike in May 1859. By 1860 Central City rivaled Denver as the leading mining town in Colorado, but by 1861 its surface diggings began to play out. Mining activity slowed down, and then word reached Denver that the Civil War had begun. Many miners left the region, some heading northwest into what is now Idaho, where gold had been discovered in September 1860. Others went home or off to fight for the North or South. While Central City suffered a decline, Denver prospered and began to mature and to emulate the orderly, patterned, and cultivated life of eastern cities, including theater.

For instance, in July 1861 two men remodeled the large second-floor room over the Apollo and renamed it the Criterion Concert Hall. V. M. Gorham organized a blackface troupe and called it the Criterion Minstrels. Gorham also brought some performers from the East, including Mademoiselle Carolista, danseuse and tightrope walker. To attract attention to the new Criterion Concert Hall, Gorham announced that if sufficient funds were raised through subscriptions, Mademoiselle Carolista would give an outdoor exhibition of her tightrope-walking skills. About $170 was raised, and at two o'clock in the afternoon on July 18, 1861, she walked across Larimer Street on a three-hundred-foot rope tied fifty feet above the ground between the Criterion Concert Hall and the New York Store. Denver residents gathered along the street to watch the "brave and noble little woman" and to applaud her success. When the new company presented its first performance on July 29, many gold seekers were among the six hundred people who crowded into the theater to be entertained by the farces *The Barber Shop, Barnum in Trouble,* and a takeoff on *La Sylphide.* Mademoiselle Carolista also performed and wheeled a wheelbarrow from one end of the hall to the other on a tightrope.[25]

When the Civil War ended, Denver had about five thousand residents. It had become a regional trading center providing the mining towns and miners with everything from furniture and food to wine and women. But the postwar economy was not strong, and by 1866 many mines had been abandoned, their machinery left to rust. However, Central City, located in the Rockies about twenty-five miles west of Denver, experienced a second life when new mining techniques were introduced and the corporations in control hired miners. The second boom at Central City also attracted gamblers, prostitutes, and saloonkeepers. New buildings were hurriedly constructed, including a theater and hotel to offer miners more ways to lose their gold dust. The new hotel was the Teller House, built in 1871 at a cost of sixty thousand dollars by Henry M. Teller. The four-story hotel was opened on June 25, 1872, and on the last day of that year the hotel planned to hold a big New Year's dinner for Central City's residents. The *Central City Register,* December 31, 1872, described plans for the dinner:

> The most elaborate bill of fare we venture to say that has been provided by any hotel west of the Mississippi River for a public dinner will be served by the Teller House tomorrow, New Year's evening at half past eight o'clock. Every description of wild and domestic meats to be found have been gathered. There are fishes, beef, veal, mutton, pork, oysters in every style, turkey, mallard duck, mountain grouse, prairie chicken, wild turkey, antelope, venison, buffalo, Rocky Mountain black bear, with entrees, vegetables, relishes, side dishes, pastries, puddings, ice-cream, jellies, and dessert, to be ornamented also with elegant pyramids of cakes and other elaborate designs in confectionery. It is intended to be the great dinner of the Territory—incomparably

Danseuse and tightrope walker Mademoiselle Carolista (top, left of center) walks across Larimer Street in Denver on a three-hundred-foot rope tied fifty feet above the ground between Criterion Concert Hall and the New York Store, July 19, 1861. It was part of a promotion for Criterion Concert Hall, and attracted a large crowd. (Courtesy Colorado Historical Society)

greater than has ever before been witnessed in the west. . . . The price is fixed at $5.00 per head or $10.00 per couple. It is expected that a large number of ladies and gentlemen will be present.

By the early 1870s, small theatrical groups were touring the mining towns on a regular basis to entertain the miners. Several of the towns had small theaters. Central City, for instance, took pride in having several theaters with names like the People's, Montana Belvedere, National, and Opera House Auditorium. But they were inadequate for large theatrical performances. The residents of Central City raised money by subscription and had an imposing opera house, 55 by 115 feet, constructed of cut native stone, very plain but imposing, with four-foot-thick walls. The stage was forty by fifty feet. The interior of the Teller Opera House, as it was called, was not gaudy. There was not much gingerbread woodwork, and the centerpiece was an open dome painted by C. H. Massman of San Francisco. The parquet and dress circle of Teller Opera House seated 426 people, while another 126 persons could be seated in the gallery. The building was finished in the spring of

1878, opening on March 4 with a dedication performance for the musicians, followed by a second dedication performance on March 5 for the actors.

The same year the Teller Opera House was opened in Central City, the cry "Silver!" echoed across the Rockies and beyond. Immensely rich silver lodes were discovered near the ruins of the old Colorado mining camp of California Gulch at the headwaters of the Arkansas River. Within days, as fortune seekers found their way, the new boomtown of Leadville was born with all the amenities found in the countless mining boomtowns that preceded it, including the ever-present trinity of gambling, drinking, and prostitution. The boom at Leadville rivaled the Pikes Peak rush of 1859, as this newspaper description of Leadville suggests:

> On all sides was a conglomerate mass of diversified humanity—men of education and culture, graduates of Harvard and Yale and Princeton, mingling with ignorant and uncouth Bull-whackers; men of great wealth mixing with adventurers of every degree without a cent in their pockets with which to pay for their night's lodging at the bit corral down the street; men of refinement jostling against cheap variety actors and scarcely less masculine actresses, dancehall herders and others with callings less genteel; representatives of the better element in all the callings of life—hopelessly entangled in throngs of gamblers, burro-steerers, thugs, bullies, drunkards, escaped convicts, dead beats and the "scum of the earth" generally.
>
> The buzz of conversation was almost deafening and kept up all through the night, for because of the scarcity of sleeping accommodations many were waiting for more fortunate and earlier comers to vacate beds at various lodgings and thus afford them an opportunity of snatching a few winks of sleep in the early morning hours . . . waiters were busy all night . . . for the throng was ever present. Meantime bartenders, nearly fainting with exhaustion, strove hard to satisfy the thirst of the multitude which eddied back and forth between the curbstone and the bar. . . . You could get a poor meal for $1.00 and possibly bad whiskey for 25 cents a swallow. Everyone kept open house but no silk hats were visible, no "boiled shirts," no four-horse sleighs, no calling cards.[26]

Miners in Leadville could visit several brothels on State Street including Red Light Hall, whose sign was a beacon. It was one of the more respectable houses, claiming to have more beautiful girls than any other establishment in Leadville, including such saloons as the Pioneer and the Bucket of Blood.

The largest gambling hall in Leadville—in fact the largest in Colorado—was C. Hall & Company on Chestnut Street. Nearby was Bill Nye's Hall of Chance, and on Harrison Street was the Texas House. For miners who did not engage in gambling or patronize prostitutes—and there were some—there were other forms of entertainment and relaxation. Weekly newspapers contain countless notices of meetings and entertainments given under the auspices of such organizations as the Masons, Order of Eastern Star, Woodmen of the World, Women of Woodcraft, Rathbone Sisters, Fraternal Order of Eagles, Elks, and the local miners' unions.

The Leadville boom also saw a resurgence of theater thanks to Horace Tabor, a native of Vermont, who came west during the middle 1850s. By 1860 he was prospecting at California Gulch and operating a small general merchandise store providing miners with supplies. Early in 1878 Tabor grubstaked two prospectors, Rische and Hook, who discovered what became known as the Little Pittsburg mine and started the Leadville boom. Tabor received a third of the riches of the mine and used his money to make additional mining investments, becoming a multimillionaire. He was an uneducated man who loved pomp and elegance. He built a fine opera house in Leadville, which opened on November 20, 1879, with a performance of *The Serious Family*, starring Jack Langhise. The following year Tabor went to Denver, gave a contractor a blank check, and told him to build the finest theater in the world. When completed, the theater stood lavishly adorned with polished cherry furnishings, red plush, damask hangings, and soft lights.

Poker Alice Tubbs, born in England, came to the United States with her parents, who settled in Colorado. Her father was a schoolteacher. She left home in the 1870s and went to South Dakota during its gold rush days. There she became a pleasure provider, a card dealer in gambling houses in Deadwood and Sturgis, and she ran a bawdy house. She smoked cigars and dealt poker with great success, but she never gambled herself or let her girls service customers on Sundays. When she got old, she retired and built a small house in Sturgis, South Dakota, where she lived a respectable life until her death in 1930. (Courtesy Western History Collections, University of Oklahoma Library)

Denver's Tabor Grand Opera House opened on September 5, 1881, with a performance of *Maritana* by Emma Abbott and Company.[27]

Another theater of note in Leadville was Vivian's Opera House. A. S. Vivian came to town in 1880, leased a building, and formed a stock company to give legitimate productions. But since he did not offer liquor, gambling, dancing, or prostitution, the venture was a failure. Vivian, a well-known ballad singer and son of an English clergyman, had arrived in New York City in 1867 and soon knew everyone of importance in the theatrical profession. Eventually he and some friends formed a social organization they called the Jolly Corks. In 1869 the name was changed to the Benevolent and Protective Order of Elks. On March 20, 1881, Vivian died suddenly in Leadville. He was buried there in Evergreen Cemetery, but in 1889 his body was removed, taken east, and reburied in Mount Hope Cemetery in Boston, Massachusetts.

DUSTY OLD ISSUES of weekly newspapers from the established mining towns of the West contain countless references to how miners spent their leisure hours. A few suggest that by the 1880s prizefighting was another popular form of entertainment. One reported a match in Silverton, Colorado, at the Walsh smelter, between two boxers—one an amateur, the other a professional—in front of a large crowd. The latter, anxious to get a return engagement, did not try hard to win. The crowd booed and hissed. The infuriated referee entered the ring, pulled his gun, and ordered the contestants to quit fooling around and fight. There ensued a quick knockout by the pro, who, as he feared, then lost any chance of being asked to return for another fight.[28]

At Cripple Creek, Colorado, residents enjoyed seeing motion pictures of the Corbett-Fitzsimmons prizefight held weeks earlier, March 17, 1897, at Carson City, Nevada. The first night the film was presented, showing "Gentleman Jim" Corbett losing to Robert "Freckled Bob" Fitzsimmons, the audience was mostly miners. But according to a Cripple Creek newspaper, at the second showing the audience included many ladies. Motion pictures were then still a novelty, and the paper described the film in some detail:

> The pictures which flash past the light at the rate of 48 each second
> form on the canvas a life-like moving picture. . . . There is no blood
> seen, and nothing to shock the nerves. The life-size pictures flit back

and forth as silent as shadows; but every motion of the big fighters is plainly seen.[29]

Only twenty miles from Pikes Peak, Cripple Creek was the last and also the richest of Colorado's major mining boomtowns. While its wealth had been overlooked in 1859 by miners seeking to find gold at the base of the famous peak, scientific advancements in mining techniques and technology had helped to locate and extract the gold by the 1890s. By 1900 Cripple Creek, with a population of more than 25,000, was Colorado's fourth largest city and the business and social center of the mining district.

Cripple Creek had the fashionable five-story National Hotel, and the town's fine department stores and shops rivaled those of Denver and Colorado Springs. Cripple Creek's opera houses played to standing-room-only audiences night after night. Streetcars moved up and down the major streets, and there were more than seventy saloons, many of them on Myers Avenue, a street devoted to pleasure. The most popular saloons were the Opera Club, Combination, Old Yellowstone, Last Chance, Terminal, Miners Exchange, Abbey, and Dawson Club. Variety theaters were also located on Myers Avenue, with names like Crapper Jack's and the Red Light. They had eight- and ten-piece bands, many dance-hall girls, and risqué burlesque shows. Before each performance the theater managers sent their bands and girls to parade up and down the street to drum up customers. Cripple Creek's parlor houses were located across the street from the saloons and variety theaters. In one block alone there were five whorehouses: the Old Homestead, the Mikado, Nell McClusky's, Royal Inn, and Laura Bell's. Four others were located within walking distance, along with many unpainted pine shacks or one-girl cribs, each operated by prostitutes with names like Doll, Dot, Doe, Frankie, Kitty, Rosy, and Eva, who came from France, Japan, China, and Mexico and included Indian and Negro women.

The Old Homestead, a two-story building at 353 Myers, had the best reputation and the highest prices. It also had electric lights, running water, a telephone, and an intercom system, things that were available in all of Colorado's larger communities by 1900. On the ground floor of the Old Homestead were a large entertainment room and several parlors, each lavishly decorated with one or more crystal chandeliers and red velvet, and warmed with fireplaces. Upstairs, however, the bedrooms were tiny, each heated by a small coal stove. Rates were steep, and only men known to the management could get in. A visit to the Old Homestead usually included dinner, with the finest food, liquor, and entertainment, before customers selected their companions for the evening.

A well-known Cripple Creek crib girl, who called herself "Leo the Lion," once stood stark naked at noon on the corner of Myers Avenue and Fourth Street. There she yelled out for everyone to hear, "I'm Leo the Lion, the queen of the row!" Some miners who knew her took her back to her crib to sleep off her midday binge. The residents tolerated Leo, but in 1914, when Cripple Creek was in decline, writer Julian Street visited the town and toured Myers Avenue for a series of travel articles he was writing for *Collier's* magazine. At one point a middle-aged woman with jet-black hair and orchid-colored cheeks, wearing a middy blouse and a white linen skirt, winked at him as she stood in the doorway of her shack. A glass sign hanging in her narrow front window read MADAME LEO. Street stopped to chat and learned that the woman was Leo the Lion. She described Cripple Creek as pretty dull, adding that she was making only two or three dollars a day. She said that she wished someone would start a club or open a dance hall across the street. As Street departed, Madam Leo urged him to send up "some nice boys." When his article was published, the residents of Cripple Creek were furious. Street had devoted his entire article to the old red-light district and his conversation with Madam Leo. The residents, however, had the last laugh when they officially changed the name of Myers Avenue to Julian Street.[30]

CHAPTER XI

Along the
✳ Rails

He that loveth pleasure shall be a poor man.
—Proverbs 21:17

B Y THE 1840s traveling for pleasure had caught the fancy of many
Americans living east of the Mississippi. Improved roads, new
turnpikes and canals, and the railroads made travel easier. Railroads especially became a popular mode of transportation in the East. Philip
Hone, a businessman and onetime mayor of New York City, noted in the
late 1840s: "There is scarcely an individual in so reduced circumstances as to
be unable to afford his 'dollar or so,' to travel a couple of hundred miles
from home, in order to see the country and the improvements which are
going on."[1]

In the West, however, traveling for pleasure was not yet in vogue. To
understand why, some background is necessary. Until 1856 there were no
railroads from west of the Mississippi River to the Rocky Mountains. East of
the Mississippi, there were about nine thousand miles of working track. In
1856, however, the Mississippi River was bridged by the Chicago and Rock
Island Railroad. By the late 1850s another line had reached the Missouri
River at St. Joseph. By then there were calls for a transcontinental railroad,
with southerners wanting a southern route and Northerners a northern one.
The Civil War, of course, reduced the number of pleasure seekers, but the
secession of the Southern states freed President Abraham Lincoln from
demands for a southern route. In 1862 he signed the Pacific Railroad Act,
authorizing a massive government loan for a new line linking Omaha,
Nebraska, and Sacramento, California. In 1863 the Central Pacific started
building eastward from the Pacific, and the Union Pacific began to lay
tracks westward from Omaha.

As the railroad pushed westward from Omaha, camps or temporary towns were established to house the construction gangs. Each morning track trains, as they were called, carried the construction workers to the end of the line. There the men worked until late afternoon, when the train returned them to the work camp, where there was little to do but eat and sleep. After the track was completed to a point about sixty miles beyond the temporary camp, the word passed quickly that it was time to move. Everyone pitched in. Tents were folded, shacks dismantled, equipment was packed and loaded on flatcars, and everything transported to the western end of the track. There, in a matter of hours, the camp reappeared.

When the line reached what is today North Platte, Nebraska, the character of the usually dull construction camp changed. Providers of pleasure arrived on the scene, built crude shacks, and pitched their tents, including a large one, a hundred feet long and forty feet wide, which held a bar, dance floor, and fancy gambling equipment. Scattered around the large tent were smaller ones, plus shacks serving as saloons, dance halls, brothels, and living quarters for the gamblers, saloonkeepers, and prostitutes. This was the beginning of what became known as a "Hell on Wheels." When the construction camp moved, so did the providers of pleasure, who set up shop nearby. These temporary towns gave birth to communities that still exist today, including North Platte, Nebraska, and Julesburg, in northeast Colorado.

Henry Stanley, a reporter for the *New York Tribune*—the same Stanley who would later locate the missionary David Livingstone in Africa—arrived in Julesburg in August 1867, soon after "Hell on Wheels." At what passed for a railroad depot, Stanley found:

> a mixed crowd, composed of gamblers, teamsters, and soldiers . . . all eager and anxious for news. Bustling through them, I found my way to the very comfortable quarters at the Julesburg House, and was fortunate enough to find a feast composed of various styles of soups, *fricandeaus,* vegetables, game in abundance, pies, puddings, raisins, apples, nuts, wine and bread at *discretion,* for the moderate sum of twelve bits. I was astonished to find such company as then sat at the table. Everybody had gold watches attached to expensive chains, and was dressed in well-made clothes, and several wore patent leather boots. I vow I thought these were great capitalists, but was astonished to find they were only clerks, ticket agents, conductors, engineers, and "sich like." These *habitués* of the Julesburg House were the upper-tendom of sin-

ful Julesburg. Dinner over, I took a stroll through its streets, and was really astonished at the extraordinary growth of the town, and the energy of the people. It was unmistakable go-ahead-it-ative-ness, illustrated by substantial warehouses, stores, saloons, piled with goods of all sorts, and of the newest fashion. As might be expected, gambling was carried on extensively, and the saloons were full.

I walked on till I came to a dance-house, bearing the euphonious title of "King of the Hills," gorgeously decorated and brilliantly lighted. Coming suddenly from the dimly lighted street to the kerosene-lighted restaurant, I was almost blinded by the glare and stunned by the clatter. The ground floor was as crowded as it could well be, and all were talking loud and fast, and mostly every one seemed bent on debauchery and dissipation. The women appeared to be the most reckless, and the men seemed nothing loth to enter a whirlpool of sin. Several of the women had what they called "husbands," and these occasional wives bore their husbands' names with as much ease as if both mayor and priest had given them a legal title. The managers of the saloons rake in greenbacks by hundreds every night; there appears to be plenty of money here, and plenty of fools to squander it.

These women are expensive articles, and come in for a large share of the money wasted. In broad daylight they may be seen gliding through the sandy streets in Black Crook dresses, carrying fancy derringers slung to their waists, with which tools they are dangerously expert. Should they get into a fuss, western chivalry will not allow them to be abused by any man whom they may have robbed. . . . The females are monstrous creatures undeserving the name of women, and their male followers are a disgrace to manhood.

The population of Julesburg is rapidly growing; and the town, like its predecessor of North Platte, may be epitomized as a jumble of commencements, always shifting, never ending.[2]

As the Union Pacific pushed into what is now Wyoming and stopped its westward building in autumn 1867 to await spring, "Hell on Wheels" moved west with the construction camp, and the town of Cheyenne was born. Built so rapidly that it earned the name "the magic city," from its start Cheyenne had a large number of saloons in tents, "where whiskey and poisonous compounds were retailed at fabulous prices, and coarse provisions commanded prices according to the size of the hungry individual's purse." A few weeks after Cheyenne was founded, Robert Hopkins and Perry Downing had a small one-story building constructed to house a saloon, at what became the corner of 16th and Ferguson Streets. And within two months the Head Quarters Saloon was constructed nearby. Thirty-six by one hundred feet in size, it was one of the largest buildings in Cheyenne and contained "several elegant and well ventilated billiard rooms and a handsome saloon." The owners hired a brass band to call attention to the establishment.

A concert hall and saloon in early Cheyenne, Wyoming. (Author's collection)

A month later most residents of Cheyenne enjoyed a prizefight between John Hardey and Enoch Winter in a ring a mile and a half from the city. The fight lasted only thirty minutes; Hardey won. Within a month the fight promoters scheduled another bout with John Hardey for November 9, 1867. His opponent was John Shannessy; each man was paid five hundred dollars. "The fight lasted one hour and forty-three minutes, during which time one hundred and twenty-six rounds were fought, closing by a 'foul' claimed by Hardey's party and allowed by the referee. Both men evinced considerable pluck and all parties were satisfied that this was one of the most honorable fights that has ever transpired."[3]

Cheyenne survived and prospered because it was about a hundred miles north of Denver. Cheyenne became a transfer point where wagon freighters picked up freight delivered by rail and drove their loads to Denver. Some of the purveyors of pleasure remained in Cheyenne, but others moved westward as the railroad resumed construction in the spring of 1868. They set up their pleasure palaces at a new construction camp, sixty miles west of Cheyenne, which grew into the town of Laramie, Wyoming.

When the Union Pacific reached Utah, the line's temporary town became known as Bear River City. Located forty miles west of modern Green River, Wyoming, Bear River City no longer exists, but in its day it was described as "the liveliest city, if not the wickedest," in the United States. The town was calm during the workday, but as darkness arrived, it came alive with dancing, singing, gambling, fighting, and wild pleasure-making. Legh R. Freeman, who published the *Frontier Index,* an end-of-track newspaper, was getting heartily sick of the vice and violence. Freeman, the son of a railroad employee, was a telegrapher at Fort Kearny when he started a newspaper there late in 1865. He moved it to nearby Kearny, Nebraska, in the spring of 1866, and later that year to North Platte. Transporting his Washington handpress by wagon, Freeman then followed the railroad westward. His paper provided news and entertainment for construction workers, and, finally, at Bear River City, Freeman lashed out editorially against the gambling interests and the lawlessness. He was instrumental in organizing a vigilante group, and in the November 6, 1868, issue of his *Frontier Index,* Freeman printed the following announcement:

> WALKING PAPERS—The gang of garroters from the railroad towns east, who are congregating here, are ordered to vacate this city or hang within sixty hours from this noon. By order of
>
> ALL GOOD CITIZENS

The vigilantes hanged three men, and the other bad characters left town. But on November 19, 1868, Freeman's enemies formed a mob, attacked Bear River City, and burned the jail and the newspaper office. Freeman was taken prisoner by the mob and was being threatened with death when "Bear River" Tom Smith, the town marshal, diverted the crowd's attention. Freeman ducked into a saloon, fled out its back door, and left town. Freeman soon ordered a new printing press, type, and other equipment from Chicago and rebuilt his newspaper in Ogden, Utah, the last "Hell on Wheels" along the Union Pacific's westward route.[4]

The railroad, which contributed to the founding of Laramie, Wyoming, and other western communities, brought eastern goods and merchandise, including bicycles. Three members of the Laramie Bicycle Club posed for this photo around the turn of the century.
(Courtesy American Heritage Center, University of Wyoming)

Bear River City, sometimes called "Bear Town," a well-known "Hell on Wheels" town located in what is now southwest Wyoming. (Courtesy American Heritage Center, University of Wyoming)

One of the last "Hell on Wheels" towns was Corinne, Utah Territory. This stereograph shows Corinne's main street. (Courtesy American Heritage Center, University of Wyoming)

This scene, titled "Sunday-night Amusements," depicts a dog
fight, one pleasure enjoyed by railroad workmen in one of the last
"Hell on Wheels" towns at Corinne, Utah. Illustration from
J. H. Beadle's The Undeveloped West, or, Five Years in the
Territories . . . , *published in 1873. (Author's collection)*

In contrast, opportunities for pleasure providers were very limited among construction workers laying tracks along the Central Pacific route east from Sacramento. Unlike the Union Pacific, which apparently condoned the "Hell on Wheels" to give its workers some diversion while crossing the unsettled plains, the Central Pacific, especially J. H. Strobridge, the road's construction superintendent, would not tolerate the temptations of the "Hell on Wheels." Most of his construction workers were Chinese—more than twelve thousand at one point—and they had their own diversions, including the occasional smoking of opium, which Strobridge opposed. Some of his workers were Irish immigrants who did enjoy an occasional spree, but Strobridge gave them few opportunities for such pleasure. He was able to restrict the movements of vice peddlers because his tank cars carried the only available water, and he discouraged the booze sellers who arrived by wagon by charging them more to water their horses than they could make selling their whiskey. If any of the vice peddlers persisted, Strobridge simply called together a few burly track hands and had them smash the whiskey barrels and send the peddlers packing.

By the time the Central and Union Pacific met and linked up at Promontory Point in Utah, on May 10, 1869, most of the gamblers, saloonkeepers, prostitutes, and other shady characters of "Hell on Wheels" had sought greener pastures elsewhere. Some had set up their establishments in Ogden, about thirty-five miles north of Salt Lake City, to provide their wares to railroad crews, freighters, and gold seekers. Ogden was a transfer point for rail freight going to Salt Lake City, and it was also a jumping-off point for the new goldfields along the Wyoming-Idaho border.

Some of the other providers of pleasure headed east to Kansas, where the Union Pacific Railway, Eastern Division, was being constructed westward from the Missouri River. Gamblers, saloonkeepers, and prostitutes focused their attentions on the cattle towns of Abilene, Solomon, Salina, Brookville, Ellsworth, and Ellis, and on the railhead towns of Newton, Wichita, Caldwell, and Dodge City, which developed along the route of the Atchison, Topeka & Santa Fe Railroad. Although the Santa Fe line reached

Much pleasure was found on May 10, 1869, when the Central Pacific and Union Pacific linked up at Promontory Point in Utah. (Courtesy Bancroft Library, University of California, Berkeley)

Dodge City in far southwest Kansas in September 1872, the remote settlement did not become a cattle town until 1877. Even before herds of Texas
longhorns began arriving in Dodge, the town gained a wild and woolly reputation as a trading and pleasure center for buffalo hunters on the southern
plains. Any excuse to celebrate turned the townspeople, including the buffalo hunters, into pleasure seekers.

In one instance, on New Year's Eve, 1872, A. R. Glazier, an engineer
with the Santa Fe Railroad, pulled his train into Dodge City late in the afternoon. After disconnecting the railroad cars, Glazier put the engine in the
roundhouse with fire and steam up. He then got his supper and returned to
the roundhouse to take a nap in the engine cab. About nine o'clock that
evening, he went to the depot for his work orders. "I lighted my lantern and
got about half way down from the roundhouse to the depot when I heard a
shot fired; then a bullet whistled very close to me. About that time Harry
Campbell, who was braking for Joe Hanson, stuck his head out of the
caboose window and said, 'You fool, put that light out; they are celebrating
down there and they will kill you; they are shooting at your light.' The light
was out before he finished the sentence.

"I crossed over behind a string of box cars, got to the depot, got my
orders, went back to the roundhouse behind the same string of cars and told
the hostler to set the table. He wanted to light the headlight for me. I told
him "No lights for me at all." I got out of the house and turned [the engine]
on the table, had the fireman throw the main line switch for me, and, after we
got onto the main line, I thought he never would get that switch closed and
get back onto the engine. His name was George Veach.

"All this time they were celebrating the incoming new year down town,
and it sounded like a battle royal. I got out about three miles from Dodge
City when I stopped and lighted my head, tail and cab lights."[5]

By 1877, the year Texas cattle began arriving in Dodge City, the town
had nineteen saloons. Its population was only twelve hundred. The town's
nicest saloon was the Saratoga, owned by Chalkley M. "Chalk" Beeson, who
loved music and exercised good taste in providing entertainment—often a
full orchestra—for his patrons. The Saratoga was high-toned compared to
Dodge City's other saloons. It attracted the town's leading citizens, railroad
men, cattle barons, and other prominent people. Beeson took the name of
his saloon from the resort community of Saratoga, New York. Other prominent saloons in Dodge City included Beatty and Kelley's Alhambra, the
Alamo, Mueller and Straeter's Old House, the rather plush Opera House
saloon, and the Longbranch, built in 1873 by Charles Bassett.

Most saloons offered drinking, gambling, and prostitutes. Early in 1879, a Dodge City newspaper editor described one such establishment as "a long frame building, with a hall and bar in front and sleeping rooms in the rear. The hall was nightly used for dancing, and was frequented by prostitutes, who belonged to the house and for benefit of it solicited the male visitors to dance. The rooms in the rear were occupied both during the dancing hours and after, and both day and night by the women for the purpose of prostitution."[6]

In Dodge City, and elsewhere in the West, pranks and practical jokes were the products of the isolated, mostly self-sufficient, socially independent, and competitive frontier society. They also relieved boredom during slow times. An early Dodge City resident recalled that one saloon owner kept a large wire cage filled with more than a dozen large rattlesnakes behind his saloon. "Now then, it was the duty of some loafer or hanger-on around the saloon to go out and hunt up a greenhorn, invite him to a drink, then tell him about the big den of rattlers, and take him out and show him the snakes, relating an interesting history of this big rattler and that rattler, how they had bitten a man who died. When he had his auditor absorbed in the story, with his eyes bulged out, and attending to nothing else but the story of the big snakes, the story teller would suddenly say: 'Bend your neck and look down there at that monster,' and when his man would bend his head and stoop over, someone would place the enormous stuffed snake on his neck, its tail and its head almost touching the ground from either side. Mr. Man, feeling the snake and, at the same time, seeing it, would give an ungodly whoop, bend his head, and keep jumping up and down, trying to shake it off over his head, instead of straightening up, as he ought to have done, when the snake would have dropped off his back. Then there would be a seance. The crowd would whoop and hollo, and the poor fellow would join them from fear and keep jumping up and down, until, finally, he would get rid of the terrible snake—it would drop off."[7]

When the cattle trade began to disappear from Dodge City in the middle 1880s, several prominent businessmen decided to concoct something new, something unusual, to attract attention to their town and to provide entertainment for everyone. A. B. Webster, a former Dodge City mayor, suggested the town hold a real Mexican bullfight. The idea triggered the imagination of the town's businessmen. They spread the word and within twenty-four hours ten thousand dollars had been raised in cash and subscriptions. But staging a bullfight in Kansas, where none had ever been held, would be no easy matter. Some residents of Dodge City had seen bullfights in Mexico, but no one knew how to set one up. The businessmen organized the "Dodge City Driving Park and Fair Association"; Webster was appointed general manager, and the group set out to organize a bullfight for the Independence Day celebration on July 4, 1884.

Through a friend in El Paso, Texas, Webster arranged for some Mexican bullfighters to come to Dodge City, and he located a dozen ferocious bulls on a ranch near Dodge. They were brought to town, and three days before the scheduled bullfight, the *Dodge City Globe* reported: "As some of them are liable to be numbered with the dead before our next issue, we deem it proper to give a short sketch of these noted animals, together with their pedigrees." The newspaper then described each bull. The best of the lot, at least in the newspaper's opinion, was "Ringtailed Snorter." The oldest of the dozen bulls, he had reportedly been in twenty-seven different fights— and won each. Another of the better bulls was "Iron Gall," described as "a famous catch-as-catch-can fighter, and very bad when stirred up." Another bull, "Klu Klux," was number seven on the list. "He is a four-year old," reported the newspaper. Everyone viewed the bulls and approved of the selection. Meantime, a handful of critics in Kansas had accused the residents of Dodge City of returning to barbarism. Rumors spread throughout Dodge City that Kansas Governor Glick in Topeka, at the other end of the state, would stop the fights. Another rumor claimed that the mayor had received a telegram from the U.S. attorney general's office that said bull-fighting was against the law in the United States. To this the mayor suppos-edly said, "Hell! Dodge City ain't in the United States!" Most residents did not take the rumors seriously until a handful of reporters from eastern newspapers arrived in Dodge to cover the bullfight and began sending their stories back. The promoters tried to set the out-of-town reporters straight on the facts in fear that their stories might cut the number of eastern visitors who were planning to come to Dodge City for the bullfights.

On July 4, 1884, however, fears were forgotten. Dodge City was full of visitors who were spending money. The festivities began at two o'clock in the afternoon, with a large parade from town to a half-mile track and a four-thousand-seat grandstand that had been constructed on forty acres of land south of town, purchased by the Dodge City Driving Park and Fair Association. The bullfight promoters and town officials led the parade, followed by the town's cowboy band and the bullfighters, who were decked out in "red jackets, blue tunics, white stockings and small dainty slippers." The grandstand soon filled with spectators. Of the four thousand paying cus-tomers, nearly fifteen hundred were women and children. One deputy sher-iff had the job of separating the soiled doves, or prostitutes, from their

(Left) The Mexican bullfighters who performed in Dodge City, Kansas, in July 1884. (Courtesy Kansas State Historical Society) (Right) The front page of the Dodge City Democrat, *June 21, 1884, announcing the "Grand Spanish Bull Fight" scheduled for early July. (Courtesy Kansas State Historical Society)*

"more respectable sisters." The sound of a bugle at 3:30 P.M. signaled the grand entry. The matadors and picadors, four afoot and one mounted, paraded into the arena. Dressed in their fighting costumes, they circled the arena, bowed to the officials, and prepared for the first bull to enter.

Again the sound of the bugle echoed across the grandstand, and the first bull entered. The animal was hit by two decorated barbs thrown into his neck. This infuriated him, and he charged. Then the matadors began to demonstrate their abilities. For thirty minutes they were in their glory. The crowd cheered time after time, but soon the bull tired. The order was given to bring on another. The second bull came out, but the crowd—anticipating more of the same—was disappointed. The second bull was a coward. He ran from the matadors and was soon taken from the arena. The third, fourth, and fifth bulls were also poor imitators of the first. The crowd began demanding that the first bull be returned. When the announcer said there was time for only one more fight that day, the crowd demanded the first bull. They yelled and screamed, and the bull was returned with the announcer saying that the animal—the last bull of the day—would be put to the sword.

The chief matador—Captain Gregorio Gallardo from Chihuahua— was given his sword. The audience became quiet. Tension gripped the audience as the advertised bloodletting was about to begin. The bull spotted the matador and charged. Gallardo deflected the bull's rush with a graceful sweep of his cape. The crowd cheered. The bull wheeled and headed again for Gallardo. Once more the crowd cheered as the animal found nothing but air. The performance continued. Once Gallardo was almost caught by the bull, but he gracefully escaped the animal's path.

Then it was time for the kill.

Bowing to the crowd, Gallardo slowly began walking toward the bull with his sword in position for the kill. The bull, standing still, watched, his eyes never leaving Gallardo. When the matador was almost upon the animal, the bull shot forward. Gallardo stepped aside. Two more times his position was not right, but the fourth time the sword found its mark. The bull stopped, staggered a step or two, sank to his knees, and a moment later rolled to the ground. The first of two days of bullfighting had ended.

The next day, July 5, the bullfights went on as scheduled. A Dodge City newspaper reported: "The second day's fighting with the exception of the killing of the last animal in the ring, was more interesting than the first." And after the fights that afternoon the businessmen, celebrating at a local saloon, agreed that the bullfights had been very successful, at least financially, for Dodge City. They were the first real bullfights held in the United States.[8]

The only other community in Kansas to rival Dodge City's reputation as a center for pleasure seekers was Phil Sheridan, named after the Civil War general, but simply called Sheridan or sometimes Sheridan City. The town began in the summer of 1868, when the Union Pacific Railway, Eastern Division, established a construction camp on the east bank of the north fork of the Smoky Hill River, thirteen miles northeast of Fort Wallace and only about fourteen miles from the Colorado border. Tents and crude shacks constituted the town's first structures, until word came that the railroad would not continue to build beyond that point. The railroad had used up its government subsidies and had to wait until it could find more money. Sheridan suddenly boomed; within two weeks it had a population of two hundred and about sixty-five businesses, many in frame structures. Sheridan quickly became a major transfer point for freight and passengers, who rode the railroad to the end of the line and then took a stagecoach farther west.

Nathan Meeker, an eastern newspaperman, visited Sheridan soon after the boom started and described the town as having "two half streets, some 300 feet apart, the railroad track being in the center. There are large commercial houses engaged in the Santa Fe trade," but, he added, the rest of the buildings in the town were "saloons and gambling establishments, more than

50 in number, all open and apparently doing good business. In almost every one there are women. Fiddles and accordions are playing, glasses klinking and there are billiard and roulette tables and other gambling devices." Meeker described the men in Sheridan as "able-bodied and strong; few are more than 35; the majority are less than 30 years old; their faces are flushed, their necks red and thick. . . . But they have a restless, uncertain look and a quickness of movement both strange and suspicious and this more so because they are connected with much that is homelike and familiar. Of course, they are well armed and very offensive or aggressive, although I have every reason to believe that they would commit murder on what we would call the slightest provocation for they have been so audacious and bold that men of property have been obliged to resolve themselves into a Vigilante Committee and hang 15 or 20."9

Sheridan was located in unorganized country, and the Vigilante Committee provided the only law and order. For the townspeople, the violence and resulting action taken by the vigilantes often provided bizarre entertainment. For instance, one day members of the Vigilante Committee arrested a bad character on some charge. He was brought before their court in a saloon crowded with onlookers. William E. Webb, visiting the town, later recalled that as the man was brought into the saloon, he yelled at the judge and called the court names. The judge restored order and then announced, "This yere court feels herself insulted without due cause and orders the prisoner strung up for contempt." The man was promptly taken from the saloon and hanged from a railroad trestle just east of town as many townspeople cheered and watched.

Webb also described another incident involving two men who found pleasure in bullying others: Gunshot Frank and Sour Bill. One day they had a quarrel. Each man got a revolver and a spade and then, with a few friends, started for a spot just outside of town. Many townspeople, anticipating pleasure in what might happen to the bullies, followed. The plan was for each man to dig a grave for the other and then have a duel. But before the digging was finished, Gunshot Frank made an impudent remark to Sour Bill, who shot him through the abdomen, killing him. Gunshot Frank's friends at once fell upon Sour Bill, one of them breaking his skull with a spade. That night, according to Webb, the two men slept in the graves that their own hands had helped to dig, and their friends celebrated in a local saloon. The bullies were two of perhaps a hundred men buried in the Sheridan cemetery. With only one or two exceptions, all of them had died violent deaths during the town's short life.10

Sheridan died about as quickly as it was born. After Congress authorized the railroad to mortgage the road and its land located between Sheridan and Denver, the railroad resumed construction westward, under the name Kansas Pacific. When the tracks reached Kit Carson, Colorado, in March 1870, the buildings, shacks, and tents of Sheridan were dismantled and shipped west on the line to Kit Carson, where a new construction camp was established. The pleasure providers followed. Within four months there were only eighty people left in Sheridan, and after the post office was closed early in 1871, Sheridan soon became a ghost town. Today the only visible reminders of Sheridan are a few depressions in a pasture located in Logan County, Kansas, about fourteen miles from the Colorado border. Even the town's cemetery is not marked.[11]

Few other western railroads experienced such problems as they built their routes across the West during the remainder of the nineteenth century. They learned how to avoid the pervasive dispensers of pleasure. For example, to the north along the St. Paul, Minneapolis & Manitoba Railroad—later the Great Northern—the railroad eliminated the need for establishing temporary towns by providing three-deck rolling bunkhouses for the laborers during the late 1880s, as the track was being laid from Minot in the Dakotas to Helena in the Montana Territory. The construction gang was guarded by soldiers, who took their band along to provide some civilized pleasures for everyone.

CHAPTER XII

Western Pleasure
♦♦ Palaces

Increased means and increased leisure are the two civilizers of man.
—Benjamin Disraeli

FOLLOWING THE CIVIL WAR many of the new rich from eastern cities began to look for pleasurable diversions that were once beyond their means. Some sought pleasure at Saratoga Springs in upstate New York, others found it at Newport, Rhode Island. These resort areas had become prominent among wealthy easterners well before the Civil War. But those who could not find space or acceptance turned westward and took the transcontinental railroad to the Pacific to view the scenery, enjoy the climate, and see the remnants of the Old West. The coach fare from Omaha to San Francisco in 1869 was $32.20, and with extra charges for over-weight luggage, a round-trip, coast-to-coast first-class railroad fare, including lodging, cost between $250 and $300, plus meals. A wealthy eastern tourist might spend several hundred dollars to cross the country, tour north-ern California, and return east. In a period when a small frame house could be rented for a few dollars a month, and teachers made little more than $200 a year, it was the wealthy and not the masses who first ventured westward by rail for pleasure.[1]

George M. Pullman's sleeping cars, sometimes described as the wealthy man's "yachts on wheels," gave travelers much pleasure in getting there. Pullman's sleeping cars were introduced in the Ohio Valley in 1865, but their use in the West did not begin until after the first transcontinental route was opened in 1869. Pullman, a New Yorker who had moved to Chicago, con-ceived the idea that railroad sleeping cars could be greatly improved, and with funds earned as an industrial contractor, he began in 1855 to develop what ten years later became the first "Pullman car," featuring convertible coach seats that would make up into lower and upper berths. Pullman's Pioneer, the first truly successful sleeping car, cost roughly twenty thousand dollars fully equipped, and it first gained national attention when it carried the body of President Abraham Lincoln from Chicago to Springfield. In 1867 the Pullman Palace Car Company was organized in the company's factory, located in south Chicago. Pullman cars soon became popular, and the basic style changed little through the remainder of the nineteenth century. Each year, however, saw some refinements and improvements, including the enclosed vestibule and the reclining seat. The Pullman sleeping cars used on the transcontinental railroad provided comfort and luxury matching the standards of the time. Pullman, who learned mechanics from his father and cabinetmaking from a brother, fitted his sleeping cars with carved and gilded walnut and etched and stained plate glass. There were silver-plated metal trappings. Seats were cushioned with thick plush material, and there were washstands of marble and walnut, damask curtains, and massive mirrors in frames of gilded walnut. The floor of each car was carpeted with the most costly Brussels, and the roof beautifully frescoed in mosaics of gold, emerald green, crimson, sky blue, violet, olive drab, and black. Each car offered private or semiprivate toilets and sleeping accommodations for about thirty passengers.[2]

When Susan Coolidge took a train west to California during the early 1870s, she recalled that her drawing room had four windows, six ventilators, a long sofa, two armchairs with movable backs, mirrors, and storage space. Between two drawing rooms was a dressing closet with toilet facilities. When bedtime came, she wrote that the porter entered and "in some mysterious way" converted the sofa and the armchairs into room beds. He gave her a batch of clean towels and left.[3]

While the Union Pacific and most other railroads purchased Pullman cars, officials of the Central Pacific thought they cost too much. They purchased sleeping cars manufactured by Jackson and Sharp Company, which contained white metallic interiors and for this reason were known as "silver palace cars." They contained single private sitting rooms, each equipped with a spittoon. John H. Beadle, a correspondent for the *Cincinnati Commercial,* wrote: "They are decidedly convenient for single gentlemen, having extensive sitting rooms at each end, in which smoking is allowed, as they can be completely shut off from the main room; but in other respects they do not appear to me as comfortable in winter as the Pullman. Different parts of the car seem to heat unequally."[4]

Until the late 1880s, most Pullman passengers had to leave their comfortable cars to mingle with the masses when the train halted at what became

*Nineteenth-century illustration of the interior of a palace-car on the
Central Pacific Railroad. (Author's collection)*

known as breakfast, lunch, or supper stops. There, the travelers were
offered "square dinners" and "elegant lunches," unless they carried lunch
baskets or had taken one of the weekly extra-fare "gilt-edged" trains, which
carried "restaurant" or dining cars. The first dining car, named Delmonico
after a well-known New York City restaurant, was placed in service on the
Chicago and Alton Railroad in 1868. By the early 1870s dining cars were
found on the first-class overland trains. Compared to the rough fare at most
western stagecoach stations, the dining cars were pleasure palaces, offering
such delights as sugar-cured ham with champagne sauce, salmon, and a
choice of vegetables, relishes, desserts, and drinks. "Fine French Wines"
cost fifteen cents extra. Between meals and sleeping, passengers could play
cards, read, talk, or view the western scenery through broad windows. And
at watering stops—most were very tiny settlements—the passengers could
see the local hotel, a saloon or two, maybe a dance hall, restaurant, and a few
usually weather-beaten frame dwellings. Into the 1870s it was not uncommon for passengers to see herds of buffalo (bison), deer, or antelope or
prairie-dog towns along the tracks.

By the late 1860s excursion trains carried parties of sightseers and
hunters westward onto the buffalo ranges from both Omaha, Nebraska, and

Kansas City, Missouri. Along the line of the Union Pacific Railway, Eastern Division (later the Kansas Pacific), passengers shot buffalo from their train cars. Perhaps the best account of such an excursion was written by E. N. Andrews, who left Lawrence, Kansas, in October 1868 on an outing organized for the benefit of a church. The train consisted of five passenger coaches, one smoking car, one baggage car, and one freight car. The party consisted of about 30 women and 250 men, including the Lawrence Cornet Band. The men had nearly eighty guns and rifles. The party spent the first night sleeping in their coach seats at Ellsworth, Kansas. At dawn the train headed west again and by evening the party reached the 325 milepost west of Kansas City, at which point they began to see thousands of buffalo grazing in the distance. During the next forty miles they never lost sight of buffalo. At the 365 milepost, they saw buffalo near the train. What happened next is told in Andrews's own words:

> Three bulls were on the left of the track, though nearly all that we had
> seen were on the right, or north of the barrier [tracks], while now on

Excursion trains carried hunters to the buffalo range in central Kansas during the late 1860s.
(Author's collection)

their southward course, feeding in their slow advance. They kept pace with the train for at least a quarter of a mile, while the boys blazed away at them without effect. It was their design to get ahead of the train and cross over to the main body of their fellows; and they finally accomplished their object. The cowcatcher, however, became almost a bull-catcher, for it seemed to graze one as he passed on the jump. As soon as the three were well over upon the right, they turned backward, at a small angle away from the train, and then it was that powder and ball were brought into requisition! Shots enough were fired to rout a regiment of men. Ah! see that bull in advance there; he has stopped a second; he turns a kind of reproachful look toward the train; he starts again on the lope a step or two; he hesitates; poises on the right legs; a pail-full of blood gushes warm from his nostrils; he falls flat upon the right side, dead. . . . The engineer was kind enough to shut off the steam; the train stopped, and such a scrambling and screeching was never before heard on the Plains, except among the red men, as we rushed forth to see our first game lying in his gore. The writer had the pleasure of first putting hands on the dark locks of the noble monster who had fallen so bravely. Another distinguished himself by mounting the fallen brave. Then came the ladies; a ring was formed; the cornet band gather around, and, as if to tantalize the spirits of all departed buffalo, as well as Indians, played Yankee Doodle. I thought that "Hail to the Chief" would have done more honor to the departed.[5]

Before Andrews and his party returned to Lawrence, they had killed more than a dozen buffalo. Shooting buffalo from trains for pleasure was banned by the Kansas Pacific in 1875.

The idea for such excursion trains originated with the Englishman Thomas Cook, who also is credited with creating the package tour. It was Cook, more than anyone else, who introduced American travel for pleasure not only to wealthy Americans but to the British middle class. He first provided chaperoned tours through the eastern United States in 1865 and early 1866. By then he recognized the potential for tour packages in the West, and after the first transcontinental railroad was completed, Cook established offices in the United States with the aim of promoting travel for pleasure. Tours conducted by Cook and others were open to persons who could afford the tariff and who could pass the most elementary tests of social acceptability. The typical tour party, often taken west in private railroad cars, usually did not exceed sixty people. They came to cherish the familiar surroundings and prearranged comforts of the railroad cars, especially after returning to them following side trips to see the Wild West. Historian Earl Pomeroy observed that such tours provided "effective insulation from the world outside. Even if the attraction of the group lay in a sense of high adventure and large undertaking, rather than in a desire to cling to some of the physical niceties of Eastern life, it kept the tourist from seeing the West as it was, and for that matter the Westerner from seeing the tourist as he was; it maintained a gulf and a contrast between tourist and resident in the eyes of each, while bringing them closer in a physical sense than most Easterners would have come without the assurances that the agencies offered."[6]

Eastern industrial magnates also frequently traveled in private cars and sometimes in special trains to see the West. Dr. William Seward Webb, president of the Wagner Palace Car Company and related by marriage to the Vanderbilts, took his family from New York City to California in 1889 in a four-car special train. Webb's party consisted of twelve persons, served by a maid, two cooks, two nurses for the children, and eight porters. One of the railroad cars had been remodeled into a nursery for Mrs. Webb and the children. Webb even hired a Pinkerton detective to guard the family at night between Kansas and California, and he had gongs installed in the cars that could be used to call the servants or help should outlaws board any car.[7]

Although many of the order files of such private car builders as Pullman, American Car & Foundry, and others were classified, and in some cases destroyed when they were no longer useful, it is known that between 1882 and 1900 Pullman built sixty-one private cars for businesses and individuals. Many of the private cars were named, and the records show the Pedford Penola was built for Jay Gould in 1886; the Oriental for Austin Corbin in 1889; the Alexander for A. A. McLeod in 1890; and the Ohio for John McLean in 1894. The cost of these cars is not known, but throughout the 1870s twenty thousand dollars bought a nice palace car with picture windows and Eastlake decor stressing square, solid, but ornate furnishings. By 1900, the going price was about fifty thousand dollars for a car equipped with Westinghouse air brakes, electric lights, and king-size brass beds in master staterooms. Even Brigham Young, head of the Mormon church, had a palace car for his travels during the 1870s. The Mormons had done contract labor for the Union Pacific as it extended its tracks into Utah, with the bill reportedly amounting to more than a million dollars. When the railroad said it could not meet the claim, the Mormons took instead six hundred thousand dollars' worth of equipment, including a railroad car that was rebuilt into a private car for Young. Angels were painted on the ceiling, and gilt and scrollwork appeared in wildest profusion. The finished car "combined the best features of business office and episcopal palace and aboard it the bearded patriarch travelled extensively and splendidly over the then existing railroads of Utah surrounded by his wives, bishops of the church, elders and other peers in saintliness until his death in 1877."[8]

Whether tourists were traveling in private palace cars or on the lowest fare possible, they could purchase printed guides to help them find pleasure as they were whisked westward over the rails. Perhaps the earliest transcontinental railroad guide was published in Chicago by George A. Crofutt, under the title *Great Trans-Continental Railroad Guide*. For passengers traveling the Union Pacific route across western Nebraska, Crofutt's guide provided background information on the towns, frequently capitalizing on the earlier and often rough nature of the settlements during the railroad's construction period. For example, Crofutt's 1869 guide contains the following note on Julesburg:

> Julesburg was the roughest of all rough towns along the Union Pacific line. The roughs congregated there, and a day seldom passed but what they "had a man for breakfast." Gambling and dance houses constituted a good portion of the town; and it is said that morality and honesty clasped hands and departed from the place. We have not learned whether they ever returned; and really we have our doubts whether they were ever there.[9]

Printed guidebooks, often containing embellished short histories and descriptions of western towns, provided romance and adventure for many western travelers, and they also provided information on how to derive pleasure from watching the countryside. Such information, which could not be extracted from indifferent conductors or other passengers, might be about points of interest, including such major stopovers as Cheyenne and Salt Lake City. Through the early 1870s Crofutt's guidebooks, and those of several imitators, even told travelers where they might see wild game.

Most coach passengers enjoyed simpler and much less luxurious accommodations than those who could afford to travel in the Pullman cars. Coach seats were more comfortable, however, than those of the Concord stagecoach. In cool or cold weather, a wood- or coal-burning stove at one end of each coach provided heat. Every train had a news or "train boy," who sold books, newspapers, lollipops, canned beans and bacon, fruit, coffee, and cigars. Even after dining cars became commonplace, the Union Pacific–Central Pacific route across Nebraska, Wyoming, and Utah to California still made short mealtime stops where hungry passengers without their own supplies of food, or who could not afford dining car prices, could rush to a depot restaurant and hurriedly eat a meal. The menus at such stops usually consisted of such mainstays as beefsteak, fried eggs, and fried potatoes. For sleeping, coach passengers stretched out as best they could in their seats and covered themselves with coats or blankets. Unlike the passengers in comfortable Pullman cars, those in the coaches usually arrived at their destination sleepy-eyed, tired, and stiff.

Railroad travelers experiencing the least pleasure were those traveling in immigrant cars, a class of rail travel created by railroad companies to meet basic travel needs and to offer the lowest possible fares for immigrants. The Central Pacific began using this class of travel in 1879. There were few comforts in the rather plain, boxlike, and poorly lighted immigrant cars. Many had upper and lower berths, but with wooden slats in lieu of upholstery, the passengers supplying either their coats or blankets. On many trains boys sold straw mattresses costing about $2.50 to make sleeping more comfortable for those who could afford them. The immigrant cars were equipped with toilet facilities and a coal-burning stove on which some immigrants also cooked. Many of them carried their own food and ate their meals aboard these cars. At some stops they could purchase milk and food from local hawkers. Since there were no curtains to divide sections of the cars, passengers lived together like one large family, often sharing their food, singing songs, joking, and sometimes fighting. In spite of the conditions, emigrants found pleasure in the promise of new homes in a new land.[10]

In 1888 Rand, McNally & Co.'s *New Guide to the Pacific Coast*, written by James W. Steele, provided readers with the concise itinerary for a trip from Kansas City, Missouri, to the Pacific Ocean, including meal stops. His words made the journey seem gracious:

> . . . the evening at NEWTON, Middle Kansas,—SUPPER. During the night the journey lies westward along the Arkansas River,—seen first at Hutchinson, Kan.,—across what were once known as "The Plains," to and across the western line of Kansas, to LA JUNTA, COLORADO. BREAKFAST, Tuesday morning.
>
> From La Junta the coaches and Pullmans going direct to the Pacific coast turn south-westward;—those for Denver, or Colorado Springs and a junction there with the Colorado Midland Railroad or the Denver & Rio Grande Railroad, going northward. During the forenoon TRINIDAD, at the foot of the Raton Range, is passed, and the

train climbs the eastern slope and passes through Raton tunnel. DINNER at the town of Raton. SUPPER at the town of LAS VEGAS, whence a branch line of six miles runs to the LAS VEGAS HOT SPRINGS. Beyond Las Vegas is passed the Glorieta Range, and immediately beyond this is the station of LAMY, whence a branch line of 17 miles goes up to the city of SANTA FE.

During the night of Tuesday, the train enters the Valley of the RIO GRANDE, passing down this valley as far as ALBUQUERQUE, where the Pacific coast cars turn westward over the Atlantic & Pacific Railroad.

Passengers for El Paso, or the interior or City of Mexico, are carried southward from Albuquerque.

WEDNESDAY: Breakfast at COOLIDGE, near the western line of New Mexico. During the forenoon pass LAGUNA, Fort Wingate, etc., and fairly enter the curious country in which there is so little, and yet so much, to interest. DINNER at HOLBROOK or WINSLOW.

During the afternoon pass Canyon Diablo, and enter the forest region about Flagstaff. SUPPER at WILLIAMS. During the night pass some of the finest mountain scenery possible to American travel; about midnight reach Peach Springs, the nearest railroad station to the GRAND CANYON, which lies directly north; and strike the down grade to the Colorado River.

THURSDAY: Breakfast at THE NEEDLES, California, at the western end of the bridge crossing the Colorado.

Here begins THE DESERT, to many travellers not the least interesting portion of the journey. DINNER at a station reached about one o'clock, and at about three o'clock p.m. arrive at BARSTOW, where cars for LOS ANGELES, SAN DIEGO and all points in Southern California turn southward to cross the San Bernardino Range through Cajon Pass. SUPPER, SAN BERNARDINO or LOS ANGELES. At San Bernardino Valley; those for San Diego direct go southward. To Los Angeles, the journey (supposing it to begin on Monday) ends on Thursday evening; to San Diego on Friday morning; to San Francisco direct, not turning off at Barstow, on Friday morning.

The distance from Kansas City to San Bernardino, 1,740 miles. To Los Angeles, 1,800 miles. To San Diego, 1,871 miles. To San Francisco (direct), 2,115 miles.[11]

For pleasure seekers heading west during the 1870s, there were few accommodations to brag about outside of San Francisco and Denver. In San

Francisco, financier William Chapman Ralston built the Palace Hotel, the largest and costliest American hotel when it opened its doors in 1875. Almost a city within itself, under a glass roof the Palace offered shops and tropical gardens arranged around a central courtyard and marble driveway in the Viennese style. Five years later the Windsor Hotel opened in Denver, and it was described as the largest and most elegant hotel between Chicago and San Francisco. Elsewhere in the West, however, hotels offered few of the amenities found in the East. The early hotels along the Pacific railroad were labeled "whitewashed Mugby Junctions" by newspaperman Henry M. Stanley, who described the proprietors as trying to outdo one another with "exorbitant charges and poor fare."[12]

To remedy the situation, increase travel, and attract more pleasure seekers, railroads encouraged eastern capitalists to invest in and to construct hotels in the West. The Southern Pacific Railroad, through its construction subsidiary, the Pacific Improvement Company, built the first of the great western tourist resorts, the Hotel del Monte, at the southern end of Monterey Bay. It opened in 1880 and provided urban comforts and graces against

The Windsor Hotel in Denver soon after it opened in 1880. Photo by William Henry Jackson.
(Courtesy Colorado Historical Society)

The Windsor's dining room. Photo by William Henry Jackson.
(Courtesy Colorado Historical Society)

a carefully refined and refashioned rural background. It was called "A Palace of Delight" and "The Queen of American Watering Places," and the hotel attracted the wealthy from San Francisco and elsewhere. There were saltwater baths and carriage drives, and writers working for the promoters made the Hotel del Monte sound like paradise:

> The hotel is first seen through a vista of trees, and, in its beautiful embowerment of foliage and flowers, resembles some rich private home in the midst of a broad park. This impression is heightened when the broader extent of avenues, lawns and flower-bordered walks come into view. The gardener's art has turned many acres into a choice conservatory, where the richest flowers blossom in profusion. Here and there are swings, croquet grounds, an archery, lawn-tennis courts and bins of fine beach sand—the latter being intended for the use and amusement of the children. The use of all these, as well as of the ladies' billiard saloon, is free to guests. In all directions there are seats for loungers. Through a vista formed by the umbrageous oaks and pines, the huge, bulbous forms of a varied family of cacti are seen.
>
> In another place is a bewildering maze. . . . The Del Monte Bathing Pavilion is situated on the beach, about eight minutes' walk

from the hotel, and is one of the largest and most complete establishments of the kind in the world. . . . Outside of this pavilion is a beautiful sandy beach, on which surf-bathing may be indulged. An adjunct of the Hotel del Monte is its 18 mile drive, over a splendidly-kept macadamized road, by way of Monterey, Pacific Grove, Cypress Grove, Carmel Bay, and the old Mission Church.[13]

Santa Barbara had the first tourist hotel in Southern California. It was called the Arlington and opened in 1874. Visitors were few, however, until the Southern Pacific completed its coast line in 1903 between Los Angeles and San Francisco. Pasadena was more fortunate. Settled by a group of people from Indiana with strong temperance views, who planned to grow oranges, the town began to attract eastern tourists during the late 1870s. They would spend the winter months eating, sleeping, and relaxing in the mild climate. With Pasadena located on the main line of the Santa Fe, the railroad donated a site along its tracks for a hotel and a main rail stop. The town provided the water. The hotel—the Raymond—was built and opened in 1886. Walter Raymond, a native of New England, was the proprietor. The hotel's staff, after working the summer season in the White Mountains of New England, returned to Pasadena for the winter season from November to May.

Promoters described the Raymond Hotel as "one of the best equipped west of New York," and they noted that it "boasts the finest scenery from its piazzas in the country. . . . Four miles from the city the Sierra Madres rise to an elevation of from six to eight thousand feet. The range abounds in canyons and drives of the greatest beauty; falls, cascades, trout streams, caves, deep gulches, trails leading to the summit, and a thousand and one novel features, affording the tourist a new pleasure every day in the year. It is this feature which has made Pasadena the great fashionable winter resort of America. Tourists do not want climate alone; they are paying for amusement, and in its drives and innumerable natural beauties Pasadena is unexcelled. Nine miles from Los Angeles, twenty from Santa Monica and sea bathing, with the finest opera house in Southern California, the tourist has every facility for pleasure and enjoyment. The hunting is good, and out door life can be counted on nearly any day in the true land of flowers."[14]

San Diego had the Hotel del Coronado. Finished in 1888, it could house more than a thousand guests. Situated on a peninsula across from San Diego, this spectacular seaside resort hotel was designed by James W. Reid and Merritt Reid. Almost everything in its appearance—cupolas, pillars, turrets, gewgaw gingerbread—suggests the richness and eclecticism of late-Victorian American architecture.[15]

COLORADO ALSO HELD great potential for pleasure traveling and resorts. The first transcontinental railroad skirted Colorado, but early visitors recognized its possibilities. Samuel Bowles, the editor of the Springfield, Massachusetts, *Republican*, traveled by train to Cheyenne in 1868, and then took a stage to Denver and toured the Colorado Rockies or "the Switzerland of America," as he described the region. Bowles recognized that Colorado could attract pleasure seekers. He wrote:

> We borrow our ideas of mountain travel and mountain heights from Switzerland and the White Mountains of New Hampshire. Among them both, vegetation ceases at about five thousand feet above the sea level, and perpetual snow reigns among the Alps at seven thousand to eight thousand feet, and would in the White Mountains if they went as high. But here in these vast mountain regions . . . the hills themselves only begin to rise from the Plains at an elevation of five thousand five hundred feet. And at that height, though the nights are always deliciously cool, the summer's days are as warm as, if not warmer than they ever are in the valleys of the New England States, and snow enough for sleighing.[16]

Once railroads arrived in Colorado, the construction of resorts moved along at a brisk pace. Although the Denver and Rio Grande Railway built the three-story frame Colorado Springs Hotel in 1871, it was not until 1883 that General W. A. J. Palmer of the Denver and Rio Grande Railroad opened the Antlers Hotel in Colorado Springs, a truly gracious hotel, under the shadow of Pikes Peak. Twelve years earlier Palmer had laid out the nearby resort community of Manitou, where visitors could seek relief for what ailed them and find pleasure in the mineral waters that flowed from the earth. Manitou became to Denver what the Hotel del Monte became to San Francisco.[17]

Georgetown, Colorado, claimed the Hotel de Paris, a small but luxurious establishment, where visitors winding their way through the Rockies on narrow-gauge lines could stop for a night or two and enjoy the dry mountain air. But in western Colorado, first-class resort accommodations did not appear until 1893, when Walter Devereux of the Colorado Midland Railroad

The bathhouse in the resort community of Manitou near Colorado Springs, where visitors could enjoy mineral water baths. Photo taken late nineteenth century. (Courtesy Colorado Historical Society)

spearheaded the construction of the five-story Hotel Colorado at Glenwood Springs. It was designed by New York architects in the Italian style, supposedly inspired by the Villa Medici in Rome. Devereux hired none other than Walter Raymond to run the hotel, which had two hundred bedrooms, many with open fireplaces. There were fifty-nine private bathrooms, besides the sixteen on each floor for general use. The bedrooms were finished in light woods, a variety of color schemes, and most had brass beds and testers, or canopies. The spacious lobby was flanked on the north and south by a court. The north court was a small interior alcove with arches. A twelve-foot-wide sheet of water dropped in a waterfall, a distance of twenty-five feet from its rear-wall rim to a pool beneath. The other court was a three-sided exterior area surrounded by wide verandas. Fronting on this south court were the ordinary dining room, the servants' dining room, the children's playrooms, the private banquet room, and the ladies' billiard room. The south court also had a large pool in its center, from which a fountain shot a jet of water a hundred feet into the air, creating an iridescent spray against the sunlight. The pools in both courts were stocked with trout. In the basement was a bar, a gentleman's billiard room, and a cold-storage compartment that could hold three hundred tons of ice.[18]

Guests and perhaps a few townsfolk posed for this photograph taken outside the Hotel de Paris in Georgetown, Colorado, late in the nineteenth century. (Courtesy Colorado Historical Society)

Equally plush, and constructed a few years after the Hotel Colorado, was Redstone Castle, twelve miles from Glenwood Springs. John Cleveland Osgood, a cousin of President Grover Cleveland, who made a fortune in Colorado iron and coal, built a forty-five room, 27,000-square-foot sandstone mansion not as a hotel but as his personal pleasure palace. He filled room after room with treasures, including Gustav Stickley chairs, English silver services, Oriental carpets, carved cherrywood sideboards, Tiffany lighting, embossed Italian leather library walls, baccarat tables for the gaming room, trophy heads, and gold-embossed leather ceilings. Some rooms had Belgian wall hangings and French silks and damasks. Located on the bank of rushing Crystal River, Redstone Castle had vast, neatly kept lawns. Osgood, then one of the nation's wealthiest industrialists, invited the famous to visit him, and they did—Teddy Roosevelt, John D. Rockefeller, J. P. Morgan, the King of Belgium, among many. It is said that Teddy Roosevelt once waited on the veranda for big game to be driven conveniently down a valley toward the castle. As he fingered his rifle trigger, Roosevelt supposedly declared, "This scenery bankrupts the English language!"[19]

Not only did the railroads encourage the building of resorts in the West, but they sought to capitalize on the western scenery and create appealing images to attract visitors seeking pleasure. The railroads, intent on transplanting the pleasures of Europe and New England, labeled California as the "Italy of America" and "the Riviera of America." Monterey Bay was called the "Naples of the New World," and Santa Cruz, "the Newport of the New World," with a climate like that of "the Isles of Greece." Colorado was described not only as "the Switzerland of America" but as "the American Alps." To counter the picturesqueness often associated with Europe, the promoters romanticized the history of the region.

Missourian John H. Tice traveled the Kansas Pacific to Denver soon after the line opened in 1870. In his book *Over the Plains and On the Mountains* (1872), Tice wrote: "There is scarcely a brook, canyon or peak, of which some Indian tale is not related, derived from the Indians themselves by the daring trappers who were domiciled amongst them. . . . If the tales of a wild hunter's life should be more desirable staple for a romance, there is no lack of them also, whether of those who long since 'have gone over the Divide,' or of those who are 'still on the Range.' "[20]

If legends and names of springs, canyons, falls, lakes, geysers, mountains, and other natural wonders did not have names, the promoters created them to satisfy the pleasure seekers. As early as the 1850s, some rock formations near present-day Colorado Springs were labeled the "Garden of the Gods." John Tice noted that the formations were in "an enclosed area of six or seven miles long and from a few rods to a quarter of a mile wide. The enclosing rock is composed of various strata, but its predominant one is red sedimentary sandstone of a brick color. The entrance has a gate-like appearance of perpendicular rocks two hundred feet high, and the wall generally is from 200 to 275 feet high, having an inclination of a few degrees from the perpendicular, but at places actually leaning over from five to ten degrees. As at the proper season this little dell is a continuous, glaring and gaudy floral plot, all the richly colored wild flowers indigenous to this region being found in it."[21]

A gathering of general railroad passenger agents in their horse-drawn vehicles touring the Garden of the Gods near Colorado Springs, Colorado, September 19, 1890. Photo by William Henry Jackson. (Courtesy Colorado Historical Society)

These ladies taking burro rides in the Garden of the Gods near Colorado Springs paused to have their photograph taken late in the nineteenth century. (Courtesy Colorado Historical Society)

The "Garden of the Gods" offers large rock formations that resemble a stag's head, birds, crawling serpents, and in one case a seal making love to a nun. One visitor around the turn of the century complained, "There is little doubt that the average tourist is so intent on finding these monstrosities, that he misses the grandeur and glory of the place!"[22]

In some instances promoters made certain that tourists would not miss the grandeur of western scenery. Near Colorado Springs a cog railway, completed in 1890, carried paying passengers to the top of Pikes Peak. Once on the barren summit, which nevertheless offered a wonderful view of the plains to the east and the mountains in all other directions, travelers could send telegrams to friends and relatives and, on descending, buy a newspaper listing their names among the day's visitors. Railways were also built to the tops of other mountains in the west including Mount Lowe, near Pasadena, in 1893, and Mount Tamalpais, northwest of San Francisco, in 1896. These mountains, along with other natural and unnatural curiosities, are still touted as places where American and foreign visitors can find pleasure, thanks in part to the efforts of the railroads and their early promoters. Ironically, however, many of the rail lines that helped to create pleasure and pleasure palaces in the West have long since stopped carrying passengers westward, or have simply ceased to exist altogether.

CHAPTER XIII

In the Desert ⚊ Southwest

Follow pleasure, and then will pleasure flee. Flee pleasure, and pleasure will follow thee.

—*Heywood*, Proverbs

WHILE THE AMERICAN explorers and travelers who first criss-crossed the desert Southwest often found pleasure in the diversions enjoyed by the Spanish and Mexicans, they also brought with them their own ideas of pleasure from the East, especially after gold was discovered in California early in 1848. Until then the village of El Paso was nothing more than a sleepy adobe village located on the Rio Grande. Within weeks, however, El Paso became a bustling stopping point for westbound gold seekers heading for California. To men who had crossed hundreds of miles of the vast dry plains of west Texas with few trees and little grass or water, El Paso must have seemed like an oasis. One California-bound traveler, C. C. Cox, wrote in his diary, "The sight of this little place is truly refreshing to the weary traveller of the plains—indeed, the cool shady avenues, fragrant breezes, delicious fruits and luxuriant appearance of everything around, makes one almost feel that he is transported to the bowers of Eden."[1]

More than four hundred wagons had passed through El Paso headed for the California goldfields by August 1849. By then many gold seekers were discouraged from continuing, having heard stories of difficult travel westward across what is now New Mexico and Arizona. Many decided to winter in El Paso and while away their time gambling, drinking, and basking in the sun. While they had no way of knowing it, they were setting the pattern for other Americans who, during the years to follow, would be enticed by the land, the sun and climate, and the feeling that since they were far from their homes, anything goes. On the site of the modern Westin Paso del Norte

Hotel was an adobe building that by 1858 was owned by Ben Dowell. It housed the post office, saloon, general store, and tables for cards, dice, and billiards, and served Mexican mescal. Later, Pass Brandy or Pass Whiskey was added to the menu of drinks. In his book *Out of the Desert*, Owen White wrote that there were twenty gamblers at Dowell's establishment. "Nobody worked, that is, nobody except Mexicans worked regularly. The 'white men' in the community did practically nothing for the very simple reason that there was nothing to do, and the very natural result of this pleasing state of affairs was that Uncle Ben Dowell's saloon sheltered the entire American male population of the town for the greater part of every day and for nearly all of every night."[2]

There was a sameness about the early saloons in El Paso and the desert regions of southwest Texas during the late nineteenth century. This photo shows the interior of Kipling's Saloon and Gambling House at Pecos, Texas. Proprietor Kipling (center) is wearing the white apron and serving drinks. (Courtesy Western History Collections, University of Oklahoma Libraries)

By 1881, when the Southern Pacific railroad arrived, El Paso had become another frontier "sin city." On the corner of just about every street in the business district was a saloon, with at least two or three more saloons between street corners. On Utah Street, now South Mesa, there were broth-

els with the madams and girls, some in palatial mansions, providing pleasures to those seeking them. More respectable forms of pleasure arrived during the 1880s when the Nellie Boyd Dramatic Company arrived to put on
plays. They were followed by variety acts, which came in by rail to perform
in the newly constructed Hill's Hall, and a dance hall called the Coliseum
was soon constructed. In 1883 Samuel Schutz, a German immigrant, built an
opera house, and others constructed the Pictorial, Gem, and National theaters. The National, however, did not last long. Henry W. Myar, a German
immigrant who came to El Paso from Arkansas, where he had made a fortune in cotton, bought the National, tore it down, and in its place erected the
Myar Opera House, which was the pride of El Paso theatergoers into the
twentieth century.[3]

The December 17, 1887, *El Paso Times* described Myar Opera House as
"first-class," and the paper publicly endorsed "the action of the managers of
our new opera house in excluding public prostitutes from the choice parts of
the theatre and limiting their attendance only to the balcony." During the
1890s, as the influence of eastern civilized life increased, El Paso citizens
concerned about their community's image as a sin city organized the Law
and Order League to clean up the town. Although not immediately successful, by the early twentieth century the movement had helped to transform El
Paso from a wide-open frontier town into a respectable city. The dance halls,
saloons, and brothels were closed in 1904, and the pleasure providers moved
across the Mexican border to Juárez, or elsewhere. The quest for illicit pleasure became more difficult.

The sleepy village of San Felipe de Albuquerque, 235 miles up the Rio
Grande in New Mexico Territory, went through similar growing pains after
the New Mexico and Southern Pacific Railroad reached there in the spring
of 1880. The prostitutes who had been following the railroad construction
crews arrived to ply their trade. The saloonkeepers and gamblers followed
and set up their businesses. Peter "Shorty" Parker may have been the town's
first pleasure provider. He claimed squatter's rights on a lot, placed a board
across two upended barrels, and opened a bar. Soon the area was dotted with
tents, false-front stores, and saloons, and a red-light district was established
along the west and south sides of the plaza in Old Town. W. T. Armstrong
established a combination saloon and brothel in a one-story adobe structure
where he employed two soiled doves called "Belle" and "Maud." The two
prostitutes remained in their rooms at the back of the saloon waiting for customers sent to them by Armstrong or his bartenders. There were also dance
halls, including the infamous Mariano Martin's Old Mexican Dance Hall,

This 1881 photo shows the interior of the ornate Senate Saloon in El Paso, Texas. (Courtesy Western History Collections, University of Oklahoma Libraries)

Madam Kate Fulton's Old Town Dance Hall, Sim Ovelin's Old Town Music Hall, and Pascual's Dance Hall. In each the house rules were, "No drinks, no dancing." First men purchased overpriced drinks for themselves and "champagne" for their partners. Once these things were done, the couples could dance to the music of a band, usually out of tune. If a customer found an appealing partner, he would make the necessary business arrangements and retire with her to a nearby room.

The various establishments offering the services of soiled doves had many nicknames, including palaces of sinful pleasure, parlor houses, gilded palaces of shame, wine rooms, mansions, cottages, and even female boardinghouses, appellations that had been used elsewhere in the West. The prostitutes were sometimes called demimondaines, ladies of the half-world, *nymphes du pavé* (street nymphs), fallen women, or inmates. Few girls used their real names, choosing instead names ending with *ie*—Mamie, Fannie, Jennie, Nettie, Mollie, Annie, Minnie, Cassie, Sadie, Janie, Marie, and Vallie.

A newspaperman from Vermont, passing through Albuquerque in 1881, was not impressed with what he saw: "The saloons, with three to ten gambling tables each, are in the lead, and the ring of bottles, the rattle of high ball, the clink of billiards and the shake of the dice, accompanied by the roundest profanity, fill the air."[4]

If the Vermont newspaperman had remained in Albuquerque, he prob-ably would have been shocked by what the *Albuquerque Morning Journal* described as a "Bold, Bad Ball." In July 1882, a madam rented a newly con-structed opera house and held a grand ball featuring the town's soiled doves. When the doors opened, there were perhaps five men for each woman. The men were "of all classes, married and single, young and old. Some stand high up on the social scale, while others are known to be thieves and black legs. The women were, in many cases, handsomely dressed, and had it not been for the blasé look which had possession of their faces, they would eas-ily pass in a ballroom which claimed more pretensions as to the characters of the people in attendance," reported the paper. The early part of the evening was quiet, but as the "young ladies" drank more and more wine and beer, the ball became wilder and wilder. When the liquid refreshments "failed to stim-ulate, drowsiness took possession of the abandoned dissipaters and they one by one turned toward the places they call home. . . . The blow out was just what it was intended to be, and for that reason it was a success. Money flowed over the bar one way, while whiskey and wine went over in the other, and while the stomachs of the rioters were being gradually filled with spir-its, their pockets were becoming empty and those of the venturesome madam correspondingly full."[5]

A second red-light district began to develop by 1882, on Copper Avenue between Third and Fourth Streets in New Albuquerque, a new town site laid out about two miles east of Old Town after the railroad arrived. Madams from Old Town began buying the most lavish dwellings available in New Town for their businesses. On March 12, 1882, the *Morning Journal* reported: "Two of the demimonde have purchased the fine new residence on the north end of Fourth Street, paying $3,000 in cash for it. They will no doubt trans-form it into a gilded palace of shame." The new red-light district became known as Hell's Half Acre, but to the uninformed the mansions were simply handsome dwellings with such tranquil and dignified names as the Gem, Rose Cottage, Vine Cottage, or with easily remembered numbers like 555, 444, 222, and 101.

In 1883 a lady traveling through New Albuquerque with some visiting journalists was given a tour of the town by a local editor, on the new horse-drawn streetcar system. As the party passed some of the attractive resi-dences in Hell's Half Acre, she asked about them. The May 19, 1883, *Albuquerque Daily Democrat* reported:

"Yes, we have many fine and substantial brick buildings of which we are justly proud." By this time the car was passing the elegant frame structures west of the Armijo house [hotel]. "And we have some imposing frame structures," continued the editor. "You may have noticed that we do not number houses here in the regular manner in which they do in eastern cities."

"I see," said the lady looking at the large golden numbers on some houses immediately in front of them.

"There," continued the lecturer on the Descent of Woman, "is 444, and then 222, and to be more irregular, there is 101, and so on. There is another thing very peculiar with our people here. In regard for their daughters they place their names in large golden letters over the door. There is, for instance, Maud and Lillie and Nellie and Maggie conspicuous on the transoms."

The visiting male journalists also taking the tour could hardly refrain from laughing. The incident had provided them with some unexpected pleasure. Fortunately for the lady visitor, the girls in the houses were not in evidence. Competition between the soiled doves was so intense that they frequently exhibited themselves to the public by riding around Albuquerque in surreys or appearing suddenly in the doorways or windows of their business establishments wearing few clothes.

By 1885, the year New Albuquerque was incorporated as a city, the red-light district in Old Town had disappeared, the brothels having moved to New Town. There Hell's Half Acre soon became too conspicuous and controversial, as civic groups planned parks, schools, and a library to make New Albuquerque more respectable in order to attract new residents and investors. A city ordinance closed Hell's Half Acre in 1914. Many of the girls left the now incorporated City of Albuquerque for the unincorporated Old Town more than a mile to the west, which had no laws against prostitution. There, in an area south of the plaza where the first brothels had appeared thirty years earlier, the girls continued to ply their trade for many years.[6]

Another town that went through many of the same gyrations as Albuquerque was Tucson, Arizona, first known by its Indian name of *Stukshon* when it was nothing more than a sleepy village in northern Mexico built around an ancient fortress. With the Gadsden Purchase, in 1853, Tucson became part of the United States. By 1855, when the overland stage began serving Tucson, Americans, including traders, land speculators, gamblers, criminals, and men with political ambitions, began to arrive. As their kind had done in El Paso and Albuquerque, they brought their particular forms of diversion and pleasure, mainly drinking, gambling, and women. Tucson soon gained a reputation as a den of iniquity. Outside their homes, saloons were about the only places townspeople could find diversion until 1870, when Carrillo Gardens, located on eight acres off South Main, opened, providing water, shade, company, and amusements. Other diversions suitable for the more upstanding citizens followed later that year, when a jolly, heavyset German, Alexander Levin, who had started a brewery in 1869, took over the Hodges Hotel on Main Street and at the same time began turning the land around his brewery into a three-acre park that provided residents with many pleasures, welcome breaks in the monotony of frontier life. In 1878 he erected Levin's Opera House, a large building available for all sorts of entertainments. The next year he built a bowling alley and shooting gallery.[7]

By then the leisurely pace of life was changing. John G. Bourke later remembered with pleasure when "nothing was done energetically" except riding and dancing, and "nothing disturbed the monotonous routine of daily life but an occasional *carreta* (horse race) or a *pelea de gallos* (cock fight)." Bourke blamed the Americans for "whipping up the pace." Even though Tucson was changed by the Americans, dancing remained a popular pastime. Bourke remembered his first Mexican ball in Tucson, and he described how the women sat on wooden benches extending around the room. The benches had no backs. To save their dresses from rubbing against the lime on the walls, the women had to "sit bolt upright," Bourke recalled. "If a gentleman wished to dance with a lady, he asked her, and she accepted or declined at her option. After each dance it was de rigueur to invite your partner to partake of 'dulces,' or refreshments, and in all cases those invitations were accepted, not that the young lady always ate what was purchased for her; frequently she would take the 'pasas' [raisins], 'bollos' [sweet cakes] or other refection, wrap them up in her handkerchief and keep them to take home. Those who wished it could have 'mescal' or 'wine.' In Arizona this 'wine' is mostly 'imported' and [it is] a viler decoction [consisting] of boiled vinegar, logwood, alum, and copper. . . .

"The ladies had a curious method of expressing their preference for a gentleman; this was done by breaking a 'cascarron,' or eggshell filled with cologne water or finely cut gold paper. The recipient of this delicate compliment had to return it in kind and then to lead the young lady to dance. The energetic musicians extorted something like music from their wheezy mouthorgans and tinkling harps. This is my recollection of a Tucson 'baile,' barren and meagre enough it looks to me now, but there was a time when my companions and myself thought nothing of staying at one of them all night and of going to six in a week if we could."[8]

There were, of course, the less refined forms of pleasure that continued to grow and prosper close by the saloon district located near the corner of Meyer Street and Congress, south of the old presidio, and also in a three-block area just north of Congress on Maiden Lane, a street originally called *Calle de la India Trista* (street of the sad Indian girl). According to legend, the street was named for an Indian maiden who once lived with a Mexican officer in the presidio. After he died, she was cast out by both her people and his. On the north side of Maiden Lane was the red-light district. Until 1880, most of the girls who worked there were of Mexican descent. One pioneer's diary tells of women named Big Refugia, Windy, and Cruz among the prostitutes; they charged anywhere from one to two dollars for their services. The pioneer, George O. Hand, saloonkeeper and former soldier, recorded the names of citizens who got drunk, and made reference to attending bull-fights, playing lotteries, and hearing preachers' sermons. On March 7, 1875, his birthday, Hand wrote in his diary:

> (Sunday). Very dull. Stores are all closed. My 45th birthday. Took a hot bath. Pat O'Meara got drunk, fell down, and someone stepped on his nose. Puppet show in the evening. Overstreet hit a Mexican and the Mexican hit Harrison with a stone, cutting his head. Took a walk after closing and got home at three in the morning (Cruz) [meaning he had visited a prostitute named Cruz].[9]

Many residents of Tucson discovered another diversion in the spring of 1876, when John P. Clum, a government agent among the Apaches, arrived in Tucson with an escort of fifty-four Apache policemen armed with government rifles. Clum and his Apaches were en route to the Chiricahua Reservation but were waiting in Tucson for the arrival of the U.S. Sixth Cavalry. Clum later wrote:

"A committee of Tucson's leading business men came to me with a request for an Apache war dance. I consulted my Indians, and found them not only willing, but enthusiastic. A load of firewood was hauled to the center of the old military plaza. As soon as it was dark, the campfire was kindled. Under a full moon, spectators filed into the plaza by the hundreds, until we had an audience of three thousand. Appeared the actors, thirty-five red-skins stripped to their waists, bodies and faces hideous with smears of war-paint; fantastic headgear; bearing lances and shields, bows and arrows, or rifles, according to the act assigned. Redskin chanters; musicians with tom-toms. First came the 'instigation scene,' in which one lithe dancer performed gracefully with lance and shield. Gradually the number of participants increased, until the campfire was circled by a score of wildly gesticulating Apaches, of ferocious aspect. The night air was vibrant with blood-curdling war-whoops. The committee had expressed its desire for a realistic spectacle, and when I observed the audience gradually retreating from the lunging, howling Apaches, I suspected that the presentation was becoming a bit too realistic. Chief Justice French edged his way to my side.

" 'Clum,' he urged, 'hadn't you better stop this before the Indians get beyond your control?'

"Adopting somewhat the style of John Paul Jones, I replied: 'Judge, we have just begun to dance.'

"Now we approached the climax, for which our audience was wholly unprepared. None of the citizens knew that I had supplied *blank* cartridges for each rifle in the custody of this apparently frantic bunch of savages. Suddenly came the sharp crack of a rifle, keen, clear, above the din of the dance. This was the signal for a chorus of super-yells; then the fusillade—nerve-racking explosions from twenty additional rifles, fired in volleys, in rapid succession. Meanwhile, the vocal efforts and athletic contortions of our redskin entertainers approached the peak of noise and confusion. To the spectators it looked as if these unleashed Apaches were running amuck. Fortunately, the old military plaza afforded ample exits for our audience, and the audience literally took to its heels. Soon we had the entire plaza to ourselves. For ten or fifteen minutes we performed, alone in our glory. But as we had arranged a full programme of events, we decided to go through with it. The show ended with a final salvo from the rifles.

"Then my redskin actors transformed themselves immediately into well-trained, decorous Apache scouts. The company formed at 'attention.' I thanked them on behalf of the departed audience, and dismissed them. Of course we all had a good laugh over the timidity of the citizens. By this time, the citizens, who had been watching the finale from behind adobe walls and deep shadows in the distance, concluded we were safe and sane, returned by groups to the plaza, and congratulated us on our very vivid and realistic portrayal."[10]

By 1877 Tucson had two breweries, two hotels, and ten saloons in which gambling went on at a furious pace, day and night. The buildings between the saloons housed most of the *nymphes du pavé*, who kept the same hours the saloonkeepers did. When the railroad arrived at Tucson in 1880, the population grew and the town experienced rapid growth. The number of saloons increased, as did the amount of gambling and the number of prostitutes. Maiden Lane flourished until the late 1890s, when the prostitutes moved from the center of town to a narrow street, between Convent and Meyer Streets, officially named Sabino Alley but called Gay Alley by the customers. Saloons and gambling continued unregulated until after 1900. Some saloonkeepers, to make their establishments appear popular, paid men to sit at the tables "to create an atmosphere of interest and sociability in the gambling room." As a group they were called "boosters," but they described themselves as the "Sons of Rest" because all of them opposed work. One Tucson resident later called them "a worthless lot . . . lazy and willing to accept things as they came."[11]

While El Paso, Albuquerque, and Tucson had reputations as illicit pleasure capitals, so did one individual named Manuel Blasos, known as Old Blazes. He toured mining camps with his own "hell on wheels," a wagon with three windows on each side, decorated like a circus bandwagon, and drawn by six plumed horses. Inside the wagon he carried whiskey, sometimes called "bug juice," and gambling equipment for roulette, faro, and dice games. Old Blazes went wherever the pickings seemed good.[12]

If there was one town in the desert Southwest that gained the reputation of being wilder than any other, it was Tombstone, Arizona, which supposedly got its name from miner Ed Schieffelin. Schieffelin, according to leg-

This is the gambling room in the Orient Saloon, Bisbee, Arizona, late in the nineteenth century. (Courtesy Western History Collections, University of Oklahoma)

end, was warned that if he kept prospecting in Apache country, the Indians would lift his scalp and all he would find would be his tombstone. After Schieffelin struck it rich, the town, laid out about a mile from the site of his mining camp, became known as Tombstone.[13]

Within weeks the new town had about forty houses, cabins, and tents and about a hundred permanent residents, plus perhaps a thousand miners camped outside town. Then came the pleasure providers. Gamblers, saloon-keepers, and others from the waning goldfields of California, many of whom had been kicked out of other places by vigilante committees, soon arrived in Tombstone to open saloons and gambling halls. Just a few months later, two out of every three buildings in the business district were saloons and gambling dens. An immense red-light district soon developed, along with churches and the town's first cemetery. Like countless other frontier towns on the far side of the Mississippi, the name Tombstone became synonymous with every form of illicit pleasure found in the West.

A major Tombstone attraction was the Bird Cage Theater, an oblong adobe structure built in 1881 and named for the birdcagelike boxes in its small auditorium. It was a combination variety house, saloon, gambling hall, and brothel, and dispensed pleasure in many forms for the unattached miners. Another well-known establishment was the Oriental Bar, although it was not as impressive as the Crystal Palace Saloon directly across the street. The Crystal Palace was perhaps the grandest saloon and gambling hall in Tombstone. It was located in a gray frame building with overhanging eaves, and night and day the tables inside offered faro, roulette, and poker. Each night after midnight the ladies arrived by carriages to drink with men, gamble, and offer their bodies to the lusty. The more respectable residents of Tombstone generally avoided these pleasure palaces, preferring to attend performances in Schieffelin Hall. Built in 1881 by Al Schieffelin, brother of Ed, it was the site of many performances by touring dramatic actors. At one point John L. Sullivan and a group of boxers performed in this hall.[14]

THE PLEASURE PALACES OF Tombstone existed and survived because of the hardships encountered by the miners and prospectors, many of whom can only be described as eccentric. They brought with them to the desert Southwest their own morals, customs, and superstitions, and they sought pleasure in the midst of their hard work. Some believed that the mines were inhabited by little people, called *Kobolds* by miners from Germany. Mexicans

This photograph shows the interior of the well-known Crystal Palace Saloon, constructed in 1881 at Tombstone, Arizona. (Courtesy Western History Collections, University of Oklahoma Libraries)

described them as *duendes,* and those of British origin called them "tommy-knockers." These mysterious little people "were inclined to mischief rather than malice" and "often carried off small tools and played pranks, and long ago it was the custom to keep them in a good humor with offerings of food." One early miner in Arizona wrote:

> *I'm a hardrock miner an' I ain't afeard of ghosts.*
> *But my neck hair bristles like a porcupine's quills*
> *An' I knock my knuckles on the drift-set posts*
> *When the tommyknockers hammer on the caps an' sills*
> *An' raise hallelujah with my pick an' drills.*[15]

Belief in the little people may, in part, be blamed on pack rats, which are indefatigable collectors. They would slip into a mining camp or mine and make off with anything they could carry, including combs, socks, can openers, scissors, and even dynamite. In their place the pack rats would leave a rock, stick, pinecone, or piece of cactus, apparently as fair exchange. Pack rats would sometimes hide objects they did not take. There are stories of pack rats placing thumbtacks in shoes and boots, and socks in coat pockets. While miners did not always look kindly on rats above ground, the rodent was not only tolerated but apparently provided some pleasure in the mines. Miners tossed them scraps of food from dinner buckets, and the rats became accurate timekeepers, appearing at mealtime, even before the miners would sit down and open their buckets. Miners who worked for a long time in the same mine got to know the rats as individuals and gave them names. The superstitious miners thought it bad luck to kill a mine rat, and a miner who did was viewed with the same scorn as a man who, aboveground, mistreated a dog. Miners said rats would give warnings of impending cave-ins and bad gas because the rodents noticed the slightest movement of the surrounding rock and scampered to places of safety.[16]

IN EL PASO, ALBUQUERQUE, Tucson, and other towns in the desert Southwest the period of illicit pleasure did not last and gave way to respectable forms of entertainment, especially after the towns grew into cities of families who wanted only the best for their children. Most every family had some musical instrument, including foot-pump organs, usually located in their sitting rooms. The lucky family that had one would often gather around the organ for music and song. In one instance an Arizona pioneer acquired a large bass drum brought west from Illinois. It was used in one northern Arizona community as a rallying symbol, around which local musicians gathered to form a town band. When someone returned home from a visit to a distant town, new songs and tunes would be brought back home, the words having been written down and the melody memorized. Children's dances were given on the afternoons of the Fourth of July and Christmas. Dances for grown-ups were held frequently on Saturday evenings. During the cooler months there were baseball games and horse races.[17]

The early issues of newspapers describe many activities enjoyed by residents. Most editors wrote about life in their communities not only to inform but to entertain their readers. While most editors were opinionated, they did seek to report factual news. And sometimes they published stories that seemed unbelievable, as in the case of one datelined Galisteo Junction, New Mexico Territory, which appeared in the *Santa Fe Daily New Mexican* on March 28, 1880. Headlined "Galisteo's Apparition, A Mysterious Aerial Phantom Appears at the Junction," it reads:

The telegraph operator there, and two or three friends, were taking a short walk before bedtime, when they were startled to hear voices evidently coming from above them. At first they thought it to be a trick of the atmosphere bringing the sounds from a nearby mountain, but on looking above them they were astonished to see a large fish-shaped balloon coming from the west.

The construction of the balloon was entirely different from anything of the kind ever seen by any of the party, being in the shape of a fish, and at one time was so low that fanciful lettering on the outside of the car, which appeared to be very elegant, was plainly seen. The air machine appeared to be entirely under the control of the occupants and was guided by a large fanlike apparatus.

The party seemed to be enjoying themselves, as laughter and occasionally strains of music were heard. A few articles were dropped from the car as the balloon passed over the Junction, but owing to the imperfect light the only thing which was found was a magnificent flower, with a slip of exceedingly fine silk-like paper, on which were some characters resembling those on Japanese tea chests. One article which from its weight when thrown from the car, seemed to be a cup or some other piece of earthenware could not be found tonight, but diligent search will be made for it in the morning. The balloon was monstrous in size, and the car, as near as could be judged, contained eight or ten persons. Another peculiar feature of the air machine was that the occupants could evidently sail at any height they chose, as soon after passing the Junction, it assumed a great height and moved off very rapidly toward the east.

The next day the newspaper reported a cup "of very peculiar workmanship, entirely different to anything used in this country" had been found where it had been dropped from the air machine. Only one other newspaper story was apparently published about the incident, and it reported that a traveler purchased the flower and cup for a vast sum of money, and that the traveler believed the air machine "must have come from Asia" and possibly from Jidda.[18]

Sometimes, when there was little happening in their towns, editors would give their readers something to talk about by using their columns to attack editors in other communities. This was one way to keep their readers reading and to provide them with some pleasure. William J. Berry, editor of the *Arizona Sentinel* at Yuma, frequently used his paper in this fashion. On one occasion he wrote the following about John Marion, editor of the *Arizona Miner* at Prescott:

We were never more puzzled in our life than we are now to account for the conduct of that cuss of the *Arizona Miner*. We have been badly, yes, most shamefully treated by him. "To prove this, let facts be submitted to a candid world."

On the completion of the line of Telegraph, connecting Yuma with Prescott, we, by the kind permission of Col. Rockwell, A.Q.M., and Commodore Haines, Superintendent, sent a congratulatory dispatch to the editor of the *Miner* announcing the joyful event. Everybody knows that this is a military telegraph, but as above stated we were permitted to send that, the first citizen telegram that ever passed over the wires. We esteemed this a high privilege, and expected and had a right to expect that it would be gladly received and courteously responded to. Was this done? No, no response ever came.

We waited several days and Commodore Haines repeatedly telegraphed to John H. Marion, and said cuss who presides over the *Miner* asking him to send response to our greeting. On the day of our going to press, last week, we particularly desired some recognition of our aforesaid telegram, that we might publish it, and Commodore Haines again telegraphed to the editor of the *Miner* asking him to send response immediately. But none came! nor has any come yet.

Now we ask all our editorial brothers and all right thinking men, "What do you think of such conduct as this?" Can anything be more uncivil or discourteous? We cannot account for it, particularly as the relations between the editor of the *Miner* and ourself have always been of the most cordial and friendly character. We fear that our worst apprehensions are realized, and that Marion's glory has departed. It may be that he is sick. If so, we take this all back. If not we mean it all, and more too. We had our fears. Take a rusty old bachelor editor and raise him to the summit of connubial felicity, and in nine cases out of ten it is more than he can stand. His brain reels, reason totters and he is a goner.

Alas, poor Marion! we ne'er shall look upon his like again! We write this more in sorrow than in anger. Adios amigo. "Sic transit gloria mundi."[19]

Not quite two years later, after a United States senator from California named Hager described the Arizona Territory as "nearly worthless country," Berry questioned what the senator knew about Arizona and answered his own question: "Nothing. He is totally ignorant of the Territory and its resources, and to make such a barefaced gratuitous lying assertion is disgraceful to the country and to his constituency."[20]

About four months later editor Berry decided to take a wife and inserted the following advertisement in his newspaper:

WANTED

A nice, plump, healthy, good-natured, good-looking, domestic and affectionate lady to correspond with, Object—Matrimony.

She must be between 22 and 35 years of age.

She must be a believer in God and immortality, but no sectarian.

She must not be a gad-about or given to scandal, but must be one who will be a help-mate and companion, and who will endeavor to make home happy.

Such a lady can find a correspondent by addressing the editor of this paper, Post Office box 9, Yuma, A.T.

Photographs exchanged!

If anybody don't like our way of going about this interesting business, we don't care. It's none of their funeral.[21]

WHILE AMERICAN FOODS could be found in the larger communities of New Mexico and Arizona, which were served by railroads, many new residents had to develop a taste for local culinary offerings, which were not Spanish but Indian-Mexican. Spaniards did not have *tamales, enchiladas, panocha, tacos,* or hot chili dishes. These were indigenous to the desert Southwest. Early U.S. settlers "found the Mexican pintobeans—*frijoles,* usually seasoned with hot peppers—and the ever-present *chili con carne.* When well-prepared, the accurately named *chili con carne (Chili* = chili; *chili con carne* = chili with meat; *chili con carne con frijoles* = chili with meat and beans) was a delicacy in its own right. . . . The best New Mexican *chili con carne* was made from a quantity of lean pork cut into one-inch squares and boiled until tender in covering water containing sage, crushed garlic, and salt. When tender, the meat was removed from the liquid stock and fried in pure lard with the addition of *chili* powder, gauged to taste by experience, and two or three tablespoons of browned flour. The meat and mixture in the frying pan were then returned to the original stock and allowed to boil down to the consistency of a medium-thick soup, which was served by itself or with rice and beans on the side. *Chili con carne* of this kind formed the center for the popular *tamale,* made in New Mexico simply by rolling a small quantity—two or three ounces—of cornmeal dough around the chili con carne, then encasing the whole in corn husks and steaming until cooked.

"The Americans also found *tortillas,* the staff of life among the Mexicans of the Southwest. Made of hand-ground blue cornmeal into round, thin, pancakelike bread, *tortillas* served at mealtime as pushers to scoop up the *frijoles,* which were then eaten, *tortilla* and all. They formed the base also for the hot *tacos, enchiladas,* and other dishes. . . . *Tacos* were made of fine *tortillas* half folded, filled with meat, and fried in deep fat. Withdrawn from the fat, the *taco* was then stuffed from the sides with chopped onions, green *chili*-pepper sauce, shredded lettuce, and grated cheese. *Enchiladas* consisted simply of *tortillas* dipped in *chili* sauce and piled one on top of another, like pancakes, with chopped onions and grated cheese sprinkled between the layers, the whole crowned with a fried egg. Both dishes were hot enough to start rivulets of perspiration down the gourmet's, and certainly the gourmand's, neck."[22]

When a new hotel, the Juniper House, opened in Prescott, Arizona, on July 4, 1864, the bill of fare displayed a reliance on local dishes:

> *Breakfast*
> *Fried Venison and Chili*
> *Bread and Coffee with Milk.*
>
> *Dinner*
> *Roast Venison with Chili*
> *Chili Baked Beans*
> *Chili on Tortillas*
> *Tea and Coffee*
> *with Milk.*

All the cooking was done under a juniper tree from which the hotel got its name.[23]

In the desert regions, like elsewhere in the West, the names of things like hotels, saloons, mountains, valleys, creeks, and streams, among many others, suggested that those doing the naming found pleasure in it. In Greenlee County, Arizona, John H. Toles Cosper, a rancher, killed between sixty and seventy rattlesnakes in a sloping valley under the Mogollon Rim. He gave it the name Rattlesnake Basin. In Yavapai County, Abraham Harlow Peeples, an early traveler, killed three antelope and then named a nearby mountain Antelope Peak. Others called a nearby valley Antelope Valley. In Coconino County, Jacob Hamblin, an early Mormon pioneer, killed a badger along one stream, which he named Badger Creek, and proceeded to a second, where he cleaned the animal and put it to boil. When he awoke the next morning expecting to find stew in his kettle, he found that the alkali in the water and the fat from the badger had combined to create soap. So he named the stream Soap Creek. In Apache County another creek, designated Freezeout, was not named for the weather. The name came from the game of freezeout poker, which cowboys once played there, and a nearby eight-thousand-foot peak was called Poker Mountain. East of Roswell, New Mexico, are the Bottomless Lakes, so named by cowboys who measured the depth of the water by tying several lariats together as a plumb line. They found no bottom and concluded that the lakes were bottomless. Hermit's Peak near Las Vegas is named for Juan Maria Agostini, who lived on the granite rise during the 1860s. Sitting Bull Falls, southwest of Carlsbad, New Mexico, is named after the Indian chief, who supposedly was in the area about 1881. In Mohave County, Arizona, Screwbean Spring was named for a lone screwbean tree found there. In Pinal County, Bulldog Mine was named for a nearby rock formation, which resembled an enormous bulldog. Show Low in northeastern Arizona was named for a game of cards played by two early settlers, C. E. Cooley and Marion Clark, who gambled for the ranch on which the town was later built. The game was seven-up, and the winner was to take the ranch. With the score five to six in Clark's favor, the last hand was dealt. Cooley played high. Clark challenged him: "Show low and take the ranch." Cooley did. Mormons later bought the ranch and established the town of Show Low.[24]

Certainly many outlaws in the Old West robbed to get easy money to buy pleasure. William Graham, known as Curly Bill Brocius, was such an outlaw. One day he and his gang rode into Bowie, Arizona, for a little fun just as the westbound passenger train arrived. The outlaws watched as the engineer used his oilcan. Curly Bill asked the engineer, "Do you want to sell this thing?" The engineer, thinking the men were cowpunchers having a little joke, did not answer. Again Curly Bill asked the question, this time shoving his six-shooter into the engineer's stomach. "I asked ya a civil question an' that's the kind of answer I want." The engineer quickly raised his hands into the air and replied, "I can't sell it, I can't, honest." Curly Bill replied, "In that case, we'll borrow the thing for a spell." Curly Bill and his men cut the locomotive off from the rest of the train, piled into the cab, and roared down the track. As the engineer rushed to the station to report the theft, the locomotive came back to the station, only to disappear again down the track before the eyes of the astounded train crew. For half an hour, while the train crew watched, Curly Bill and his gang raced the engine up and down, blowing the whistle. They then backed the locomotive into the station, climbed down, walked leisurely to their horses, mounted, and rode at a walk out of town. They had had their fun.[25]

CHAPTER XIV

In the Pacific ⌐⌐ Northwest

But pleasures are like poppies spread,
You seize the flower, its bloom is shed;
Or like the snow falls in the river
A moment white, then melts forever.

—*Robert Burns*

OR THE EARLY SETTLERS who made their homes in Oregon, there were only simple pleasures, and they were found in social activities. Although dull when compared to many pleasures of today, they were eminently satisfactory for the pioneers of the 1840s, who had followed the Oregon Trail from Missouri to the promised land and learned to do without. For most settlers the greatest pleasure lay in finally reaching the gently rolling hills, smooth, rich-soiled valleys, and densely wooded forests of the immense area called Oregon, which then included the modern states of Washington and Oregon as well as parts of Idaho and western Montana.

The destination of most early immigrants was Oregon City, a settlement of about a hundred buildings located alongside a waterfall on the east bank of the Willamette River. Here they found about six hundred inhabitants, some of whom could guide them, offer practical help and advice, and acquaint them with conditions. The immigrants also found two churches, four general stores, two gristmills, some sawmills, two taverns, a hatter, a tannery, cabinetmakers, silversmiths, tailor shops, two blacksmiths, one doctor, three lawyers, and even a printing office that published a newspaper, the *Oregon Spectator,* twice a month.

While a few immigrants settled in and around Oregon City, most of those with families chose to farm because they could take any of the unsettled land between the 49th parallel to the north and the 42nd parallel to the south, and from the Pacific Ocean on the west to the Rocky Mountains on the east. It was a vast region, but most men with families chose the Willamette Valley, which was in stark contrast to the barren prairies and plains and rugged Rocky Mountains they had traversed getting there. The settlers built their homes, tilled the soil, and got by the best they could, infatuated by the land that seemed so full of promise.

Others, especially unattached men, were attracted by the densely wooded forests where they found jobs as lumberjacks. In the 1820s the Scottish scientist David Douglas, a botanist sent to America by the Royal Horticultural Society, arrived by ship in the Puget Sound area. Douglas soon identified what became known in his honor as the Douglas fir, a lumberman's dream. Mature Douglas firs have thick trunks, grow up to heights of a hundred feet and more, and contain straight-grained, tough wood ideal for use in heavy-duty construction. Douglas also discovered sugar pines, with light but durable wood excellent for doors, window sashes, and shingles, and western white pines, sometimes called Idaho pines, used in making fruit and vegetable crates, and the ponderosas, or western pines, which often grow more than 150 feet in height. Settlers could build their houses from ponderosa, which provided strong, fine-grained wood.

Long before immigrants arrived from the East during the 1840s in search of farms, the business of lumbering provided jobs for newcomers, especially single men, who wandered from one logging camp to another in search of work. They would cut and move on, and, like unattached men elsewhere in the West, they sought pleasure wherever they could. Unfortunately there was little diversion in the logging camps aside from playing cards, hunting, and fishing. Whiskey and women were not permitted in most camps, although the former was smuggled in to lumberjacks willing to pay the price. In one instance, also, some prostitutes claiming to be magazine saleswomen arrived in a logging setup north of Washington Territory's Olympic Peninsula and established themselves in a cabin down the road from the camp. On the surface they appeared respectable, but when lumberjacks visited the cabin to buy subscriptions to eastern magazines, they not only received the magazines, but for a little more money they also enjoyed the company of the women.

While most of the new arrivals in the region chose either logging or farming, one early pioneer, Charles E. Pickett, decided that physical labor in the new land was not for him. A cultivated and educated Virginian who arrived in 1843, Pickett became involved in the political entanglements of the early settlements. He felt that as an intellectual, he could contribute more by

This cabin on Martin Creek in Washington's Cascade Mountains housed a theater and cafe offering lumberjacks home cooking. A steak cost 35 cents. (Courtesy Washington State Historical Society)

using his mind than his muscles. Incensed that missionaries had made excessive land claims, he decided to have a little fun and staked a claim on their land by way of a challenge. Only then did he use his muscles to clear much of his 640-acre claim, building a log cabin and planting a vegetable garden. Some missionaries brought suit against him, but he remained and lived on his claim alone until he won title to the land. Having won, he had had his fun. He gave up the claim and in 1845 started a biweekly newspaper, which he called the *Flumgudgeon Gazette and Bumble Bee Budget,* subtitled "A Newspaper of the Salmagundi Order, Devoted to Scratching and Stinging the Follies of the Times." Pickett listed the editor as "The Curtail Coon." What made this first newspaper in the Pacific Northwest different was that, since no press was available, Pickett wrote it out in longhand. Twelve issues have survived, each throwing jabs at any evil Pickett wished to attack. However, Pickett soon tired of Oregon and left, eventually ending up in San Francisco where he edited a newspaper that was printed on a press.[1]

The first actual printed newspaper in Oregon was the *Oregon Spectator* at Oregon City, published on February 5, 1846, by John Fleming, who had migrated westward from Ohio. This was about two years before Oregon Territory was formed in 1848. The first newspaper in what would become

Holidays, especially Christmas, were times of celebration. Artist Paul Frenzeny produced this sketch for Leslie's *magazine, under the title "Christmas in the Oregon Mountains—The Backwoodsman's Christmas Frolic."*

Washington Territory was the *Columbian*; it was pulled from the forms of a seventy-year-old Ramage press (a small hand-press named for its inventor, Adam Ramage) at Olympia on September 11, 1852, and "published every Saturday at $5 a year." The *Columbian* successfully campaigned for the formation of Washington Territory, which occurred in 1853, and then promoted Olympia as the territorial capital. These newspapers and others that followed were very welcome, because reading matter was scarce. Few books had been brought by the settlers from the East, and the cost of ordering books and magazines was prohibitive. Most had brought their family Bibles, which were read over and over again until the pages wore thin.

The old saying "Necessity is the mother of invention" could easily have been coined in nineteenth-century Oregon. For the settlers, privation was the stepmother of substitutes, and finding good substitutes brought satisfaction. People who had worn out their last pair of boots used leather and their ingenuity to make new foot coverings. Since foundries and ironworks were unknown, the settlers found substitutes for hinges, nails, stoves, and other iron implements they needed. When it came to coffee, however, men and women long accustomed to the drink were hard pressed to find an acceptable substitute. Some pioneers roasted barley as an alternative, while others used dried, roasted peas or oats. Yet another innovator fixed bran in such a manner that when cooked it tasted very much like coffee. The recipe: "1 gallon of bran, 2 tablespoons molasses, scalded and parched in the oven until it is somewhat brown and charred. Bran treated this way and cooked the same as coffee provided a very tasty drink." Otto Mauermann, who grew up in what became Lewis County, Washington, recalled:

> My mother made coffee from dried peas, which she roasted. The night after father came home with the stove, when we sat down to supper and tasted our coffee, our eyes must have stuck out in amazement. We asked, "Mother, what makes the coffee taste so funny?" We were told that father had brought home some "Indian salt". It was sugar, the first we boys had ever tasted. We expressed the wish that the Indians would bring some more of it.[2]

Once trading posts were established, coffee and other goods were available for those who had money or something to barter. A post established in 1858 by Marcel Chappellier on a road linking Cowlitz Landing to Olympia was typical. The drug department shelves held "items like camphor, soothing syrup, toothache drops and 'pain killer,' epsom salts, blister plaster, matches, toothbrushes, and a number of the patent-medicine remedies so popular in those days. In the general department the customer could secure hoops, needles, buttons, gloves, farm tools, butcher knives, candle molds, mirrors, seeds for planting, and so forth. Not to be overlooked was liquor. Magazines and newspapers were also carried. A good deal of the business was conducted by barter or on credit, as currency was scarce. The Indians were credited for hauling freight, for skins, for fish, and for wages, in return for which they would be given whatever goods they needed. White settlers traded oats, eggs, butter, bacon, hay, and whatever else was of general use."[3]

Rosa Ellen Flynn, in recalling her early life in what is now Clark County, Washington, remembered:

> We always had plenty of food. We killed four or five hogs a year, smoked the hams, made barrells of sauer kraut. We had two cows and some chickens. Our work wasn't as hard then as now. We raised wonderful vegetables in those days, and were not bothered by worms in our gardens. We bought only flour and sugar. We planted a big orchard on our farm, including apples, pears, cherries, gooseberries and strawberries.[4]

Another pioneer, Charrie Mears, remembered: "What delicious doughnuts we used to make, dropping them into boiling bear grease, our only shortening."[5]

Settlers used almost any occasion as an excuse for a dance. Once the time and place were set, word was passed, and on the appointed day settlers from miles around—not only young people but whole families—headed for the farm where the dance was to be held. When going to a dance, a young man would usually call for his date on horseback, often bringing another horse with a sidesaddle for her. When they reached the site of the dance, it was a thrill for most girls to slide off the horse into the arms of the young man. George Lamb, who settled in what is now Clallam County, Washington, provided a more vivid description of the "hardships" endured by settlers going to dances. He wrote:

> Gallant husbands and beaus carried the shoes and "party gowns" of their wives and sweethearts, while these ladies accompanied them on foot or horseback, dressed in old kitchen clothes, or even the men's overalls and boots. Many a toilette has been made by these pioneer ladies by the light of smoky lanterns in a barn or other out building on the farm where the dance was to be held in order that milady might appear fresh and clean and lovely when she entered the "ballroom."

Not infrequently the strong men of those days were compelled to ford creeks and swampy places carrying their ladies in their arms.[6]

When a family arrived at a dance, the babies were bedded down in the wagons and the older children watched from the benches around the largest room in the cabin until they, too, were sent off to bed in the wagons while the adults went on dancing to the music of a fiddler and perhaps an accordion player, and occasionally a banjo picker. Such musical instruments were brought west by the settlers, along with Jew's harps, mouth organs, and melodeons. But by far the most popular instrument for dancing was the fiddle, and a fiddler who could play a dance tune such as "Old Dan Tucker" or "Turkey in the Straw" was always in demand. At Olympia, which became a thriving frontier settlement in about 1851, three brothers named Cornell gained much popularity as dance fiddlers, and Oliver Shead achieved a fine reputation as one who could call the quadrille dance changes.[7]

The success of a dance depended upon the caller and the fiddler—if they were good, two of the most important people in any community. A good caller was usually a personable, glib-tongued fellow with strong lungs, who was rated by the dancers on the new figures or movements he could improvise. A good fiddler was one who could liven up the dance by a little clowning. Some could toss their fiddles in the air or flip them upside down without losing a beat. Others waved their instruments backward over their heads while they played.

The dances were generally called in rhyme and had their own terminology. The words to one old-time quadrille were:

> Balance one—balance all eight
> Swing on the corner like swinging on a gate;
> Now swing your own if not too late,
> Left alamand—right to your partner and hand over hand,
> All the way 'round; promenade eight when you get straight,
> First lady out to right, swing that gent with right hand 'round,
> Partner by left with left hand 'round,
> Lady in the center and seven hands 'round (circle)
> Bird hop out and crow hop in
> Seven hands up and around again.

When the fiddler could no longer make a tune, or the caller's voice was gone, or the dancers were exhausted, the dance would end and everybody would head for home. If the young people had enough energy, they would sing as the wagons carrying the families wandered through the dark to the scattered farms. The songs they sang were often the plain, sometimes morbid popular tunes, including "Do They Miss Me at Home," "The Dying Nun," "Foot-steps That Never Come," "Somebody's Waiting for Me," or "Little Nell of Narragansett Bay."[8]

Perry Sims, a pioneer who settled in what became Okanogan County, Washington, remembered:

There were no old people in the country. One missed them among the young married couples. It was rather sweet to see an old man or woman. Dances were the most fun of all. I would yank my horse out of the mud by day and if at home at night, would play the fiddle for dances, and what was more, the people danced to what was played. . . . The Devil's Dream, Arkansas Traveler, Old Zip Coon, Tassels on My Boots, these were some of the old time favorites. Surprise parties were in vogue. Once I stood on my doorstep and wondered at all the dust in the canyon. It was my birthday and every white man and woman in the settlement was coming to honor my day.[9]

When settlers living along the coast wanted to have a dance, it was not uncommon for them to get together in a sailboat, take a violinist along, and stop in at some logging camp along Puget Sound and dance all night, then come back by boat the next day.[10]

Except among certain religious groups, dances were considered proper and respectable. They were always chaperoned, and the steps generally required no closer proximity than a momentary touching of hands. In the few movements when the gentleman had to put his arm briefly around the lady's waist, he found her so completely encased in whalebone and steel under layers of clothing that, as one person recalled, "any sensual stimulation resulting from the contact must have been purely psychological."[11]

Between dances, people found pleasure in visiting neighbors on weekends. During the early years homesteads were miles apart, and to fill the need for social contact "Saturday-night week ends," as they were called, became almost an institution in some areas of the Northwest. "The family started out in a straw-filled wagon on a Saturday evening after the chores were done. When the neighbor's house was reached, it was generally bedtime for the children, who were promptly disposed of, and then the older folks settled down for a gab fest. The favorite theme of conversation for years after settlement was crossing the plains, and, as time passed, the embellishments became so numerous that the teller himself could hardly distinguish fact from fiction. Sunday was devoted to the time-honored custom of amusing the children and to the big dinner."[12]

Pioneer children in the Pacific Northwest seem to have been no different from children elsewhere in the nineteenth-century American West. At home or during recess at school, they played such games as blindman's buff, hopscotch, run sheep run, pom pom pull away, duck on a rock, old cat, ante over, drop the handkerchief, and ball. J. T. Alexander of Lewis County, Washington, remembered: "During my school days the most popular games were ball and ante-over. Anything was used for a ball, usually a home-made yarn affair, with a rock wound in heavy material to lend weight. I saved my money for quite a while to buy a [real] ball, and when father and I went to Seattle, he gave me my money (about 50 cents), and loaned me an additional 25 cents so I could buy the ball I wanted. It was of solid rubber, and I had to save for quite a time to repay the loan."[13]

Another pioneer, Loren Bingham Hastings, who was born at Port Townsend, Washington, in 1853, reminisced about the pleasure he had found as a boy in "bow-and-arrow hunting with other lads and some Indian children, picnics in the woods (not too far from home), blackberrying, fishing and swimming." Very early on, Hastings decided he wanted to go to sea, "and badgered many a sailor to explain to me the various rigs that gave to ships the names of schooner, sloop, bark, etc." He also recalled occasional traveling shows appearing at the local IOOF (Independent Order of Odd Fellows) hall. In 1868 Hastings delighted in what he remembered seventy years later as "the finest singing" he ever heard from ten Negroes billed as "Songbirds of the South—But Recently Released from Slavery." When his father consented to his having a shotgun, he found much enjoyment in hunting for blue grouse, ducks, and geese, which were very plentiful.[14]

It was only natural for settlers to want churches and schools, and when there were a sufficient number of families in a neighborhood, a school would be built that might also double as a church on Sundays. These mostly one-room structures soon became the center of social activities, including dances, the "singing school" (or what was later called a community sing), spelling bees, and box socials, to which each lady brought a supper in a shoebox or similar receptacle. Each box was auctioned to the highest bidder, who had the privilege of sharing the box with the donor. Such auctions often made considerable money for the church or school organization sponsoring them. When young men learned which box had been made up by the prettiest unattached girl, they often bid high in order to have the honor of sitting with her and eating her sandwiches, cake, and whatever else she had prepared. At one such box social, a girl's sweetheart bid against a burly logger. The logger bid the most. When the angry girl refused to share the lunch, the logger gave her a spirited talk and told her he did not like quitters. The girl went home in tears, so angry because her sweetheart had not tried to beat up the logger that she would not permit him to accompany her. The outcome: Three months later she married the logger.[15]

Schoolhouses were also used for dances. The benches and tables would be pushed back against the wall, and the orchestra seated on a slightly raised platform, on which the teacher's desk usually stood during the week and the preacher stood on Sunday mornings. At the opposite end of the room a table was set with simple but abundant food, to be attacked at midnight. The newer, European-style dances, such as the waltz, had not yet filtered out to the countryside, and square dances were still good enough. Among the simple games sometimes played at these affairs, a popular one was accompanied by the tune and words of "Weevilly Wheat":

> *Your weevilly wheat isn't fit to eat*
> *And neither is your barley;*
> *We'll have the best of Boston wheat*
> *To bake a cake for Charley.*
>
> *Chorus:*
> *Oh, Charley, he's a fine young man*
> *And Charley, he's a dandy,*
> *And Charley loves to kiss the girls*
> *Whenever they come handy.*[16]

On beautiful Whidbey Island, the second largest in the United States, in Puget Sound, settlers enjoyed many of the same pleasures as those elsewhere in old Oregon. Flora A. P. Engle remembered: "Father, mother and the children would get into the big wagon and jog and bump over the rough roads after the farm horses six or seven miles—a long way then—to spend the day and possibly the night with a neighbor. Hospitality was unbounded and every man was the close friend and comrade of his neighbor. Sunday was the day for 'visiting out' and it was no uncommon thing for a family to entertain a dozen guests over the weekend. Picnics were popular, and to these lunches were taken—usually in clothes baskets or trunks. Games were played in the woods and the forest rang with shouts of good-natured raillery. How they did eat—those stalwart men! They had good times in spite of their hardships and they were happy and healthy. The people of the settlement were like one large family and a spirit of kindliness and neighborliness pervaded the atmosphere from one end of the island to the other. What was of interest to one was of equal interest to all. The afflictions of one household became a common cause of sorrow and the good fortune of a neighbor brought rejoicing to all.

"On those rare occasions when people gathered together, whether at Quarterly Meeting or at a dance in a new barn or at the county hall, everybody danced, from gray-haired men to little girls of six. When a candidate for office came to the island to speak, everybody attended to hear him exalt his own party and abuse the opposing party. Other entertainments were virtually unknown, though there were occasional Christmas and Fourth of July celebrations."[17]

Christmas and Fourth of July celebrations were commonplace throughout Old Oregon. In Kittitas County, Washington, Mrs. R. M. Osborn remembered seeing her first Christmas tree when she was nine years old in Mill's general store. "It was called a Christmas exhibition. Everybody turned out to make this a real Christmas. There were no Christmas tree ornaments. String pop corn did double duty. Every child had a present and a big bag of candy. My sister and I received a red heart-shaped pin cushion and were speechless with joy. There was a big supper and speeches and songs later. My sister and I were part of the entertainment, rendering a duet called 'Dying Californian's Last Request' taught us by our father. Save that we knew the song and squeezed the last bit of sentiment out of it, there was no particular reason for singing the ballad as first aid for Christmas cheer."[18]

Orpha Higgins Sutton remembered celebrations on Christmas Eve. "Many neighbors came to the home and from the large front room the furniture would be moved out of doors in rain or snow. The folks would dance and make merry until the morning hours."[19]

Jennie S. Tyler, who moved with her parents to Washington Territory from Dakota Territory in 1877, remembered:

On Christmas we always had a tree. Once the Indians sent me a hundred little dolls. They had bought them from a store at Neah Bay. We divided them among all the neighbors for Christmas. We made all our presents. Covered cardboard with bright cloth was used for the boxes and the little dolls were dressed. We had a fine Christmas dinner with

The photographer's caption—"A Merry Christmas"—seems to suggest these men enjoyed the holiday playing cards. This late-nineteenth-century photo, probably posed, was taken somewhere in Washington State. Notice the corncob pipes the men are smoking. (Courtesy Washington State Historical Society)

all kinds of meat, ducks, geese, chickens, plenty of eggs and lots of cream, with cakes and strawberry pie. We lived high. We had elk meat and venison often. Then in the evening we had dancing in one of the larger houses and brother played the violin.[20]

The Fourth of July was celebrated with equal vigor. Matilda A. Hotaling of Grant County, Washington, remembered everybody went to town on Independence Day. "The little taverns were crowded. Mothers took their children and all took turns in staying with them in a separate room while the others dance."[21] In Yakima County, Washington, James H. Purdin remembered "the marvelous parades, the display of flags, lemonade stands, patriotic speeches, and last but not least, the 'plug uglies' clowning through the streets."[22]

Despite the popularity of dancing, the settlers still sought other forms of entertainment. By the 1860s traveling performers began to arrive in the two largest towns, Portland and Seattle, which could easily be reached by water. Among the first theatrical musicians were blackface minstrels. In 1864 the Taylor Brothers, singers and dancers, and Tom Lafont, the great "American

Horse-drawn sleighs pause in the snow-covered woods somewhere in Oregon in February 1902.
(Courtesy Oregon Historical Society)

Mocking Bird," a noted whistler, appeared at Yesler's Hall in Seattle. The same year Bob Ridley gave a banjo recital. In 1860 the violinist Barney appeared with Herman the magician, and returned frequently.[23]

In more difficult-to-reach settlements such as Challam Bay, Pysht, or Neah Bay, some third-rate company might occasionally arrive by boat for two or three nights' stay. The company usually included a magician, a black-face comedian with a banjo, and a Dutch comedian with a pillow under his vest. Everyone came to these performances, but during the long intervals between such appearances, and to satisfy the pioneers' longing for make-believe, amateur theatricals were given two or three times a year in a church or hall. If the memories of pioneers may be trusted, these were even better than the performances given by so-called professionals, and included such farces as *Box and Cox* and *The Dutchman's Predicament,* and such dramas as *Ten Nights in a Barroom, Under the Gaslight,* and *The Mistletoe Bough.* In the last-named a beautiful maiden, hiding from her sweetheart in an old chest, was locked in and her poor bones were not found for years and years. In the meantime her sweetheart had withered away until he was nothing more than a shadow.

Occasionally the local talent even performed some of Shakespeare's comedies. George Lamb, a Clallam County pioneer, recalled that he once tried to present *East Lynn,* but he could not, since no woman in the community would consent to play Lady Isabelle Vane, the female lead, who, Lamb recalled, "deserted her good husband, eloped with a rascal, and (whisper it), had a child which had to take its mother's name because legally it had no father."[24]

Politics of the cracker-barrel variety, with free and open discussion, was another form of entertainment for many settlers. Unlike some other areas of the West, where settlers were not active in politics, in Oregon and Washing-

These bartenders and patrons of a Tacoma, Washington, saloon posed for the photographer around the turn of the century. (Courtesy Washington State Historical Society)

ton nearly every man knew on which side of the fence his neighbor stood. No local issue was too small not to be a matter of intense concern. Torchlight parades, noisy rallies, and much oratory usually accompanied campaigns, with the climax occurring on election day. For Clarence J. Houser, born near Seattle in 1864, one election day was particularly memorable. Two men—Robinson and Cassidy—threatened to fight each other; Al Whitson broke his leg; a team ran away scattering a load of lumber; and an Indian woman "got drunk and hollered and raised a big fuss. It was a red-letter day, still remembered for its excitement."[25]

While most settlers loved the land for its natural beauty, one pioneer found pleasure in fashioning nature into even more beauty that gave pleasure to others. He was John Bennett, born in Glasgow, Scotland, in 1818. As a young man he came to the United States with his parents after acquiring an exceptional education in botany. He traveled extensively, and at one point was hired to plan and plant the beautiful grounds around a polytechnic institute in Peoria, Illinois. After gold was discovered in California, he headed west to seek his fortune. Like so many others he was disappointed, and, in 1858, at the age of forty, he settled on Puget Sound. He thought the climate ideal for growing things. Having no money to buy land, he found a job and worked about two years until he had enough money to buy some land in Whatcom County, near Sehome. There he made his home and established a nursery and gardens. He had brought with him a chest filled with roots, bulbs, and seeds of fruits, flowers, grains and grasses, which he had gathered in his wanderings over the world. John Bennett's home soon became the showplace of Whatcom County: "The Bennett pear, Bennett's Champion plum, and several varieties of apples, as well as many varieties of flowers" were created by him for the pleasure and welfare of local residents. People from all over the region came to visit John Bennett's garden.

Lottie Roeder Roth, who often visited, remembered:

We entered this old fashioned garden by mounting six or eight steps to a platform on the fence, and descending on the other side in the same way. I can smell the mint now as it grew under those stairs and gave off its odor as we brushed against it. Honeysuckles and sweet briars covered the cottage by the stairs. Lilacs, snowballs, flowering almond, laburnum, hollyhocks, wallflowers, and every old fashioned flower attainable was there. . . . What a beautiful picture it is to recall—that dear old gentleman with his broad visored cap, fringed by bright brown curls, his knees all padded to protect him from the dampness of the earth, for no matter what help he had, Mr. Bennett had to get down and love and care for all the plants, and listen to the small, still message from each. In a voice in which was mingled manhood, intelligence, kindness, and music (I have never heard a voice like Mr. Bennett's beautiful Scotch accent), he would tell us most interesting facts of his travels, of trees and plants secured in various countries—it haunts me still like some beautiful melody.[26]

Another interesting pioneer was Charles Hildebrand, who settled at Oyster Bay in Mason County near the south end of Puget Sound and found pleasure in the bagpipe. Frank Mossman, who knew Hildebrand, remembered him as "a long, lean, hungry-looking man, who wore long hair down his back, and a buckskin suit. He was a perfect picture of Buffalo Bill gone to seed. He had a bagpipe and was a fine player. When he first played this moaning instrument upon his arrival, he was a mile across the waters. When he began moaning before pulling out some of the minor keys of the bagpipe, I thought it was another sick Indian across the bay, and by the sounds, the Indian would die before morning, but there were few smarter men in Mason County than Bagpipe Charley. He claimed to have been chief piper for Queen Victoria, and he evidently wore the same suit of buckskin he had worn before the Queen. Charley had been in many Indian wars, carried dispatches for Generals Reno and Custer, and had been in the Modoc war in Southern Oregon and Northern California, where he had exchanged shots with Shagnasty Jim. Charley sold his oyster holdings for a cool hundred thousand dollars, later, and we lost track of him."[27]

The recollections of the pioneers contain many stories of the simple pleasures enjoyed by the early settlers. Grace Gatch, who lived in Seattle, remembered her father's pleasure in teaching her sisters a lesson in knowing right from wrong. During the early years, when there was no postal delivery in Seattle, everyone went down to the post office for the mail. "Strange as it seems, it was a common practice in those days for women to be allowed to go to the head of the line, such was the gallantry of the men. . . . My father noticed that his little girls, Ruth and Gay, would come into the house with the mail, reading the postal cards. To him, this was a reprehensible habit and he chided them about it, but without result, as he observed. So he decided upon a more drastic method. A few days later these little girls came back from the post office to their home with the mail and scared looks on their faces. They handed their father the mail, and among the letters was a postal card which they had evidently read. The words on the postcard:

> *What are these little girls doing?*
> *They are reading a postal card.*
> *Is the postal card addressed to them?*
> *No. It is addressed to their father.*

The lesson was effective and the father had a good laugh."[28]

BY THE 1860s PORTLAND had become a frontier "city," with a population of about four thousand, many of whom were transients going to or coming from the goldfields or logging camps. These transients were mostly single men who craved more stimulating pleasure than that offered by churches or the more respectable organizations. The businessmen of Portland were practical and sought to give their customers what they wanted. As one student of Portland's history wrote: "So they set themselves to see that the demands for new commodities should be supplied to the sweeping, transient population—a population that remembered San Francisco and Spain and New Orleans and Vienna and London and Peking and countless other places, and that did not remember New England. There arose saloons that were far more sinful than the one-billiard-table establishment of Jim Fruiht and Donald Stewart. (They brought the first billiard table to Portland by boat in 1851.) There were hurdy-gurdy houses and dance halls and temples of Aphrodite that far overshadowed the simple efforts at disorderliness that poor old Madame Hamilton brought up from San Francisco a decade before. Satan claimed the transient population for his own."[29]

Portland was a city of contrasts. Lavish living, social graces, and Victorian behavior characterized the society of the city's permanent residents, who sought to emulate and even outdo Boston. Many of them had amassed great fortunes during the town's early years, and they displayed their wealth perhaps more ostentatiously than people anywhere else in the nation at that time. Portland had a horse-drawn trolley, and gaslights had been installed in the business area about 1860. But what went on on the other side of Portland, on Skidroad, or in the North End as it was also known, was ignored by respectable residents. In the area close to Skidroad one could find any kind of pleasure that money could buy, in the bars, gambling houses, theaters,

The Columbia Saloon in Portland, Oregon, around the turn of the century. (Courtesy Oregon Historical Society)

penny arcades, and shooting galleries, or in booths of fortune tellers, phrenologists, astrologists, herb doctors, and patent-medicine men located around Second and Third Streets and Burnside. There one could likewise find lumberjacks, sailors, rivermen, miners, and visiting young experimenters from rural areas in Oregon and Washington amusing themselves. And there also were small-town moralists who came to see how horrible it all was and to report to their congregations back home.

Portland's Skidroad dated back to the days when logs were dragged by horses, mules, or oxen from where they were felled to waiting ships on the Columbia River. It was only logical that lumberjacks would follow such a road to Portland in search of pleasure, and it was along this road that saloons, houses of prostitution, gambling halls, and other pleasure palaces were established. Although the first Skidroad supposedly was created on Puget Sound in the early 1850s, such roads existed throughout timber regions. Where they entered the larger communities, saloons and other pleasure palaces were

The Gem saloon in Portland, Oregon, early in this century. (Courtesy Oregon Historical Society)

established to cater to lumberjacks. In time the term "Skidroad" was corrupted and became "Skid Row," meaning a district anywhere with cheap
saloons and flophouses frequented by vagrants and alcoholics.

One sight every Portland visitor wanted to see was August Erickson's
saloon, with its six-hundred-foot bar, supposedly the longest bar in the
world at the time. Behind the bar were sufficient bartenders and enough
whiskey to satisfy a thousand drinking men at one time. A man could buy the
biggest scuttleful of beer in the United States for a nickel in Erickson's
saloon, and a man could also find pleasure by spending his money on women
and gambling. Erickson's also featured a museum filled with more-or-less
Rabelaisian objets d'art and curiosities. On the stage was an orchestra with
lady musicians gowned in rose pink, seated behind brass rails that were
charged with enough electricity to stop the most amorous lumberjack or
sailor who might decide he wanted to be better acquainted with them.[30]

At the nearby variety theaters, the ladies of the night took their turns on
the stages and then worked the boxes, where they shocked many a customer

by offering beer at a dollar a bottle. One floor below, a half gallon of beer cost only five cents. Nearly all the saloons had rooms where women of almost every nationality and color plied their trade. There also were crib houses for transients, and octoroon sporting houses catering exclusively to white patrons and charging anywhere from five to ten dollars, with city health authorities requiring that the prostitutes have periodic medical examinations. Just beyond Skidroad one could find higher-class gambling establishments and the house of Madame Fanshawe, located at Broadway and Morrison, and half a dozen other famous houses and madames, whose histories are inextricably interwoven into a comical story of political machinations gone awry. When the mayor appointed a vice commission to survey the town, its report included a full-page map of the city, with the streets erased but with dots showing where prostitutes could be found. Almost overnight, reproductions of the maps were being sold, along with compasses for eager men seeking pleasure.[31]

The wide-open pleasure palaces of Portland gradually became more discreet after business leaders decided to hold the Lewis and Clark Centennial World's Exposition in 1905, and after Tom Word was elected sheriff on his pledge to close the gambling houses. Portland needed to change its image for the exposition. Saloons remained open, but the girls were moved upstairs. Most of the houses of prostitution closed, and the women scattered among the hotels, apartment houses, and rooming houses of the city, where they continued their calling provided they could afford to pay for temporary protection from the law. On the surface it appeared only respectable pleasures flourished, with elaborate masquerade and fancy-dress balls and theatrical and musical performances. Society long remembered a Marie Antoinette fête held at the Marquam Grand Theater, when a stately minuet was danced, its participants in regalia complete with swords and powdered wigs.[32]

Seattle, to the north in Washington, had grown faster than Portland. Seattle's businessmen also sought to give customers what they wanted. The city fathers, realizing that their city offered the only red-light district in Washington, set aside a large restricted area for the benefit of transients. Under Mayor Tom Humes, the city established a policy of passive consent, resulting in the influx of countless gamblers, thieves, and procurers. One journalist wrote about what he called slavery among the Japanese women in Seattle, who lived in rows of one-story cottages by the waterfront in an area called Whitechapel. In addition to the Japanese, there were women from China, Mexico, and France, as well as American women, black and

Jack Benton and Clay Grater play poker with another, unidentified man in an Ashwood, Oregon, saloon. (Coutesy Oregon Historical Society)

white. In 1910, when Hiram Gill ran for mayor, he did so on the promise to keep Seattle an open town. But an investigation soon disclosed what everyone knew: Conditions in the red-light district were awful. A newspaper demanded Mayor Gill's recall, and he lost. There was a mass exodus from the red-light district, and the unholy alliance between the mayor and the pleasure providers was broken.[33]

By the end of the first decade of the twentieth century, Seattle and Portland were no longer cities of open sin. Since they set the tone in their respective states, other communities in Oregon and Washington that had been pale imitations of Seattle and Portland also became more respectable, at least on the surface. Civilization, or what passed for it, had arrived.

Afterword

*If there were not happiness on earth, the creation would be a monstrosity,
and Voltaire would have been right when he called our planet the latrine of
the universe.*

—*Giovanni Jacopo*

B Y THE BEGINNING OF the twentieth century the isolation and
self-contained lifestyle that once existed in many areas of the American West had disappeared. The vast region west of the Mississippi
River had been pierced by the telegraph, railroad, and the mail, bringing
improved communication, better transportation, and the products and ideals
of America's industrialization in the East. The frontier had been replaced by
farms, thriving villages, and busy towns and cities, and with them churches
and schools. With these institutions of civilized life, brought from the East,
came Puritan prejudices and orthodoxy that lingered in the minds of farmers
and the residents of small towns, who were trying to find their places in the
sun as respectable and accepted Christian members of their communities.

Gambling, prostitution, and drinking were publicly frowned on. Bearbaiting and buffalo hunting were no longer accepted. Smalltown residents,
especially businessmen, who found pleasure in hunting and fishing, usually
rested on the Sabbath for fear of arousing the ire of local clergy or for fear
that their business opportunities might suffer if they broke with the religious
and moral standards of their community. Organized sports met with resistance in many rural areas, although some pioneers refused to give up horse
racing and cockfights. In areas where such diversions were banned, some
farmers even questioned the morality and propriety of speed trials of horses
at local agricultural fairs.

Acceptable forms of diversion in rural areas and small towns were family outings; ice-cream and church socials; musical performances, including

band concerts and dances; attending performances of traveling theatrical and variety shows, including circuses and Wild West shows; and the playing of the more genteel games described in books and magazines published in the East. Many people in the West found much pleasure reading the *Saturday Evening Post,* with articles written by such popular authors as Joseph Conrad, O. Henry, Jack London, Robert Chambers, and Stewart Edward White. The *Post* reinforced the conservatism and the growing middle-class sanity of the economically and morally controlling class in towns not only in the West but elsewhere in the United States. It avoided the sensational and the esoteric and stressed American nationalism, business, and material success. The magazine assumed accepted morals and mores without question. While trying to reflect life, especially in the East, the *Post* and other magazines helped to create the same life in the West.

Western women found enjoyment and helpful information in magazines written for them, especially the *Ladies' Home Journal,* whose editor, Edward Bok, sought to provide articles that were intimate and designed to change American home life for the better. Articles advised women about affairs of the heart and told them how to dress, conduct themselves, feed their families, and even bring up their children. And the *Ladies' Home Journal* also strove to effect changes in home architecture and interior decoration.

Many men in the West read *Forest and Stream,* a weekly publication on hunting and fishing, that helped to transform what had been the business of making a living on the frontier into the avocation of "sportsmen," or, as Aldo Leopold later described them, "trophy-hunters who must possess, invade, and appropriate." Enjoy the outdoors they did.

The bar and barbershop crowd read the pink pages of the *National Police Gazette,* filled with illustrated stories about spicy vice, sex, murders, other crimes, and theater and sports, especially boxing. The cover illustration on each issue was designed for shock value, often women with bare ankles, sometimes drinking.

As many western towns grew into cities during the early twentieth century, Puritan prejudices eased as a clearly defined middle class emerged and sought to carry forward the traditions and ideals of democracy. Although prejudice against pleasure still existed among puritanical factions, religious opposition softened as citizens in the growing number of western cities sought to replace rural pastimes no longer available. New diversions emerged, including amusement parks, and public dance halls were reestablished, as were beer gardens. Horse racing was revived, along with other spectator sports. People began to find pleasure in watching and listening instead of participating.

The products of technological change also provided new diversions for people in the West. After George Eastman invented a flexible paperback film in 1884 and designed a small box camera called a Kodak that cost twenty-five dollars, many people in the West found pleasure in amateur photography. This diversion only gained in popularity after Eastman designed cheaper and simpler cameras—the pocket Kodak in 1895 and the Brownie in 1900.

Another product of technology was the phonograph. Although late in 1877 Thomas Edison thought his invention only useful as a dictaphone—he recorded the human voice on tinfoil, clumsily wrapped around a small drum—the substitution of a wax cylinder and later wax disks created a new industry and brought recorded music into homes everywhere. Edison also played a significant role in creating motion pictures, having produced the first silent movie, *Record of a Sneeze*, in 1894. Two years later the first movie theater, Vitascope Hall, opened in New Orleans. The first movie theater west of the Mississippi, the Nickel Theatre, was opened in Lawrence, Kansas, in 1903 by Clair and and Mary "Vivian" Patee. Within a few years countless other movie houses had opened throughout the West providing still another form of entertainment. Even before the first talking feature film, *The Jazz Singer*, starring Al Jolson, was filmed in 1927 in Hollywood, California, that western city had become the movie capital of the world.

While Americans early in the twentieth century continued to find pleasure traversing the vast distances in the West by railroad, the arrival of the automobile gave people the opportunity to explore beyond the railroad tracks to the outermost limits of good roads. After Henry Ford produced the first Model T—fifteen million of them in 1908—Americans began motoring through the West, retracing the routes of their ancestors and enjoying the beauty of the western landscape.

A new form of home entertainment began to develop in 1906, soon after Reginald Fessenden broadcast the first voice radio transmission from his experimental station at Brant Rock, Massachusetts. Immediately after World War I radio broadcasting began to grow, and by the start of 1923, radio stations across the nation were broadcasting programs and attracting listeners. In the West stations were located in San Francisco, Sacramento, and Los Angeles; Colorado Springs; Astoria, Corvallis, and Medford, Oregon; Oklahoma City; Albuquerque; Kansas City, Missouri; St. Louis; Wichita; Phoenix; Norfolk, Nebraska; and Great Falls, Montana. Network radio began in 1926, and soon Americans were enjoying the "Cliquot Club Eskimos," "Amos 'n' Andy," and numerous variety, dramatic, news, and information programs.

The arrival of radio brought a new form of pleasure into western homes early in the twentieth century. This photo was taken in Abilene, Kansas, about 1910. (Courtesy Kansas State Historical Society)

The arrival of radio marked the beginning of an era when canned entertainment could be delivered to American homes. Since then technology has given us countless new ways of seeking pleasure, ways that were not even dreamed of by the pioneers. In addition to movies, radio, and records, we have television, home videos, compact discs, computer games, the Las Vegas and Atlantic City pleasure palaces that any American can reach within hours by jet plane, and countless other ways easily and often effortlessly to fill our nonworking hours, provided that there is money to pay the cost. Americans are told by moneymaking pleasure providers that these new forms of pleasure are satisfying, but are they? Many of the pleasures enjoyed by the pioneers during the nineteenth century may have been more enjoyable than the ways Americans now fill their increasing number of leisure hours. The pioneers often created their own entertainment as their ancestors had done for generations before. The pioneers also actively participated in most of them. Then, too, their pleasures were for the most part simple diversions from the normal functions of their lives.

If the countless pleasures available today are not satisfying, perhaps the blame rests with the providers, not the seekers. In any event, the pleasures Americans created and enjoyed in the nineteenth century American West helped to shape the national character. Modern pleasure providers have changed and are changing that character. Whether or not the changes are for the good will be answered by generations to come.

Notes

CHAPTER I   EARLY EXPLORERS AND TRAVELERS

1. David Freeman Hawke, *Everyday Life in Early America* (New York: Harper & Row, 1988), p. 96.
2. Benjamin Franklin, "Advice to a Young Tradesman," as reprinted in Louis B. Wright and H. T. Swedenberg, editors, *The American Tradition: National Characteristics, Past and Present* (New York: F. S. Crofts & Co., 1941), p. 102.
3. James Truslow Adams, *America's Tragedy*, as cited in Jay B. Nash, *Philosophy of Recreation and Leisure* (Dubuque, Iowa: Wm. C. Brown Co., 1960), pp. 22–23.
4. Charles G. Clarke, *The Men of the Lewis and Clark Expedition, a Biographical Roster of the Fifty-one Members and a Composite Diary of Their Activities from All Known Sources* (Glendale, Calif.: Arthur H. Clark Co., 1970), pp. 94–95.
5. Ibid., p. 151.
6. Ibid., p. 113.
7. Ibid., p. 127.
8. Ibid., p. 129.
9. Zebulon Montgomery Pike, *Exploratory Travels Through the Western Territories of North America: Comprising a Voyage From St. Louis, on the Mississippi, to the Source of That River, and a Journey Through the Interior of Louisiana, and the North-Eastern Provinces of New Spain* (Denver: W. H. Lawrence & Co., 1889), p. 179. Reprint of the first English edition of Pike's 1810 work, published in London in 1811.
10. Ibid., p. 158.
11. Ibid., p. 197.
12. Ibid., p. 217.
13. Donald Jackson, editor, *The Journals of Zebulon Montgomery Pike With Letters and Related Documents* (Norman: University of Oklahoma Press, 1966), vol. 1, p. 387.
14. Edwin James, "Account of an Expedition from Pittsburgh to the Rocky Mountains Performed in the Years 1819, 1820 . . . under the command of Maj. S. H. Long, of the U.S. Top. Engineers," in Reuben Gold Thwaites, editor, *Early Western Travels 1748–1846* (Cleveland: Arthur H. Clark Co., 1904), vol. 15, p. 275.
15. Ibid., p. 274.
16. John Bradbury, *Travels in the Interior of America, in the Years 1809, 1810, and 1811 . . .* (London: 1819), as reprinted in Thwaites, *Early Western Travels 1748–1846*, vol. 5, p. 39.
17. Ibid., pp. 262–263.
18. John C. Frémont, *Report of the Exploring Expedition to the Rocky Mountains in the Year 1842 . . .* (Washington, D.C.: Gales and Seaton, Printers, 1845), p. 23.

19.   Thwaites, *Early Western Travels 1748–1846*, vol. 16, p. 83.

20.   Kate Leila Gregg, editor, *The Road to Santa Fe: The Journal and Diaries of George Champlin Sibley and Others pertaining to the Surveying and Marking of a Road from the Missouri Frontier to the Settlements of New Mexico 1825–1827* (Albuquerque: University of New Mexico Press, 1952), pp. 71–72.

21.   Ibid., p. 134.

22.   James O. Pattie, *The Personal Narrative of James O. Pattie* (Philadelphia and New York: J. B. Lippincott Co., 1962), pp. 109–110. Reprint of the 1831 first edition, unabridged, and with an introduction by William H. Goetzmann.

23.   Harrison Clifford Dale, editor, *The Ashley-Smith Explorations and the discovery of a Central Route to the Pacific, 1822–1829 with the Original Journals* . . . (Glendale, Calif.: Arthur H. Clark Co., 1941), p. 217.

24.   Albert Pike, *Prose Sketches and Poems, Written in the Western Country* (Albuquerque: Calvin Horn Publishers, 1967), pp. 148–149, 157. Although his writings were fictional, Pike based them on his personal experiences in New Mexico.

25.   *New Mexico: A Guide to the Colorful State, Compiled by Workers of the Writers' Program of the Work Projects Administration in the State of New Mexico* (New York: Hastings House, 1940), pp. 130–131.

26.   Josiah Gregg, *Commerce of the Prairies: Or the Journal of a Santa Fe Trader, During Eight Expeditions Across the Great Western Prairies, and a Residence of Nearly Nine Years in Northern Mexico* (New York: Henry G. Langley, 1844), vol. 1, pp. 242–243.

27.   Ibid., pp. 239–240.

28.   [William Brisbane Dick], *The American Hoyle: or, Gentleman's Hand-Books of Games* . . . (New York: Dick and Fitzgerald, Publishers, 1864), p. 456. See also Robert K. DeArment, *Knights of the Green Cloth: The Saga of the Frontier Gamblers* (Norman: University of Oklahoma Press, 1982), pp. 395–396. DeArment describes monte as being played with a deck of forty cards, and he uses the word "gate" instead of "port." In his description of the game, he writes, "If the gate matched a card in the layout, the dealer paid all bets made on that card. In some cases, payoffs were made for the simple matching of suits. Odds heavily favored the dealer in this game, but crooked gamblers often reduced the players' slim chances of winning to absolute zero by manipulation of the deck."

CHAPTER II   AMONG THE MOUNTAIN MEN

1.   George F. Ruxton, *Adventures in Mexico and the Rocky Mountains* (New York: Harper & Brothers, 1848), pp. 205–208.

2.   Ibid., p. 200.

3.   George Bird Grinnell, "Bent's Old Fort and Its Builders," *Collections of the Kansas State Historical Society, 1919–1922* (Topeka: B. P. Walker, State Printer, 1923), pp. 56, 61.

4.   Washington Irving, *The Adventures of Captain Bonneville* (Paris: Baudry's European Library, 1835), pp. 154–155.

5.   Ruxton, *Adventures in Mexico and the Rocky Mountains*, pp. 236–237.

6.   John K. Townsend, *Narrative of a Journey Across the Rocky Mountains, to the Columbia River, and a Visit to the Sandwich Islands, Chile, &C., with a Scientific Appendix* (Philadelphia: Henry Perkins, 1839), pp. 75–76.

7. Francis F. Victor, editor, *The River of the West. Life and Adventure in the Rocky Mountains and Oregon: Embracing Events in the Life-Time of a Mountain-Man and Pioneer* . . . (Hartford and Toledo: R.W. Bliss and Co., 1870), pp. 110–112.

8. Rufus Sage, *Wild Scenes in Kansas and Nebraska, and the Rocky Mountains, Oregon, California, New Mexico, Texas, and the Grand Prairies; or, Notes by the Way* . . . (Philadelphia: G. D. Miller, Publisher, 1855), pp. 132–133.

9. Victor, *The River of the West*, p. 51.

10. Ruxton, *Adventures in Mexico and the Rocky Mountains*, pp. 236–237.

11. Ibid., p. 255.

12. William T. Hamilton, *My Sixty Years on the Plains Trapping, Trading, and Indian Fighting* (New York: Forest and Stream Publishing Co., 1905), pp. 99–101.

13. Townsend, *Narrative of a Journey Across the Rocky Mountains*, pp. 77–78.

14. John Bradbury, *Travels in the Interior of America, in the Years 1809, 1810, and 1811; Including a Description of Upper Louisiana, Together with the States of Ohio, Kentucky, Indiana, and Tennessee, with the Illinois and Western Territories* . . . (Liverpool, England: Printed for the Author, by Smith and Galway . . . , 1817), p. 178.

15. Henry Drummond Dee, "An Irishman in the Fur Trade: The Life and Journals of John Work," *British Columbia Historical Quarterly*, vol. 7 (Oct. 1943), pp. 237–238.

16. Work H. Gray, "Journal of W. H. Gray," *Whitman College Quarterly* (June 1913), pp. 59–61.

17. Irving, *The Adventures of Captain Bonneville*, pp. 154–155.

18. William Drummond Stewart, *Edward Warren* (Missoula, Mont.: Mountain Press Publishing Co., 1986), pp. 172–173. Reprint of the 1854 first edition published in London.

19. Sigmund G. Spaeth, *A History of Popular Music in America* (New York: Random House, 1948), pp. 50, 56–64, 72–73.

20. Ruxton, *Adventures in Mexico and the Rocky Mountains*, pp. 236–237.

21. [Dick], *The American Hoyle*, pp. 57–82. For comparative purposes, the forty-eighth printing of *Hoyle's Rules of Games* (New York: New American Library, 1963) was also consulted.

22. Ibid., pp. 146–151.

23. Sage, *Wild Scenes in Kansas and Nebraska*, p. 135.

24. Hamilton, *My Sixty Years on the Plains*, p. 68. See also the recollections of mountain man Osborne Russel, *Journal of a Trapper* (Lincoln: University of Nebraska Press, 1955), pp. 55, 109.

25. J. Cecil Alter, *James Bridger, Trapper, Frontiersman, Scout and Guide* (Salt Lake City: 1925), pp. 402–403.

26. Henry Inman, *The Old Santa Fe Trail* (New York: Macmillan, 1897), pp. 330–331.

27. Victor, *The River of the West*, pp. 137–140.

28. Ibid., pp. 169–170.

CHAPTER III   AMONG THE INDIANS

1. James Willard Schultz, *Recently Discovered Tales of Life Among the Indians* (Missoula, Mont.: Mountain Press Publishing Co., 1988), p. 35. This work contains reprints of Schultz's writings as they first appeared in *Forest and Stream* magazine between 1880 and 1894.

2. Richard Irving Dodge, *The Plains of the Great West and Their Inhabitants* . . . (New York: G. P. Putnam's Sons, 1877), p. 347.

3. Chief Buffalo Child Long Lance, *Long Lance* (New York: Farrar and Rinehart, Inc., 1928), pp. 30–31.

4. George Bird Grinnell, *When Buffalo Ran* (New Haven, Conn.: Yale University Press, 1920), pp. 21–22.

5. Long Lance, *Long Lance*, pp. 32–33.

6. Schultz, *Recently Discovered Tales*, p. 35.

7. Ibid., pp. 35–36.

8. Robert H. Lowie, *Indians of the Plains* (Garden City, N.Y.: American Museum of Natural History, 1963), p. 134. This work was first published in 1954 as an anthropological handbook by the American Museum of Natural History.

9. Ibid., p. 132.

10. Richard Irving Dodge, *Our Wild Indians: Thirty-Three Years' Personal Experience Among the Red Men of the Great West* (Hartford, Conn.: A. D. Worthington and Co., 1883), pp. 325–327.

11. Dodge, *The Plains of the Great West*, pp. 320–321.

12. Henry A. Boller, *Among the Indians, Eight Years in the Far West, 1858–1866* (Chicago: The Lakeside Press, 1959), p. 166. This reprint edition was edited by Milo Milton Quaife.

13. Ibid., p. 202.

14. Ibid., p. 66.

15. Dodge, *The Plains of the Great West*, p. 344.

16. Boller, *Among the Indians*, p. 71.

17. Ibid., pp. 69–70.

18. Dodge, *Our Wild Indians*, pp. 336–337.

19. Ibid., p. 343.

20. Alice Marriott and Carol K. Rachlin, *American Indian Mythology* (New York: Thomas Y. Crowell Co., 1968), p. 16.

21. Dodge, *Our Wild Indians*, p. 337.

CHAPTER IV   ALONG THE RIVERS

1. Estwick Evans, "A Pedestrious Tour, of Four Thousand Miles, Through the Western States and Territories, During the Winter and Spring of 1818 . . . ," in Reuben Gold Thwaites, editor, *Early Western Travels 1748–1846* (Cleveland: Arthur H. Clark Co., 1904), vol. 8, pp. 335–336, 341.

2. Thomas Ashe, *Travels in America, Performed in the Year 1806* (London: 1809), p. 311.

3. Evans, "A Pedestrious Tour," pp. 336–337.

4. Albert A. Fossier, *New Orleans, the Glamour Period, 1800–1840* (New Orleans, American Printing Co., 1957), p. 453.

5. Ibid., p. 459.

6. Ibid., p. 381.

7. Timothy Flint, *The History and Geography of the Mississippi Valley* (Cincinnati: E.H. Flint, 1833), vol. 1, p. 270.

8. Herbert Asbury, "French Quarter," pp. 94–101, as cited in Michael Allen, *Western Rivermen, 1763–1861* (Baton Rouge: Louisiana State University Press, 1990), p. 129.

9. Fossier, *New Orleans, the Glamour Period, 1800–1840*, p. 385.

10. Ibid., pp. 463–464.

11. Ibid., p. 465.

12. Jim Marshall, *Swinging Doors* (Seattle: Frank McCaffrey Publishers, 1949), p. 42.

13. Arthur Singleton [Henry C. Knight], *Letters from the South & West* (Boston: Richardson & Lord, 1824), p. 125.

14. Thomas Hamilton, *Men and Manners in America*, vol. 1 (Edinburgh: William Blackwood, 1833), p. 204.

15. Ibid., pp. 208–209.

16. Samuel Parker, *Journal of an Exploring Tour Beyond the Rocky Mountains* . . . (Ithaca, N.Y.: Published by the author, 1838), pp. 22–24.

17. Flint, *The History and Geography of the Mississippi Valley*, p. 309.

18. James B. Finley, *The Autobiography of Rev. James B. Finley; or, Pioneer Life in the West* (Cincinnati: 1853), p. 66.

19. *Missouri Republican* (St. Louis), April 12, 1841.

20. Charles Dickens, *American Notes and Pictures from Italy* (Oxford: Oxford University Press, 1957), pp. 174.

21. Ruxton, *Adventures in Mexico and the Rocky Mountains*, p. 303.

22. Ibid.

23. Marshall, *Swinging Doors*, p. 67.

24. William Clark Kennerly, as told to Elizabeth Russell, *Persimmon Hill, A Narrative of Old St. Louis and the Far West* (Norman: University of Oklahoma Press, 1948), pp. 180–181.

25. Ibid., pp. 178–179.

26. Ibid., pp. 182–183.

27. Flint, *The History and Geography of the Mississippi Valley*, vol. 1, pp. 162–163.

28. Ibid., p. 145.

29. Robert Baird, *View of the Valley of the Mississippi, or the Emigrant's and Traveller's Guide to the West* (Philadelphia: H.S. Tanner, 1834), p. 342.

30. Parker, *Journal of an Exploring Tour*, pp. 21–22.

31. J. E. Alexander, *Transatlantic Sketches* (Philadelphia: Key & Biddle, 1833), pp. 248–249. See also Flint, *The History and Geography of the Mississippi Valley*, p. 236.

32. Tyrone Power, *Impressions of America During the Years 1833, 1834, and 1835* (Philadelphia: Carey, Lea & Blanchard, 1836), vol. 2, pp. 125–126.

33. Richard Cobden, *American Diaries* (Princeton: Princeton University Press, 1952), p. 121.

34. Hamilton, *Men and Manners in America*, vol. 1, pp. 89–91.

35. George B. Merrick, *Old Times on the Upper Mississippi* (Cleveland: Arthur H. Clark Co., 1909), p. 157.

36. Baird, *View of the Valley of the Mississippi*, pp. 347–348.

37. Marian Murray, *From Rome to Ringling, Circus!* (New York: Appleton-Century-Crofts, 1956), pp. 169–170.

38. Duncan Emrich, *It's An Old Wild West Custom* (Surrey, England: The World's Work Ltd., 1951), p. 69.

39.   Hamilton, *Men and Manners in America,* vol. 1, p. 22.

40.   Parker, *Journal of an Exploring Tour,* p. 22.

41.   Joseph H. Ingraham, *The South-West. By a Yankee* (New York: Harper & Brothers, 1835) as cited in Warren S. Tryon, editor, *A Mirror for Americans* (Chicago: University of Chicago Press, 1952), vol 2, p. 320.

42.   Francis Parkman, *The Journals of Francis Parkman* (New York: Harper & Brothers, 1947), vol. 2, pp. 415–416.

CHAPTER V   WITH THE EMIGRANTS

1.   Catherine Margaret Haun, "A Woman's Trip Across the Plains in 1849," manuscript, HM 538, Henry E. Huntington Library, San Marino, Calif.

2.   Oregon Pioneer Association, 35th Annual Reunion, *Transactions* (Portland: Oregon Pioneer Association, 1907), p. 161.

3.   George Keller, *A Trip Across the Plains and Life in California* (Oakland, Calif.: Biobooks, 1955), pp. 8, 12, 23.

4.   Ibid., pp. 3–4.

5.   Margaret A. Frink, "Adventures of a Party of Gold-seekers" in Kenneth L. Holmes, editor, *Covered Wagon Women, Diaries & Letters from the Western Trails, 1840–1890* (Glendale, Calif.: Arthur H. Clark, 1983), vol. 2, p. 60.

6.   Haun, "A Woman's Trip."

7.   Marian Russell, *Land of Enchantment, Memoirs of Marian Russell Along the Santa Fe Trail* . . . (Albuquerque: University of New Mexico Press, 1981), p. 20.

8.   Jesse Applegate, *A Day with the Cow Column in 1843* (Chicago: Caxton Club, 1934), pp. 19–21.

9.   G. W. Thissell, *Crossing the Plains in '49* (Oakland, Calif.: privately printed, 1903), pp. 108–111.

10.   Ibid., pp. 168–169.

11.   Spaeth, *A History of Popular Music in America,* pp. 65–135. See also Ronald L. Davis, *A History of Music in American Life: The Formative Years, 1620–1865* (Lalabar, Fla.: Robert Krieger Publishing Co., 1982), vol. 1, pp. 77–94.

12.   John D. Unruh, Jr., *The Plains Across: The Overland Emigrants and the Trans-Mississippi West, 1840–60* (Urbana: University of Illinois Press, 1979), p. 143.

13.   Joel Palmer, *Journal of Travels Over the Rocky Mountains, To the Mouth of the Columbia River* . . . (Cincinnati: J.A. & U.P. James, 1850), p. 23.

14.   Irene D. Paden, editor, *The Journal of Madison Berryman Moorman, 1850–1851* (San Francisco: California Historical Society, 1948), pp. 17, 19, 34.

15.   Unruh, *The Plains Across,* pp. 132, 134.

16.   Ibid., pp. 260–261.

17.   Ibid., p. 291.

18.   Thissell, *Crossing the Plains in '49,* pp. 77–78.

19.   Paden, *The Journal of Madison Berryman Moorman,* pp. 48–49.

20.   Ibid., pp. 49–50.

21.   T. S. Kenderdine, *A California Tramp and Later Footprints; or, Life on the Plains and in the Golden State Thirty Years Ago* (Newtown, Pa.: Published by the author, 1888), pp. 109–110.

22.   Thissell, *Crossing the Plains in '49*, pp. 33–37.

23.   John F. Lewis Diary, 1849, 1852–54, manuscript and typescript in Beinecke Rare Book and Manuscript Library, Yale University, New Haven, Connecticut.

CHAPTER VI   AMONG THE SOLDIERS

1.   Elvid Hunt, *History of Fort Leavenworth, 1827–1927* (Fort Leavenworth, Kans.: 1926), p. 34.

2.   Frémont, *The Exploring Expedition to the Rocky Mountains*, pp. 31–32, 41, 106–107.

3.   New York *Tribune*, Dec. 4, 1847, quoting the St. Louis *Era*. See also Frank S. Edwards, *A Campaign in New Mexico with Colonel Doniphan* (Philadelphia: Carey and Hart, 1847), pp. 24–36. See also George R. Gibson, "Journal of a Soldier under Kearny and Doniphan, 1846–1847," in Ralph P. Bieber, editor, *The Southwest Historical Series* (Glendale, Calif.: Arthur H. Clark Co., 1935), vol. 3, pp. 124–165.

4.   David Michael Delo, *Peddlers and Post Traders: The Army Sutler on the Frontier* (Salt Lake City: University of Utah Press, 1992), p. 97.

5.   Kennerly, *Persimmon Hill*, p. 192.

6.   Ibid., p. 191.

7.   Ibid., p. 190.

8.   Ibid., p. 193.

9.   Percival G. Lowe, *Five Years a Dragoon ('49 to '54) and Other Adventures on the Great Plains* (Kansas City, Mo.: Franklin Hudson Publishing Co., 1906), p. 49.

10.   Ibid., pp. 57–58.

11.   Dodge, *The Plains of the Great West*, pp. 71–72, 99.

12.   Lowe, *Five Years a Dragoon*, pp. 124–125.

13.   William N. Bischoff, editor, *We Were Not Summer Soldiers: The Indian War Diary of Plympton J. Kelly, 1855–1856* (Tacoma: Washington State Historical Society, 1976), p. 81.

14.   George A. Armes, *Ups and Downs of an Army Officer* (Washington, D.C.: 1900), p. 505.

15.   "Journal of Pvt. George Gibbs," as cited in *The Great Platte River Road: The Covered Wagon Mainline via Fort Kearny to Fort Laramie* (Lincoln: Nebraska State Historical Society, 1969) vol. 25, p. 493, compiled by Merrill J. Mattes.

16.   Dodge, *The Plains of the Great West*, pp. 92–93.

17.   Joel A. Allen, "History of the American Bison," *Ninth Annual Report of the U.S. Geological and Geographical Survey for 1875* (Washington, D.C.: Government Printing Office, 1877), pp. 471–472. See also David Dary, *The Buffalo Book* (Chicago: Swallow Press, 1974), pp. 255–256.

18.   Chris Emmett, *Fort Union and the Winning of the Southwest* (Norman: University of Oklahoma Press, 1965), pp. 141–144.

19.   Percy M. Ashburn, *A History of the Medical Department of the U.S. Army* (Boston: Houghton Mifflin, 1929) p. 112.

20.   Margaret I. Carrington, *Absaraka (Ab-sa-ra-ka) Home of the Crows* (Chicago: The Lakeside Press, R. R. Donnelley & Sons, 1950), pp. 204–205. A reprint of the 1868 first edition.

21.   Lydia Spencer Lane, *I Married a Soldier* (Albuquerque: University of New Mexico Press, 1987), p. 28. A reprint of the 1893 first edition.

22. Ibid., pp. 30–31.

23. Ibid., p. 183.

24. Frances M. A. Roe, *Army Letters from an Officer's Wife, 1871–1888* (New York and London: D. Appleton and Company, 1909), p. 42.

25. Lambert Bowman Wolf, "Extracts from Diary of Captain Lambert Bowman Wolf," *Kansas Historical Quarterly,* vol. 1, no. 3 (May 1932), p. 198.

26. Frances Anne Mullen Boyd, *Cavalry Life in Tent and Field* (Lincoln: University of Nebraska Press, 1982), pp. 289–291. A reprint of the 1894 first edition.

27. Thomas Railsback, "Military Bands and Music at Old Fort Hays, 1867–1889," *Journal of the West,* vol. 22, no. 3 (July 1983), pp. 28–35. For a more complete examination of military bands, see Thomas C. Railsback, "Military Bands and Music in the Frontier West, 1866–1891," unpublished thesis, Fort Hays (Kansas) State University, 1978.

28. Martha Summerhayes, *Vanished Arizona: Recollections of My Army Life* (Chicago: The Lakeside Press, R. R. Donnelley & Sons, 1939), pp. 284–287. A reprint of the 1908 first edition.

29. Ibid., pp. 284–287.

30. Samuel June Barrows, "The Northwestern Mule and His Driver," *Atlantic Monthly,* May 1875.

31. James H. Bradley, "Journal of James H. Bradley, the Sioux Campaign of 1876 Under the Command of General John Gibbon," in *Contributions to the Historical Society of Montana* (Helena: Historical Society of Montana, 1896), vol. 2, pp. 209–210.

32. Summerhayes, *Vanished Arizona,* pp. 314–315.

CHAPTER VII   IN COW COUNTRY

1.   Robert Glass Cleland, *The Cattle on a Thousand Hills: Southern California, 1850–1870* (San Marino, Calif.: Huntington Library, 1941), pp. 44–45.

2.   John C. Ewers, editor, *Adventures of Zenas Leonard Fur Trader* (Norman: University of Oklahoma Press, 1959), p. 109.

3.   Ibid., pp. 109–111.

4.   J. Frank Dobie, *A Vaquero of the Brush Country* (Dallas: Southwest Press, 1929), pp. 95–96.

5.   Lake Porter, "Played the Fiddle on Herd at Night," in J. Marvin Hunter, editor, *The Trail Drivers of Texas* (Nashville: Cokesbury Press, 1925), p. 838.

6.   Dobie, *A Vaquero of the Brush Country,* pp. 138–139.

7.   From prepared remarks delivered by the author at the 7th Annual Cowboy Songs and Range Ballads Seminar, Buffalo Bill Historical Center, Cody, Wyoming, April 7, 1989.

8.   Dobie, *A Vaquero of the Brush Country,* p. 180.

9.   George W. Saunders, "Reflections of the Trail," in J. Marvin Hunter, editor, *The Trail Drivers of Texas* (Nashville: Cokesbury Press, 1925), p. 436.

10. Dobie, *A Vaquero of the Brush Country,* p. 268.

11. [Dick], *The American Hoyle,* pp. 394–397.

12. J. L. McCaleb, "My First Five-Dollar Bill," in J. Marvin Hunter, editor, *The Trail Drivers of Texas* (Nashville: Cokesbury Press, 1925), pp. 485–486.

13. Ibid., pp. 486–487.

14. Joseph Snell, *Painted Ladies of the Cowtown Frontier* (Kansas City, Mo.: Kansas City Posse of the Westerners, 1965), p. 13.

15. E. C. Abbott and Helena Huntington Smith, *We Pointed Them North: Recollections of a Cowpuncher* (New York: Farrar and Rinehart, 1939), pp. 123, 126.

16. [Dick] *The American Hoyle*, pp. 480–481.

17. J. Evetts Haley, *Charles Goodnight, Cowman & Plainsman* (Boston and New York: Houghton Mifflin, 1936), pp. 220–221.

18. Philip Ashton Rollins, *The Cowboy* (New York: Charles Scribner's Sons, 1922), p. 185.

19. "Big Cowboy Ball," in Hunter, *The Trail Drivers of Texas*, p. 226.

20. Jim Marshall, *Swinging Doors* (Seattle: Frank McCaffrey Publishers, 1949), p. 109. See also DeArment, *Knights of the Green Cloth*, p. 132.

21. Agnes Wright Spring, *The Cheyenne Club, Mecca of the Aristocrats of the Old-Time Cattle Range* (Kansas City, Mo.: Don Ornduff, 1961), pp. 2–7.

22. David Dary, *Cowboy Culture* (New York: Alfred A. Knopf, 1981), p. 273.

23. Tom Lea, *The King Ranch* (Boston: Little, Brown and Co., 1957), vol. 1, pp. 344–345.

24. Chris Emmett, *Shanghai Pierce: A Fair Likeness* (Norman: University of Oklahoma Press, 1953), p. 7.

25. Theodore Roosevelt, *The Wilderness Hunter* (New York: G. P. Putnam's Sons, 1893), p. 24.

26. Esther McWilliams, *Eaton's Ranch* (Wolf, Wyo.: privately printed, 1982), pp. 3–5, 42.

27. M. S. Robertson, *Rodeo: Standard Guide to the Cowboy Sport* (Berkeley, Calif.: Howell-North, 1961), pp. 11–59.

28. Donald E. Green, *Panhandle Pioneer: Henry C. Hitch, His Ranch, and His Family* (Norman: University of Oklahoma Press, 1979), pp. 53–55.

CHAPTER VIII   ON THE HOMESTEAD

1. Under the Homestead Act of 1862, any person could file for 160 acres of federal land, or 80 acres if taken in more favorable locations, such as within a railroad land grant. To file, one had to be a U.S. citizen, or have filed papers of intention to become one; be twenty-one years old or the head of a family; or have served fourteen days in the U.S. Army or Navy. The person filing could never have fought for any country against the United States. This proviso excluded some Mexicans, Canadians, and Britons, as well as many residents of the South; but Congress altered the law in 1866 to make Confederate veterans eligible for homesteads. A fee of eighteen dollars was charged for each 160 acres. Fourteen dollars was paid at filing. From the date of filing, the person was given six months to make improvements on the homestead. The person also had to reside on the land for five successive years from the date of the first papers. If originally a foreigner, the person had to provide evidence after that five years of having since become a citizen of the United States. Any time after five years but within seven and one-half years, the person could pay the remaining four dollars of his or her fee and take out final papers to receive a patent on the land. The final process was called "proving up" on the homestead and consisted of providing evidence from two witnesses that the conditions had been fulfilled. If a homesteader did not wish to wait five years, a commutation clause in the filing papers allowed the

purchase of 160 acres for $1.25 an acre after six months' residence and rudimentary improvements.

2. Roger Welch, *Sod Walls: The Story of the Nebraska Sod House* (Broken Bow, Nebr.: Purcell's, Inc., 1968), pp. 143–146.

3. Everett Dick, "Sunbonnet and Calico, The Homesteader's Consort," *Nebraska History,* vol. 47, no. 1 (1966), pp. 3–13.

4. Evan Jefferson Jenkins, *The Northern Tier: Or, Life Among the Homestead Settlers* (Topeka: Geo. W. Martin, Kansas Publishing House, 1880), pp. 16–18.

5. Anne E. Bingham, "Sixteen Years on a Kansas Farm, 1870–1886" in *Collections of the Kansas State Historical Society, 1919–1922* (Topeka: Kansas State Historical Society, 1923), vol. 15, pp. 521–522.

6. Minnie Dubbs Millbrook, *Ness Western County Kansas* (Detroit: Millbrook Printing Co., 1955), pp. 243–244.

7. Hamlin Garland, *A Son of the Middle Border* (New York: Macmillan, 1923), pp. 31–32.

8. Amy Lathrop, *Tales of Western Kansas* (Norton, Kans.: privately printed, 1948), pp. 44–45.

9. Jenkins, *The Northern Tier,* p. 18.

10. Garland, *A Son of the Middle Border,* p. 47.

11. John R. Craddock, "The Cowboy Dance," in *Publications of the Texas Folk-Lore Society,* vol. 2 (1923), pp. 34–35.

12. John Greenway, *Folklore of the Great West* (Palo Alto, Calif.: American West Publishing Co., 1969), pp. 426–427.

13. B. A. Botkin, editor, *A Treasury of Western Folklore* (New York: Bonanza Books, 1980), p. 461.

14. Everett Dick, *The Sod-House Frontier 1854–1890* (Lincoln, Nebr.: Johnsen Publishing Co., 1954), p. 372.

15. Greenway, *Folklore of the Great West,* p. 431–432.

16. T. S. Denison, *Pranks and Pastimes* (Chicago: T.S. Denison & Co., 1888), p. 9.

17. Ibid., p. 10.

18. Jenkins, *The Northern Tier,* pp. 152–159.

19. Dick, *The Sod-House Frontier,* pp. 305–314.

20. Francis J. Swehla, "Bohemians in Central Kansas," in *Collections of the Kansas State Historical Society, 1913–1914* (Topeka: Kansas State Historical Society, 1915), vol. 13, pp. 486–487.

21. Alan W. Farley, "The Pioneers of Kansas," *The Trail Guide,* vol. 11, no. 2 (June 1966), p. 13.

CHAPTER IX   IN THE PRAIRIE TOWNS

1. Horace Greeley, *An Overland Journey, From New York to San Francisco, in the Summer of 1859* (New York: C.M. Saxton, Barker and Co., 1860), p. 39.

2. White Cloud (Kansas) *Chief,* Sept. 10, 1857.

3. Ibid., Jan. 5, 1860.

4. Holton (Kansas) *Recorder,* Oct. 4, 1888.

5. Leavenworth (Kansas) *Weekly Herald,* Dec. 10, 1859.

6. Hope (Kansas) *Dispatch*, Nov. 12, 1886.

7. Girard (Kansas) *Press*, Feb. 24, 1876.

8. *Sumner County Press* (Wellington, Kans.), Jan. 8, 1874.

9. *The Commonwealth* (Topeka, Kans.), Apr. 28, 1877.

10. Garland, *A Son of the Middle Border*, pp. 166–167.

11. David Dary, "When Fish Grew Big in Kansas," *Kansas City Star, Star Magazine*, Feb. 4, 1973.

12. David Dary, *More True Tales of Old-Time Kansas* (Lawrence: University Press of Kansas, 1987), pp. 233–234.

13. Ibid., p. 235.

14. David Dary, *True Tales of Old-Time Kansas* (Lawrence: University Press of Kansas, 1984), pp. 266–278.

15. [Eugene Fitch Ware], *Rhymes of Ironquill* (Topeka, Kans.: Kellam Book and Stationery Co., 1889), p. 20.

16. Oscar Wilde, "Impressions of America," in *Works* (New York: G. P. Putnam's Sons, 1916), vol. 14, p. 217.

17. Frank M. Lockard, *The History of the Early Settlement of Norton County, Kansas* (Norton, Kans.: Norton Champion, 1894), pp. 155–156.

18. Dick, *The Sod-House Frontier*, p. 374.

19. Millbrook, *Ness Western County Kansas*, p. 244.

20. T. A. McNeal, "When Kansas Was Young," *Topeka Capital*, May 9, 1923.

21. Gay MacLaren, *Morally We Roll Along* (New York: 1938), pp. 78, 151, 169.

22. *Appleton's Journal*, Aug. 14, 1869.

23. Millbrook, *Ness Western County Kansas*, p. 242.

24. Ralph Waldo Emerson, "Nature," in Charles W. Eliot, editor, *Essays and English Traits*, vol. 5, *The Harvard Classics* (New York: P. F. Collier and Son, 1909), pp. 233–248.

25. Will E. Stoke, *Episodes of Early Days* (Great Bend, Kans.: Published by the author, 1926), pp. 16–19.

26. Ibid., pp. 116–118.

CHAPTER X   IN THE MINING REGIONS

1. Leonard Kip, *California Sketches with Recollections of the Gold Mines* (Los Angeles: N. A. Kovach, 1946), pp. 35–36. A reprint of the rare 1850 first edition published in Albany, New York.

2. Richard A. Dwyer and Richard E. Lingenfelter, editors, *The Songs of the Gold Rush* (Berkeley and Los Angeles: University of California Press, 1964), pp. 6–7, 17.

3. Kip, *California Sketches*, p. 36.

4. Ibid., pp. 36–37.

5. Franklin Langworthy, *Scenery of the Plains, Mountains and Mines* (Princeton: Princeton University Press, 1932), pp. 192–193. Edited by Paul C. Phillips, this is a reprint of the 1855 first edition.

6. Dwyer and Lingenfelter, *The Songs of the Gold Rush*, p. 126.

7. Donald Dale Jackson, *Gold Dust* (New York: Alfred A. Knopf, Inc., 1980), pp. 241–242.

8. Douglas E. Kyle, *Historic Spots in California* (Stanford: Stanford University Press, 1990), pp. 77–79.

9. George R. MacMinn, *The Theater of the Golden Era in California* (Caldwell, Idaho: The Caxton Printers, Ltd., 1941), pp. 163–164, 233–234.

10. Olive Woolley Burt, *American Murder Ballads and Their Stories* (New York: Oxford University Press, 1958), pp. 177–178.

11. Albert Dressler, editor, *California's Pioneer Circus* (San Francisco: Albert Dressler, 1926), pp. 36, 40.

12. *Argonaut* (San Francisco), Dec. 21, 1878.

13. The known California songbooks published between 1852 and 1861 are: George Fawcett, *Songs of the Miners* (San Francisco: 1852). No copy is known to have survived but newspaper accounts indicate it was published; D. G. Robinson, *Comic Songs; or Hits at San Francisco.* (San Francisco: San Francisco Commercial & Job Office, 1853); John A. Stone, *Put's Original California Songster* (San Francisco: Appleton and Co., 1855); David E. Appleton, *California Songster* (San Francisco: Noisy Carriers Book and Stationery Co., 1855); *A California Song Book* (San Francisco: 1855); Mart Taylor, *The Gold Diggers' Song Book* (Marysville, Calif.: Marysville Daily Herald Printer, 1856); Thomas Maguire, *San Francisco Minstrel's Song Book* (San Francisco: Monson and Valentine, 1856); John A. Stone, *Put's Mountain Songster* (San Francisco: Appleton and Co., 1857): apparently reissued by the same publisher in 1858 under the title *Put's Golden Songster: Number Two*; Mart Taylor, *Local Lyrics & Miscellaneous Poems* (San Francisco: Hutchings and Rosenfeld, 1858); J. E. Johnson, *Johnson's Original Comic Songs* (San Francisco: Presho and Appleton Co., 1858); John A. Stone, *Put's Golden Songster: Number Three* (San Francisco: Appleton and Co., 1858); John A. Stone, *Pacific Song Book* (San Francisco: Appleton and Co., 1861).

14. Dwyer and Lingenfelter, *The Songs of the Gold Rush*, p. 53.

15. Mitford M. Mathews, *Dictionary of Americanisms* (Chicago: University of Chicago Press, 1952), vol. 1, p. 550.

16. Samuel L. Clemens (Mark Twain), *Roughing It* (New York: Harper, 1899), vol. 2, pp. 27–28.

17. Herbert Asbury, *Sucker's Progress* (New York: Dodd, Mead and Co., 1938), p. 316.

18. Wells Drury, *An Editor on the Comstock Lode* (New York: Farrar and Rinehart, Inc., 1936), pp. 88, 91.

19. Ibid., pp. 299–300.

20. J. N. Flint, "The Comstock in the Early Days," San Francisco *Call*, July 28, 1889.

21. George Williams III, *The Red-Light Ladies of Virginia City, Nevada* (Riverside, Calif.: Tree by the River Publishing, 1984), pp. 5–30. See also Douglas McDonald, *The Legend of Julia Bulette and the Red-Light Ladies of Nevada* (Las Vegas: Nevada Publications, 1980), n.p.

22. Libeus Barney, *Early-Days Letters from Auraria (Now Denver)* (Bennington, Vt.: Bennington *Banner*, 1858–1860), p. 85.

23. Albert D. Richardson. *Beyond the Mississippi: From the Great River to the Great Ocean. Life and Adventure on the Prairies, Mountains, and Pacific Coast* (Hartford, Conn.: American Publishing Co., 1867), pp. 187–188.

24. Melvin Schoberlin, *From Candles to Footlights* (Denver: Old West Publishing Co., 1941), pp. 22–23.

25. Ibid., pp. 68–69.
26. *Herald-Democrat* (Leadville, Colo.), Jan. 1, 1891.
27. Schoberlin, *From Candles to Footlights*, pp. 261–262. See also Lewis Cass Gandy. *The Tabors: A Footnote of Western History* (New York: Press of the Pioneers, 1934).
28. Muriel Sibell Wolle, *Stampede to Timberlin: The Ghost Towns and Mining Camps of Colorado* (Denver: Sage Books, 1949), p. 425.
29. Leland Feitz, *Myers Avenue: A Quick History of Cripple Creek's Red-Light District* (Denver: Golden Bell Press, 1967), pp. 5–30.
30. Ibid.

CHAPTER XI   ALONG THE RAILS

1. Philip Hone, *The Diary of Philip Hone, 1828–1851* (New York: Dodd, Mead and Co., 1889), p. 415.
2. Henry M. Stanley, *My Early Travels and Adventures in America and Asia* (New York: Charles Scribner's Sons, 1905), vol. 1, pp. 164–167.
3. E. H. Saltiel and George Barnett, *History and Business Directory of Cheyenne and Guide to the Mining Regions of the Rocky Mountains* (New Haven: Yale University Library, 1975), pp. 7, 9, 17, 19. Facsimile of the rare 1868 first edition.
4. Thomas H. Heuterman, *Movable Type: Biography of Legh R. Freeman* (Ames: Iowa State University Press, 1979), pp. 49–54.
5. L. L. Waters, *Steel Trails to Santa Fe* (Lawrence: University of Kansas Press, 1950), pp. 150–151.
6. Dodge City (Kansas) *Globe*, Feb. 17, 1879.
7. Robert Wright, *Dodge City, The Cowboy Capital* (n.p.: n.d. [Wichita, Kans.: 1913]), pp. 248–249.
8. Dary, *True Tales of Old-Time Kansas*, pp. 189–197.
9. New York *Tribune*, Dec. 11, 1869.
10. William E. Webb, "Air Towns and Their Inhabitants," *Harper's Magazine*, vol. 51 (November 1875), pp. 828–835.
11. Dary, *More True Tales of Old-Time Kansas*, pp. 94–99.

CHAPTER XII   WESTERN PLEASURE PALACES

1. Earl Pomeroy, *In Search of the Golden West: The Tourist in Western America* (New York: Alfred A. Knopf, Inc., 1957), p. 7.
2. Joseph Husband, *The Story of the Pullman Car* (Chicago: A. C. McClurg and Co., 1917), pp. 5–40.
3. Susan Coolidge, "A Few Hints on the California Journey," *Scribner's Monthly*, vol. 6 (May 1873), p. 28.
4. J. H. Beadle, *The Undeveloped West; Or, Five Years in the Territories* . . . (Philadelphia: National Publishing Co., [1873]), pp. 743–744.
5. E. N. Andrews, "A Buffalo Hunt by Rail," *Kansas Magazine*, May 1873, pp. 453–454.
6. Pomeroy, *In Search of the Golden West*, pp. 15–16.
7. William Seward Webb, *California and Alaska* . . . , 2nd ed. (New York: G. P. Putnam's Sons, 1891), pp. vi–vii, 2–4, 14.

8.   Lucius Beebe, *Mansions on Rails, the Folklore of the Private Railway Car* (Berkeley, Calif.: Howell-North, 1959), pp. 10–15, 101, 373–374.

9.   Bill Dadd [pseud. H. Wallace Atwell], *Crofutt's Great Trans-Continental Railroad Guide . . . from the Atlantic to the Pacific Ocean* (Chicago: G. A. Crofutt and Co., 1869), p. 45.

10. Oscar O. Winther, *The Transportation Frontier, Trans-Mississippi West 1865–1890* (New York: Holt, Rinehart and Winston, 1964), pp. 123–125.

11. James W. Steele, *Rand, McNally & Co.'s New Guide to the Pacific Coast, Santa Fe Route. California, Arizona, New Mexico, Colorado and Kansas* (Chicago and New York: Rand, McNally & Co., 1888), pp. 197–198.

12. Stanley, *My Early Travels*, vol. 1, p. 146.

13. Stanley Wood, *Over the Range to the Golden Gate, A Complete Tourist's Guide . . .* (Chicago: R. R. Donnelley & Sons, 1891), p. 211.

14. Pomeroy, *In Search of the Golden West*, pp. 17–19.

15. Wood, *Over the Range . . .* , p. 261.

16. Samuel Bowles, *The Switzerland of America. A Summer Vacation in the Parks and Mountains of Colorado* (Springfield, Mass.: Samuel Bowles and Co., 1869), pp. 45–46.

17. Pomeroy, *In Search of the Golden West*, pp. 20–26.

18. Caroline Bancroft, *Glenwood's Early Glamor* (Denver: Bancroft Booklets, 1958), pp. 13–15.

19. Martie Sterling, "Colorado's Redstone Castle is Royal Mountain Peace," *Kansas City Star*, Sept. 11, 1988.

20. John H. Tice, *Over the Plains and On the Mountains; or, Kansas, Colorado, and the Rocky Mountains; Agriculturally, Mineralogically and Aesthetically Described* (St. Louis: "Industrial Age" Printing Co., 1872), pp. 213–215.

21. Ibid., p. 199.

22. Pomeroy, *In Search of the Golden West*, pp. 54–55.

CHAPTER XIII   IN THE DESERT SOUTHWEST

1.   Mabelle E. Martin, editor, "From Texas to California in 1849—Diary of C. C. Cox," *Southwestern Historical Quarterly*, vol. 29 (Oct. 1925), pp 130–131.

2.   Paul Horgan, *Great River: The Rio Grande in North American History*, 2 vols. (New York & Toronto: Rinehart & Co., Inc., 1954), pp. 786–787. See also Owen White, *Out of the Desert—the Historical Romance of El Paso*. (El Paso: McMath Co., 1923), pp. 50–52.

3.   Donald V. Brady, "The Theatre in Early El Paso," *Southwestern Studies*, no. 13 (1966), pp. 5–24.

4.   C. M. Chase, *The Editor's Run in New Mexico and Colorado* (Montpelier, Vt.: Argus and Patriot Steam Book and Job Printing House, 1882), pp. 138–139.

5.   *Albuquerque Morning Journal*, Aug. 1, 1882.

6.   Byron A. Johnson and Sharon P. Johnson, *Gilded Palaces of Shame: Albuquerque's Redlight Districts 1880–1914* (Albuquerque: Gilded Age Press, 1983), pp. 57–73.

7.   C. L. Sonnichsen, *Tucson: The Life and Times of an American City* (Norman: University of Oklahoma Press, 1982), pp. 84, 88.

8.   Lansing B. Bloom, editor, "Bourke on the Southwest IV," and "Bourke on the Southwest II," *New Mexico Historical Review*, vol. 9, no. 3 (1934), pp. 76–77, 284–285.

9. Sonnichsen, *Tucson*, pp. 88–91.

10. Woodworth Clum, *Apache Agent: The Story of John P. Clum* (Boston and New York: Houghton Mifflin, 1936), pp. 173–174.

11. Sonnichsen, *Tucson*, pp. 104, 122–123.

12. Emrich, *It's An Old Wild West Custom*, p. 68.

13. Ibid., pp. 28–36.

14. *Arizona: A State Guide, Compiled by Workers of the Writers' Program of the Work Projects Administration in the State of Arizona* (New York: Hastings House, 1940), p. 245.

15. Ibid., p. 164.

16. Ibid., pp. 165, 387–388.

17. James R. Jennings, *Arizona Was the West* (San Antonio: Naylor Co., 1970), pp. 143–144.

18. Peter Hertzog, *Frontier Humor* (Santa Fe: Press of the Territorian, 1966), pp. 18–19.

19. *Arizona Sentinel*, Nov. 22, 1873.

20. Ibid., Mar. 20, 1875.

21. Ibid., July 10, 1875

22. Emrich, *It's an Old Wild West Custom*, pp. 177–179.

23. Jo Ann Schmitt, *Fighting Editors* (San Antonio: Naylor Co., 1958), p. 29.

24. Will C. Barnes, *Arizona Place Names* (Tucson: University of Arizona Press, 1960), pp. 19, 62, 170, 222, 291, 331–332. See also T. M. Pearce, editor, *New Mexico Place Names: A Geographical Dictionary* (Albuquerque: University of New Mexico Press), pp. 21, 70, 156, and *New Mexico: A Guide to the Colorful State, Compiled by Workers of the Writers' Program of the Work Projects Administration in the State of New Mexico* (New York: Hastings House, 1940), p. 449.

25. *Arizona: A State Guide*, p. 436. See also Bill O'Neal, *Encyclopedia of Western Gunfighters* (Norman: University of Oklahoma Press, 1979), pp. 122–123.

CHAPTER XIV   IN THE PACIFIC NORTHWEST

1. Sidney Warren, *Farthest Frontier: The Pacific Northwest* (New York: Macmillan, 1949), pp. 190–191.

2. *Told by the Pioneers* (Olympia, Wash.: Work Projects Administration, 1937, 1938), vol. 3, pp. 63, 117, 156.

3. Warren, *Farthest Frontier*, pp. 66–67.

4. *Told by the Pioneers*, vol. 3, p. 167.

5. Ibid., p. 172.

6. Ibid., p. 184.

7. *Washington: A Guide to the Evergreen State Compiled by Workers of the Writers' Program of the Work Projects Administration in the State of Washington* (Portland, Oreg.: Binfords & Mort, 1941), p. 136.

8. Warren, *Farthest Frontier*, pp. 82–83.

9. *Told by the Pioneers*, vol. 3, p. 186.

10. Ibid., p. 156.

11. Warren, *Farthest Frontier*, pp. 82–83.

12. Ibid., p. 83.

13. *Told by the Pioneers*, vol. 3, p. 189.

14. Ibid., vol. 2, p. 125.
15. Ibid., vol. 3, p. 185.
16. Warren, *Farthest Frontier,* pp. 134–135.
17. *Told by the Pioneers,* vol. 2, pp. 120–121.
18. Ibid., vol. 3, pp. 53–54.
19. Ibid., p. 157.
20. Ibid., pp. 37–39.
21. Ibid., p. 163.
22. Ibid., pp. 55–57.
23. *Washington: A Guide to the Evergreen State,* p. 136.
24. *Told by the Pioneers,* vol. 3, pp. 184–185.
25. Ibid., p. 81.
26. Ibid., pp. 26–28.
27. Ibid., vol. 2, pp. 221–222.
28. Ibid., vol. 3, p. 139.
29. Dean Collins, "Portland: A Pilgrim's Progress," in Duncan Aikman, editor, *The Taming of the Frontier* (New York: Minton, Balch & Co., 1925), p. 165.
30. Ibid., pp. 179–180.
31. Warren, *Farthest Frontier,* pp. 136–137.
32. Ibid., p. 135.
33. Ibid., pp. 137–140.

BIBLIOGRAPHY

UNPUBLISHED MANUSCRIPTS

Haun, Catherine Margaret. "A Woman's Trip Across the Plains in 1849." Manuscript, HM 538, Henry E. Huntington Library, San Marino, California.

Lewis, John F. "Diary, 1849, 1852–54." Manuscript and typescript in Beinecke Rare Book and Manuscript Library, Yale University, New Haven, Connecticut.

UNPUBLISHED THESIS

Railsback, Thomas C. "Military Bands and Music in the Frontier West, 1866–1891. Fort Hays (Kans.) State University, 1978.

BOOKS

Abbott, E. C., and Helena Huntington Smith. *We Pointed Them North: Recollections of a Cowpuncher.* New York: Farrar and Rinehart, 1939.

Aikman, Duncan, editor. *The Taming of the Frontier.* New York: Balch & Co., 1925.

Alexander, J. E. *Transatlantic Sketches.* Philadelphia: Key & Biddle, 1933.

Allen, Michael, editor. *Western Rivermen, 1763–1861.* Baton Rouge: Louisiana State University Press, 1990.

Applegate, Jesse. *A Day with the Cow Column in 1843.* Edited by Joseph Schafer. Chicago: Caxton Club, 1934.

Armes, George A. *Ups and Downs of an Army Officer.* Washington, D.C.: Privately printed, 1900.

Asbury, Herbert. *Sucker's Progress.* New York: Dodd, Mead and Co., 1938.

Ashburn, Percy M. *A History of the Medical Department of the U.S. Army.* Boston: Houghton Mifflin, 1929.

Ashe, Thomas. *Travels in America, Performed in the Year 1806, For the Purpose of Exploring the Rivers Allegheny, Monongahela, Ohio, and Mississippi, and Ascertaining the Produce and Condition of their Banks and Vicinity.* London: Printed for Richard Phillips, 1808.

Baird, Robert. *View of the Valley of the Mississippi: or, The Emigrant's and Traveller's Guide to the West.* Philadelphia: Published by H. S. Tanner, 1832.

Bancroft, Caroline. *Glenwood's Early Glamour.* Denver: Bancroft Booklets, 1958.

Barnes, Will C. *Arizona Place Names.* Tucson: University of Arizona Press, 1960.

Beadle, J. H. *The Undeveloped West; or, Five Years in the Territories* . . . Philadelphia: National Publishing Co., [1873].

Beebe, Lucius. *Mansions on Rails, the Folklore of the Private Railway Car.* Berkeley, Calif.: Howell-North, 1959.

Bischoff, William N., editor. *We Were Not Summer Soldiers: The Indian War Diary of Plympton J. Kelly, 1855–1856.* Tacoma: Washington State Historical Society, 1976.

Botkin, B. A., editor. *A Treasury of Western Folklore.* New York: Bonanza Books, 1980.

Bowles, Samuel. *The Switzerland of America. A Summer Vacation in the Parks and Mountains of Colorado.* Springfield, Mass.: Samuel Bowles and Co., 1869.

Boyd, Frances Anne Mullen. *Cavalry Life in Tent and Field.* Lincoln: University of Nebraska Press, 1982.

Bradbury, John. *Travels in the Interior of America, in the Years 1809, 1810, and 1811; Including a Description of Upper Louisiana, Together with the States of Ohio, Kentucky, Indiana, and Tennessee, with the Illinois and Western Territories* . . . Liverpool: Printed for the author, by Smith and Galway, 1817.

Burt, Olive Woolley. *American Murder Ballads and Their Stories.* New York: Oxford University Press, 1958.

Carrington, Margaret I. *Absaraka (Ab-sa-ra-ka) Home of the Crows.* 1868 reprint. Chicago: The Lakeside Press, R. R. Donnelley & Sons, 1950.

Chase, C. J. *The Editor's Run in New Mexico and Colorado.* Montpelier, Vt.: Argus and Patriot Steam Book and Job Printing House, 1882.

Clarke, Charles G. *The Men of the Lewis and Clarke Expedition.* Glendale, Calif.: Arthur H. Clark Co., 1970. A biographical roster of the fifty-one members and a composite diary of their activities.

Cleland, Robert Glass. *The Cattle on a Thousand Hills: Southern California, 1850–1870.* San Marino, Calif.: The Huntington Library, 1941.

Clemens, Samuel L. (Mark Twain). *Roughing It.* New York: Harper & Brothers, 1899.

Clum, Woodworth. *Apache Agent: The Story of John P. Clum*. Boston & New York: Houghton Mifflin, 1936.

Cobden, Richard. *American Diaries*. Princeton: Princeton University Press, 1952.

Dadd, Bill [pseud. H. Wallace Atwell]: *Crofutt's Great Trans-Continental Railroad Guide . . . from the Atlantic to the Pacific Ocean*. Chicago: G. A. Crofutt and Co., 1869.

Dary, David. *The Buffalo Book*. Chicago: Swallow Press, 1974.

————. *Cowboy Culture*. New York: Alfred A. Knopf, Inc., 1981.

————. *True Tales of Old-Time Kansas*. Lawrence: University Press of Kansas, 1984.

————. *More True Tales of Old-Time Kansas*. Lawrence: University Press of Kansas, 1987.

Davis, Ronald L. *A History of Music in American Life: The Formative Years, 1620–1865*. Lalabar, Fla.: Robert Krieger Publishing Co., 1982.

DeArment, Robert K. *Knights of the Green Cloth: The Saga of the Frontier Gamblers*. Norman: University of Oklahoma Press, 1982.

Delo, David Michael. *Peddlers and Post Traders: The Army Sutler on the Frontier*. Salt Lake City: University of Utah Press, 1992.

Denison, T. S. *Pranks and Pastimes*. Chicago: T. S. Denison & Co., 1888.

Dial, Scott. *Saloons of Denver*. Ft. Collins, Colo.: The Old Army Press, 1973.

[Dick, William Brisbane]. *The American Hoyle: or, Gentleman's Hand-Books of Games . . .* New York: Dick and Fitzgerald, Publishers, 1864.

Dickens, Charles. *American Notes and Pictures from Italy*. Oxford: Oxford University Press, 1957.

Dobie, J. Frank. *A Vaquero of the Brush Country*. Dallas: Southwest Press, 1929.

Dodge, Richard Irving. *The Plains of the Great West and Their Inhabitants . . .* New York: G. P. Putnam's Sons, 1877.

————. *Our Wild Indians: Thirty-three Years' Personal Experience Among the Red Men of the Great West*. Hartford, Connecticut: A. D. Worthington and Co., 1883.

Dressler, Albert, editor. *California's Pioneer Circus*. San Francisco: Albert Dressler, 1926.

Drury, Wells. *An Editor on the Comstock Lode*. New York: Farrar and Rinehart, Inc., 1936.

Dwyer, Richard A., and Richard E. Lingenfelter, editors. *The Songs of the Gold Rush.* Berkeley and Los Angeles: University of California Press, 1964.

Edwards, Frank S. *A Campaign in New Mexico with Colonel Doniphan.* Philadelphia: Carey and Hart, 1847.

Eliot, Charles E., editor. *The Harvard Classics.* 50 vols. New York: P.F. Colliers and Son, 1909–1910.

Emmett, Chris. *Shanghai Pierce: A Fair Likeness.* Norman: University of Oklahoma Press, 1953.

————. *Fort Union and the Winning of the Southwest.* Norman: University of Oklahoma Press, 1965.

Emrich, Duncan. *It's An Old Wild West Custom.* Surrey, England: The World's Work Ltd., 1951.

Ewers, John C., editor. *Adventures of Zenas Leonard, Fur Trader.* Norman: University of Oklahoma Press, 1959.

Feitz, Leland. *Myers Avenue: A Quick History of Cripple Creek's Red-Light District.* Denver: Golden Bell Press, 1967.

Finley, James B. *The Autobiography of Rev. James B. Finley; or, Pioneer Life in the West.* Cincinnati: [n.p.], 1853.

Flint, Timothy. *The History and Geography of the Mississippi Valley.* 2 vols. Cincinnati: E. H. Flint, 1828.

Fossier, Albert A. *New Orleans, the Glamour Period, 1800–1840.* New Orleans: American Printing Co., 1957.

Frémont, John C. *Report of the Exploring Expedition to the Rocky Mountains in the Year 1842 . . .* Washington, D.C.: Gales and Seaton, Printers, 1845.

————. *The Exploring Expedition to the Rocky Mountains, Oregon and California.* Buffalo: Geo. H. Derby and Co., 1850.

Garland, Hamlin. *A Son of the Middle Border.* New York: Macmillan, 1923.

Greeley, Horace. *An Overland Journey, from New York to San Francisco, in the Summer of 1859.* New York: C. M. Saxton, Baker and Co., 1860.

Green, Donald E. *Panhandle Pioneer: Henry C. Hitch, His Ranch, and His Family.* Norman: University of Oklahoma Press, 1979.

Greenway, John. *Folklore of the Great West*. Palo Alto, Calif.: American West Publishing Co., 1969.

Gregg, Kate Leila, editor. *The Road to Santa Fe: The Journal and Diaries of George Champlin Sibley and Others Pertaining to the Surveying and Marking of a Road from the Missouri Frontier to the Settlements of New Mexico, 1825–1827*. Albuquerque: University of New Mexico Press, 1952.

Haley, J. Evetts. *Charles Goodnight, Cowman & Plainsman*. Boston and New York: Houghton Mifflin, 1936.

Hamilton, Thomas. *Men and Manners in America*. 2 vols. Edinburgh: William Blackwood, 1833.

Hamilton, William T. *My Sixty Years on the Plains Trapping, Trading, and Indian Fighting*. New York: Forest and Stream Publishing Co., 1905.

Harrison, Clifford Dale, editor. *The Ashley-Smith Explorations and the Discovery of a Central Route to the Pacific, 1822–1829, with the Original Journals* . . . Glendale, Calif.: Arthur H. Clark Co., 1941.

Hawke, David Freeman. *Everyday Life in Early America*. New York: Harper & Row, 1988.

Hertzog, Peter. *Frontier Humor*. Santa Fe: Press of the Territorian, 1966.

Heuterman, Thomas H. *Movable Type: Biography of Legh R. Freeman*. Ames: Iowa State University Press, 1979.

Holmes, Kenneth L. *Covered Wagon Women, Diaries & Letters from the Western Trails, 1840–1890*. 11 vols. Glendale, Calif.: Arthur H. Clark Co., 1983.

Hone, Philip. *The Diary of Philip Hone, 1828–1851*. New York: Dodd, Mead and Co., 1889.

Horgan, Paul. *Great River: The Rio Grande in North American History*. New York and Toronto: Rinehart & Co., Inc., 1954.

Hunt, Elvid. *History of Fort Leavenworth, 1827–1927*. Fort Leavenworth, Kans., 1926.

Hunter, J. Marvin, editor. *The Trail Drivers of Texas*. Nashville: Cokesbury Press, 1925.

Husband, Joseph. *The Story of the Pullman Car*. Chicago: A. C. McClurg and Co., 1917.

Inman, Henry. *The Old Santa Fe Trail*. New York: Macmillan, 1897.

Irving, Washington. *The Adventures of Captain Bonneville*. Paris: Baudry's European Library, 1835.

Jackson, Donald Dale, editor. *The Journals of Zebulon Montgomery Pike with Letters and Related Documents.* 2 vols. Norman: University of Oklahoma Press, 1966.

———. *Gold Dust.* New York: Alfred A. Knopf, Inc., 1980.

Jenkins, Evan Jefferson. *The Northern Tier: or, Life Among the Homestead Settlers.* Topeka, Kans.: Geo. W. Martin, Kansas Publishing House, 1880.

Jennings, James R. *Arizona Was the West.* San Antonio: Naylor Co., 1970.

Johnson, Byron A., and Sharon P. Johnson. *Gilded Palaces of Shame: Albuquerque's Redlight Districts, 1880–1914.* Albuquerque: Gilded Age Press, 1983.

Keller, George. *A Trip Across the Plains and Life in California.* Oakland, Calif.: Biobooks, 1955.

Kenderine, T. S. *A California Tramp and Later Footprints; or, Life on the Plains and in the Golden State Thirty Years Ago.* Newtown, Pa.: Published by the author, 1888.

Kennerly, William Clark, as told to Elizabeth Russell. *Persimmon Hill, A Narrative of Old St. Louis and the Far West.* Norman: University of Oklahoma Press, 1948.

Kip, Leonard. *California Sketches with Recollections of the Gold Mines.* 1850 reprint. Los Angeles: N. A. Kovach, 1946.

Kyle, Douglas E. *Historic Spots in California.* Stanford: Stanford University Press, 1990.

Lane, Lydia Spencer. *I Married a Soldier.* 1893 reprint. Albuquerque: University of New Mexico Press, 1987.

Langworthy, Franklin. *Scenery of the Plains, Mountains and Mines.* Princeton: Princeton University Press, 1932.

Lathrop, Amy. *Tales of Western Kansas.* Norton, Kans.: Privately printed, 1948.

Lockard, Frank M. *The History of the Early Settlement of Norton County, Kansas.* Norton, Kans.: Norton Champion, 1894.

Lowe, Percival G. *Five Years a Dragoon ('49 to '54) and Other Adventures on the Great Plains.* Kansas City, Mo.: Franklin Hudson Publishing Co., 1906.

MacLaren, Gay. *Morally We Roll Along.* Boston: Little, Brown and Co., 1938.

MacMinn, George R. *The Theater of the Golden Era in California.* Caldwell, Idaho: Caxton Printers, Ltd., 1941.

Marshall, Jim. *Swinging Doors.* Seattle: Frank McCaffrey Publishers, 1949.

Mathews, Mitford M. *Dictionary of Americanisms.* Chicago: University of Chicago Press, 1952.

Mattes, Merrill J. *The Great Platte River Road: The Covered Wagon Mainline via Fort Kearny to Fort Laramie.* Lincoln: Nebraska State Historical Society, 1969.

Mazzulla, Fred, and Jo Mazzulla. *Brass Checks and Red Lights.* Denver: Published by the authors, 1966.

McDonald, Douglas. *The Legend of Julia Bulette and the Red-Light Ladies of Nevada.* Las Vegas: Nevada Publications, 1980.

McWilliams, Esther. *Eaton's Ranch.* Wolf, Wyo.: Privately printed, 1982.

Merrick, George B. *Old Times on the Upper Mississippi.* Cleveland: Arthur H. Clark Co., 1909.

Millbrook, Minnie Dubbs. *Ness Western County Kansas.* Detroit: Millbrook Printing Co., 1955.

Murray, Marian. *From Rome to Ringling, Circus!* New York: Appleton-Century-Crofts, 1956.

Nash, Jay B. *Philosophy of Recreation and Leisure.* Dubuque, Iowa: Wm. C. Brown Co., 1960.

O'Neal, Bill. *Encyclopedia of Western Gunfighters.* Norman: University of Oklahoma Press, 1979.

Oregon Pioneer Association, *35th Annual Reunion, Transactions.* Portland: 1907.

Paden, Irene D., editor. *The Journal of Madison Berryman Moorman, 1850–1851.* San Francisco: California Historical Society, 1948.

Palmer, Joel. *Journal of Travels over the Rocky Mountains, to the Mouth of the Columbia River* . . . Cincinnati: J. A. & U. P. James, 1850.

Parker, Samuel. *Journal of an Exploring Tour Beyond the Rocky Mountains* . . . Ithaca, N.Y.: Published by the author, 1838.

Parkman, Francis. *The Journals of Francis Parkman.* 2 vols. New York: Harper & Brothers, 1947.

Pattie, James O. *The Personal Narrative of James O. Pattie.* 1831 reprint, with an introduction by William H. Goetzmann. Philadelphia and New York: J. B. Lippincott Co., 1962.

Pearce, T. M., editor. *New Mexico Place Names: A Geographical Dictionary.* Albuquerque: University of New Mexico Press, 1965.

Pike, Albert. *Prose Sketches and Poems, Written in the Western Country.* Albuquerque: Calvin Horn Publishers, 1967.

Pike, Zebulon Montgomery. *Exploratory Travels Through the Western Territories of North America: Comprising a Voyage from St. Louis, on the Mississippi, to the Source of That River, and a Journey Through the Interior of Louisiana, and the North-Eastern Provinces of New Spain.* 1810 reprint, Denver: W. H. Lawrence & Co., 1889.

Pomeroy, Earl. *In Search of the Golden West: The Tourist in Western America.* New York: Alfred A. Knopf, Inc., 1957.

Power, Tyrone. *Impressions of America During the Years 1833, 1834, and 1835.* Philadelphia: Carey, Lea & Blanchard, 1836.

Richardson, Albert D. *Beyond the Mississippi: From the Great River to the Great Ocean* . . . Hartford, Conn.: American Publishing Co., 1867.

Robertson, M. S. *Rodeo: Standard Guide to the Cowboy Sport.* Berkeley, Calif.: Howell-North, 1961.

Roe, Frances M. A. *Army Letters from An Officer's Wife, 1871–1888.* New York and London: D. Appleton and Co., 1909.

Rollins, Philip Ashton. *The Cowboy.* New York: Charles Scribner's Sons, 1922.

Roosevelt, Theodore. *The Wilderness Hunter.* New York: G. P. Putnam's Sons, 1893.

Russel, Osborne. *Journal of a Trapper.* Lincoln: University of Nebraska Press, 1955.

Russell, Marian. *Land of Enchantment, Memoirs of Marian Russell Along the Santa Fe Trail* . . . Albuquerque: University of New Mexico Press, 1981.

Ruxton, George F. *Adventures in Mexico and the Rocky Mountains.* New York: Harper & Brothers, 1848.

Sage, Rufus. *Wild Scenes in Kansas and Nebraska, and the Rocky Mountains, Oregon, California, New Mexico, Texas, and the Grand Prairies; or, Notes by the Way* . . . Philadelphia: G. D. Miller, Publisher, 1855.

Saltiel, E. H., and George Barnett. *History and Business Directory of Cheyenne and Guide to the Mining Regions of the Rocky Mountains.* 1868 reprint. New Haven: Yale University Library, 1975.

Schmitt, Jo Ann. *Fighting Editors.* San Antonio: Naylor Co., 1958.

Schoberlin, Melvin. *From Candles to Footlights.* Denver: Old West Publishing Co., 1941.

Singleton, Arthur [Henry C. Knight]. *Letters from the South & West.* Boston: Richardson & Lord, 1824.

Snell, Joseph. *Painted Ladies of the Cowtown Frontier.* Kansas City, Mo.: Kansas City Posse of the Westerners, 1965.

Sonnichsen, C. L. *Tucson: The Life and Times of an American City.* Norman: University of Oklahoma Press, 1982.

Spaeth, Sigmund G. *A History of Popular Music in America.* New York: Random House, 1948.

Spring, Agnes Wright. *The Cheyenne Club, Mecca of the Aristocrats of the Old-Time Cattle Range.* Kansas City, Mo.: Don Ornduff, 1961.

Stanley, Henry M. *My Early Travels and Adventures in America and Asia.* New York: Charles Scribner's Sons, 1905.

Steele, James W. *New Guide to the Pacific Coast, Santa Fe Route. California, Arizona, New Mexico, Colorado and Kansas.* Chicago and New York: Rand, McNally & Co., 1888.

Stewart, William Drummond. *Edward Warren.* Missoula, Mont.: Mountain Press Publishing Co., 1986.

Stoke, Will E. *Episodes of Early Days.* Great Bend, Kans.: Published by the author, 1926.

Summerhayes, Martha. *Vanished Arizona: Recollections of My Army Life.* 1908 reprint. Chicago: The Lakeside Press, R. R. Donnelley & Sons, 1939.

Thisswell, G. W. *Crossing the Plains in '49.* Oakland, Calif.: Privately printed, 1903.

Thwaites, Reuben Gold, editor. *Early Western Travels, 1748–1846.* 32 vols. Cleveland: Arthur H. Clark Co., 1904–1907.

Tice, John H. *Over the Plains and on the Mountains: or, Kansas, Colorado, and the Rocky Mountains* . . . St. Louis: "Industrial Age" Printing Co., 1872.

Townsend, John K. *Narrative of a Journey Across the Rocky Mountains, to the Columbia River, and a Visit to the Sandwich Islands, Chili, &C., with a Scientific Appendix.* Philadelphia: Henry Perkins, 1839.

Trienens, Roger J. *Pioneer Imprints from Fifty States.* Washington, D.C.: Library of Congress, 1973.

Tryon, Warren S., editor. *A Mirror for Americans.* Chicago: University of Chicago Press, 1952.

Unruh, John D., Jr. *The Plains Across: The Overland Emigrants and the Trans-Mississippi West, 1840–60.* Urbana: University of Illinois Press, 1979.

Victor, Frances F., editor. *The River of the West. Life and Adventure in the Rocky Mountains and Oregon: Embracing Events in the Life-Time of a Mountain-Man and Pioneer.* Hartford, Conn., and Toledo, Ohio: R. W. Bliss and Co., 1870.

[Ware, Eugene Fitch]. *Rhymes of Ironquill.* Topeka, Kans.: Kellam Book and Stationery Co., 1889.

Warren, Sidney. *Farthest Frontier: The Pacific Northwest.* New York: Macmillan, 1949.

Waters, L. L. *Steel Trails to Santa Fe.* Lawrence: University of Kansas Press, 1950.

Webb, William Seward. *California and Alaska . . .* New York: G. P. Putnam's Sons, 1891.

Welch, Roger. *Sod Walls: The Story of the Nebraska Sod House.* Broken Bow, Neb.: Purcell's, Inc., 1968.

White, Owen. *Out of the Desert—the Historical Romance of El Paso.* El Paso: McMath Co., 1923.

Williams, George, III. *The Red-Light Ladies of Virginia City Nevada.* Riverside, Calif.: Tree by the River Publishing, 1894.

Winther, Oscar O. *The Transportation Frontier, Trans-Mississippi West, 1865–1890.* New York: Holt, Rinehart & Winston, 1964.

Wolle, Muriel Sibell. *Stampede to Timberlin: The Ghost Towns and Mining Camps of Colorado.* Denver: Sage Books, 1949.

Wood, Stanley. *Over the Range to the Golden Gate, A Complete Tourist's Guide . . .* Chicago: R. R. Donnelley & Sons, 1891.

Work Projects Administration. *Told by the Pioneers: Reminiscences of Pioneer Life in Washington.* 3 vols. Olympia: Washington State Historical Society, 1937.

————. *Arizona: A State Guide . . .* New York: Hastings House, 1940.

————. *New Mexico: A Guide to the Colorful State . . .* New York: Hastings House, 1940.

————. *Washington: A Guide to the Evergreen State . . .* Portland, Ore.: Binfords & Mort, 1941.

Wright, Louis B., and H. T. Swedenberg, editors. *The American Tradition: National Characteristics, Past and Present.* New York: F. S. Crofts & Co., 1941.

Wright, Robert. *Dodge City, The Cowboy Capital.* Wichita, Kans.: Published by the author, 1913.

ARTICLES

Andrews, E. N. "A Buffalo Hunt By Rail." *Kansas Magazine,* May 1873.

Barrows, Samuel June. "The Northwestern Mule and His Driver." *Atlantic Monthly,* May 1875.

Bingham, Anne E. "Sixteen Years on a Kansas Farm, 1870–1886." In *Collections of the Kansas State Historical Society, 1919–1922.* Vol. 15. Topeka: B. P. Walker, State Printer, 1923.

Bloom, Lansing B., editor. "Bourke on the Southwest," *New Mexico Historical Review* [of the University of New Mexico], vol. 9, no. 3 (1934).

Bradley, James H. "Journal of James H. Bradley, the Sioux Campaign of 1876 Under the Command of General John Gibbon." In *Contributions to the Historical Society of Montana.* Helena: Historical Society of Montana, 1896.

Brady, Donald V. "The Theatre in Early El Paso." *Southwestern Studies,* IV, no. 1, Monograph 13. El Paso: Texas Western Press, 1966.

Coolidge, Susan. "A Few Hints on the California Journey." *Scribner's Monthly,* May 1873.

Craddock, John R. "The Cowboy Dance." *Publications of the Texas Folk-Lore Society,* vol. 2, 1923.

Dary, David. "When Fish Grew Big in Kansas." *Kansas City Star, Star Magazine,* Feb. 4, 1973.

Dee, Henry Drummond. "An Irishman in the Fur Trade: The Life and Journals of John Work." *British Columbia Historical Quarterly,* vol. 7 (Oct. 1943).

Dick, Everett. "Sunbonnet and Calico, The Homesteader's Consort." *Nebraska History,* vol. 47, no. 1 (1966).

Farley, Alan W. "The Pioneers of Kansas." *The Trail Guide,* vol. 11, no. 2 (1966).

Gray, Work H. "Journal of W. H. Gray." *Whitman College Quarterly* (June 1913).

Grinnell, George Bird. "Bent's Old Fort and Its Builders." In *Collections of the Kansas State Historical Society, 1919–1922,* vol. 15. Topeka: B. P. Walker, State Printer, 1923.

Martin, Mabelle E., editor. "From Texas to California in 1849—Diary of C. C. Cox." *Southwestern Historical Quarterly* (Oct. 1925).

Root, George A., editor. "Extracts from Diary of Captain Lambert Bowman Wolf." *Kansas Historical Quarterly,* vol. 1, no. 3 (May 1932).

Sterling, Martie. "Colorado's Redstone Castle Is Royal Mountain Peace." *Kansas City Star,* Sept. 11, 1988.

Swehla, Francis J. "Bohemians in Central Kansas." In *Collections of the Kansas State Historical Society, 1913–1914.* vol. 13. Topeka: Kansas State Printing Plant, 1915.

Webb, William E. "Air Towns and Their Inhabitants." *Harper's Magazine,* vol. 51 (Nov. 1875).

NEWSPAPERS AND PERIODICALS

Albuquerque Daily Democrat, May 19, 1883.

Albuquerque Morning Journal, March 12 and Aug. 1, 1882.

Appleton's Journal, Aug. 14, 1869.

Arizona Sentinel, Nov. 22, 1873, and Nov. 20, 1873.

Argonaut (San Francisco), Dec. 21, 1878.

Call (San Francisco), July 28, 1889.

Central City (Colorado) *Register,* Dec. 31, 1872.

Columbian (Olympia, Wash.), Sept. 11, 1852.

Commonwealth (Topeka, Kans.), Apr. 28, 1877.

Dispatch (Hope, Kans.), Nov. 12, 1886.

Dodge City (Kansas) *Democrat,* June 21, 1884.

El Paso Times (Texas), Dec. 17, 1887.

Herald-Democrat (Leadville, Colo.), Jan. 1, 1891.

Junction City (Kansas) *Union,* Apr. 4, 1874.

Larkin (Kansas) *Eagle,* May 20, 1879.

Missouri Republican (St. Louis), Apr. 12, 1841.

Oregon Spectator (Oregon City), Feb. 5, 1846.

Press (Girard, Kans.), Feb. 24, 1876.

Recorder (Holton, Kans.), Oct. 4, 1888.

Rocky Mountain News (Denver), Sept. 27, 1872.

Santa Fe Daily New Mexican, March 28, 1880.

Smith County Pioneer (Smith Center, Kans.), Feb. 19, 1914.

Sumner County Press (Wellington, Kans.), Jan. 8, 1874.

Tribune (New York), Dec. 11, 1869.

Weekly Herald (Leavenworth, Kans.), Dec. 10, 1859.

White Cloud (Kansas) *Chief*, Sept. 10, 1857, and Jan. 5, 1860.

GOVERNMENT REPORT

Allen, Joel A. "History of the American Bison." In *Ninth Annual Report of the U.S. Geological and Geographical Survey for 1875*. Washington, D.C.: Government Printing Office, 1877.

Index

PERMISSIONS ACKNOWLEDGMENTS

Grateful acknowledgment is made to the following for permission to reprint previously published material:

California Historical Society: Excerpts from *The Journal of Madison Berryman Moorman, 1850–1851*, edited by Irene D. Paden (California Historical Society, 1948). Reprinted by permission of the California Historical Society.

The Arthur H. Clark Company: Excerpts from *The Men of the Lewis and Clark Expedition* by Charles G. Clarke (The Arthur H. Clark Company, Glendale, CA, 1970). Reprinted by permission of the publishers, The Arthur H. Clark Company.

Henry Holt and Company, Inc.: Excerpts from *Long Lance* by Chief Buffalo Child Long-Lance, copyright © 1928 by Cosmopolitan Book Corporation, copyright © 1956 by Holt, Rinehart and Winston. Reprinted by permission of Henry Holt and Company, Inc.

Simon & Schuster Inc.: Excerpts from *A Son of the Middle Border* by Hamlin Garland (Macmillan, New York, 1962). Reprinted by permission of Simon & Schuster Inc.

Texas Folklore Society: "The Cowboy Dance" by J. R. Craddock, from *Coffee in the Gourd* (Publications of the Texas Folklore Society II, 1923). Reprinted by permission of the Texas Folklore Society, Stephen F. Austin State University, Nacogdoches, TX.

Topeka Capital-Journal: Excerpt from "When Kansas Was Young" by T. A. McNeal (*Topeka Capital*, May 9, 1923). Reprinted by permission of the *Topeka Capital-Journal*.

University of California Press: Excerpts from "Oh, California" by John Nichols, "Hangtown Gals" and "Seeing the Elephant" by David G. Robinson, from *Songs of the Goldrush*, edited by Richard Dwyer et al., copyright © 1964 by The Regents of the University of California. Reprinted courtesy of the University of California Press.

University of Oklahoma Press: Excerpts from *Persimmon Hill: A Narrative of Old St. Louis and the Far West* by William Clark Kennerly as told to Elizabeth Russell, copyright © 1948 by the University of Oklahoma Press; excerpts from *Adventures of Zenas Leonard, Fur Trader*, edited by John C. Ewers, copyright © 1959 by the University of Oklahoma Press. Reprinted by permission of the University of Oklahoma Press.

University of Texas Press: Excerpts from *A Vaquero of the Brush Country* by J. Frank Dobie, copyright © 1929, 1957, 1985. Reprinted by permission of the University of Texas Press.

Vanguard Press: Poem and excerpt of text from *It's an Old Wild West Custom* by Duncan Emrich, copyright © 1949 by Duncan Emrich. Reprinted by permission of Vanguard Press, a division of Random House, Inc.

A NOTE ON THE TYPE

Pierre Simon Fournier *le jeune*, who designed the type used in this book, was both an originator and a collector of types. His services to the art of printing were his design of letters, his creation of ornaments and initials, and his standardization of type sizes. His types are old style in character and sharply cut. In 1764 and 1766 he published his *Manuel typographique*, a treatise on the history of French types and printing, on typefounding in all its details, and on what many consider his most important contribution to typography—the measurement of type by the point system.

Composed by North Market Street Graphics, Lancaster, Pennsylvania
Printed and bound by Quebecor Printing Martinsburg,
Martinsburg, West Virginia
Designed by Robert C. Olsson